Experience Psychology!

A LABORATORY GUIDE TO

PSYCHOLOGICAL SCIENCE

LAFAYETTE COLLEGE, THIRD EDITION

Carolyn A. Buckley

Lafayette College
Easton, PA

Kendall Hunt
p u b l i s h i n g   c o m p a n y

Cover image © Shutterstock
With SD Curve Art by Lauren Berry, Lafayette Class of 2014, used with permission

www.kendallhunt.com
Send all inquiries to:
4050 Westmark Drive
Dubuque, IA 52004-1840

Copyright © 2013, 2017, 2019 by Carolyn A. Buckley

ISBN 978-1-7924-0472-6

DEDICATED TO:

ALL FORMER LAFAYETTE COLLEGE STUDENTS IN PSYC 110L
IN GRATITUDE FOR ALL THEY'VE TAUGHT ME ABOUT LEARNING

AND TO YOU, THIS SEMESTER'S STUDENTS
FOR GIVING ME OPPORTUNITIES TO LEARN MORE

TABLE OF CONTENTS

APPLICATIONS

GLOSSARY OF TERMS AND EXAMPLES

CHAPTER 3   77
Summarizing Data and Generating Hypotheses

CONCEPTS

APPLICATION

GLOSSARY OF TERMS AND EXAMPLES

CHAPTER 4   103
Correlational Research: Testing Relationships

CONCEPTS

APPLICATIONS

GLOSSARY OF TERMS AND EXAMPLES

CHAPTER 5   139
Experimental Research I: Testing Causal Relationships

CONCEPTS

APPLICATIONS

GLOSSARY OF TERMS AND EXAMPLES

CHAPTER 6   183
Experimental Research II:
Matched Samples & Within-Participants Research

CONCEPTS

APPLICATIONS

GLOSSARY OF TERMS AND EXAMPLES

CHAPTER 7   217
Quasi-Experimental Research

CONCEPTS

APPLICATIONS

GLOSSARY OF TERMS AND EXAMPLES

CHAPTER 8   249
Advanced Topics and Animal Research

CONCEPTS

APPLICATIONS

GLOSSARY OF TERMS AND EXAMPLES

APPENDIX A – INFORMATION & APA STYLE GUIDE

APPENDIX B - ANSWERS TO REVIEW QUESTIONS

REFERENCES

ACKNOWLEDGMENTS

INTRODUCTION: AN OPEN LETTER TO STUDENTS

Dear Introductory Psychology Student,

Before you begin this course, it may help to consider an important question. Circling the emoji that matches your answer will help you understand your feelings and deal with them more effectively, so don't just point to one; actually circle it, and be honest with yourself. How excited are you about doing research in psychology?

| Not one bit | Only a little | Somewhat | Moderately | Mostly | A lot |

This might seem obvious, but it's good to explicitly recognize: The further your answer falls toward the right, the easier it will be for you to learn a lot in this course. If your emoji falls to the left, the course will be more difficult for you. There's no way around that. You can still learn a lot, but you will have to work harder to motivate yourself to do some things that you might have no internal desire to do. Of course, your answer might change as the semester proceeds -- you might end up being sad to see psych lab end! Either way, it's good to know where you stand as you begin. If your only reason for being here is to get a grade or fulfill a requirement, this will be harder for you than for the students who are looking for a learning experience, because this course is designed to be a learning experience. It focuses on the research skills behind the content of psychology. To pick up those skills, you need to engage with the material.

There's an old joke about a woman returning from work who asks her husband what he did all day at home. He replies, "I taught the cat how to do the dishes." "Really? Wow!" his wife says, as she goes to the kitchen. She returns a moment later and asks, "Why are the dirty dishes still in the sink?" Her husband replies, "I said I taught him. I didn't say he learned it."

If you found that joke even a little funny, that's probably because the implication that teaching can be done without learning is so contrary to the way people think that the punchline is a surprise. And yet, the same teaching, in a single classroom, can lead to some students learning a lot, and others learning less. Why? Many factors affect how much students learn, and not all of them are under the teacher's control. I am passionate about teaching and always eager to help students with diverse learning styles and interests learn how psychological research is done. My goal is for everyone to learn a LOT. I work at this every day (including weekends) to find and apply the best ways of teaching, so that students get to experience the best learning opportunities I can offer. But I can't force you to take advantage of those opportunities. This is a laboratory class, which means we learn by trying things. There is always some instruction before you try, but in each lab, you're going to have to try some things on your own, and that works best if you pay attention to the instructions and put sincere, internally motivated effort into the tasks. I firmly believe that building research skills, like any other skill, requires practice, and practice is useless without trying. For me, trying something out is the best, most rewarding part of learning any skill, and *learning* is why we're all here.

I am excited to have this opportunity to try things out alongside you because I have always found that learning something new brings great joy to my life, especially when it becomes useful later on. May you find much in this course to bring you joy!

Sincerely,

Carol Buckley

Lafayette College, June 2019

ABOUT THIS BOOK AND THIS COURSE: THINGS YOU SHOULD KNOW

In order to make the most of our time in lab, the same information must be provided to everyone before labs meet. Although technology is improving, there is still no better, more consistent way to do that than with a textbook. The pages are perforated because you will have to tear out and hand in some of them in lab, so purchasing a used copy or sharing with a friend are not good options. For these reasons and more…

This book is required reading, and is required IN LAB every week.

I know it's a pain having to bring your book to lab every week. But there is good news. First, the price of this book reflects a royalty-free discount. As the author and the person who requires you to purchase the book, I feel it is unethical for me to earn royalties on each sale. I have therefore negotiated with the publisher so that the amount I would make in royalties (12% of the wholesale price, or about $5.00 per book) has instead been deducted from the publisher's price, with the savings passed on to you. More importantly, the book has been designed to be maximally useful to you in multiple ways, with several unique design features:

1. Each chapter is made up of two sections: **Concepts** and **Applications**.

   a. **Concept** sections provide the information students need for a fundamental understanding of how psychological science works. Concepts may refer to the philosophy of science, ways of summarizing data related to psychology, or types of research. The associated terminology is carefully chosen and explained in enough detail to prepare you for advanced courses in research design, but this is not meant to be a comprehensive course in research methods. Statistical concepts are explained similarly, on a conceptual level, without reference to complex formulae or advanced frequency distributions, but with enough information to introduce you to the ways in which statistics can be used to make more objective decisions about data. Another important goal is to clarify basic factors that affect the trustworthiness of statistical information.

   b. **Applications** are hands-on research projects or activities to give you practice applying the concepts by doing different kinds of research. Each application includes its own brief background and procedure. Some of the background information will overlap with other applications, but this is necessary to allow flexibility in course assignments and associated readings. Some background information will also overlap with typical lecture textbook content, which may improve your performance on lecture exams.

2. **Focus your learning where you need it.** Lists of learning objectives are a popular textbook feature at the beginning of textbook chapters because research in educational psychology has shown that students learn more when they are informed of the goals of a lesson before the lesson begins (Klauer, 1984). The problem is that most students don't read them. This book tackles that problem by making the lists practical and time-saving with an interactive worksheet in a chart format. Each section starts with a chart that lists content you should learn and/or skills you should master as you read about the concepts or complete the research application. It's like taking a personal mini-quiz with no actual answers required, no grades, and no pressure. Instead, you think about the questions and rate how well you think you can answer them before you do the reading, on a scale from 1 (I don't know) to 4 (I already know this). This helps you to figure out where to focus your attention as you read the assignment, so you can skim quickly through what you already know and slow down to learn more effectively what you don't already know. The worksheet design also invites you to return to it for review after reading each section and/or doing research, which should help you figure out what you have learned and what you still need to learn. Doing so is an excellent way to prepare for actual quizzes and lab assignments. As the author of this book and coordinator of this course, collecting these charts anonymously may also help me in future course-related decisions.

3. **Glossaries**: Rather than include one large (and largely ignored) glossary in the back of the text, important terms are included in a detailed glossary with examples at the end of each chapter. This specialized glossary includes every bold, italicized term introduced in that chapter, its definition, page number on which the term was introduced, and at least one example. When these terms appear again in later chapters, the chapter or page numbers will be provided so that you can easily relocate their glossary entries, if needed. In many cases, you will also find references to pages in your lecture textbook (Myers & DeWall, 2018) where you can read more on the topic or see more examples.

4. **Practice**: Throughout this book, you will find questions that check your understanding of the concepts and terms, with a list of correct answers to these questions in Appendix B.

Read all assigned pages and bring this book to every lab session!

SUCCESS

© Creativa/Shutterstock. Modified by C. Buckley

WHAT SHOULD YOU EXPECT TO LEARN IN LAB?

Image © Creativa/Shutterstock, Inc

The main goal of the lab portion of this course is to give you **hands-on experience with the science of psychology—and the psychology of science.** You'll learn how ideas in psychology are developed, scientifically tested, supported or refuted, and communicated; that is, how psychologists think. As you read about and discuss research, and then design and do your own research, you will learn the basics in the art and practice of psychological science. Moreover, psychology is not unique among sciences, so you will also learn about the art and practice of science, in general.

You will complete several research projects on a variety of topics, most of which we hope you will find interesting, but don't think that this is all psychology has to offer! The field is so incredibly diverse that it would be overwhelming to cover even one-tenth of the *topics* that psychologists study. Instead, we focus on five basic *types* of research psychologists use: exploratory, descriptive, correlational, experimental, and quasi-experimental. These terms are applied in a categorical sense to describe the tools psychologists use, but it's important to realize that research in psychology does not always fit neatly into one category or another, and even the categories themselves are not mutually exclusive. This will become clearer as you do each type of research.

This course should help you become a more knowledgeable consumer of scientific information. Our goal is not to turn you into a professional scientist, but to provide you with introductory-level knowledge and skills that can be applied to problems in psychology or any other science. By completing the research projects in this lab, you will gain a sense of familiarity with the processes used to gather the information you read about in your lecture textbook, as well as popular science articles in newspapers, magazines, and on the Internet. You'll be better able to understand and critically interpret them. Whether this is your first college level science lab or your fifth, you should expect to learn new things about the philosophy and practice of science.

Although research in psychology often uses high-tech equipment and cutting-edge software to measure behavior and cognition, it is also possible to do some research in this field using the stuff of everyday life—simple computers, cell phones, paper and pencil. Freedom from complicated equipment means we can focus more of our attention on research design and the logic of hypothesis testing, rather than learning how to use equipment (that will most likely be outdated in a few years!). This lab is about designing and interpreting research that addresses questions related to human behavior and the behavior of other animals. It's about creative problem-solving.

Even if you took a psychology course in high school, you can still expect this course to expose you to new ways of thinking about it, and even about other sciences. In the past few decades, research comparing the impact of various areas of science on all other areas has revealed psychology's status as a "hub science," along with math, physics, chemistry, and biology (Cacioppo, 2007). A hub science is one that is cited frequently by scientists in other fields as they write about their own work. Because psychology has such a huge and diverse sphere of influence and applicability, learning the basic methods of psychological science can help you in many other walks of life, not the least of which is simply being a critical consumer of scientific information.

In conclusion, you should expect to learn something of value, regardless of your level of experience with psychology and/or other sciences.

IMPORTANT NOTICE ABOUT YOUR...

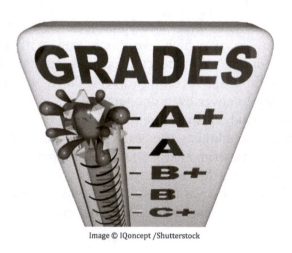

Image © IQoncept /Shutterstock

Grades in lecture and lab are combined into one grade for this whole course (Psyc 110). Your work in lecture and lab may earn up to 1000 points: 650 points for lecture and 350 for lab.

To pass Psyc 110, you must pass BOTH lecture AND lab (i.e., earn at least 60% of the points required for each portion).

In other words, you must earn at least 210 points in lab AND at least 390 points in lecture in order to pass this whole course. It is possible to get an A in lab and still fail Psyc 110 (if you get less than 390 points in lecture), or to get an A in lecture and still fail Psyc 110 (if you get less than 210 points in lab).

You can earn a bonus point on your first quiz if you sign below to confirm that you have read and understood the important information above regarding grades in Psychology 110 and 110L. To earn the point, take a picture of this page with your signature and email it to your Psychology Lab Assistant (PLA), whose email address you will find on your course syllabus.

_____
by signing on this line, I confirm that I have read and understand the information on this page regarding grades

What you learn is way more important than your grade, but there is a causal relationship: More learning generally leads to higher grades. There are three purposeful ways for you to learn in lab: **Participation, Problem Solving, and Writing.** The next few pages describe what these things are and why these are the main focus of this lab. Your syllabus tells you how your performance in these three areas affects your grade.

PARTICIPATION in lab is not just a matter of raising your hand and speaking. Virtually every introductory psychology textbook, including yours, starts with at least one chapter on scientific reasoning and the science of psychology. That chapter forms the basis for the rest of the information in the book. Everything we know about sleep and dreaming, memory, personality, and many other topics, was derived through scientific reasoning and research. Although we believe you will find most of the information in your psychology textbook to be fascinating and enduring in its usefulness, we harbor no illusions that you will remember all of it 10 years from now. We do hope that by participating in the process of scientific reasoning and research, you may at least remember how such information can be obtained and how to assess the scientific validity of new ideas to which you will inevitably be exposed throughout your lifetime.

This lab focuses on the process of psychological research. Participation in lab means being engaged in that process.

Image © sheelamohanachandran/Shutterstock

In this lab, we will be doing real research to answer real questions. In order to obtain enough data, we will work in teams, some with as few as two people, some involving the whole class, and some combining data from all sections of lab. To have the best chance at getting meaningful results, everyone has to be prepared and contributing to the process. *Your classmates will be counting on you to think clearly, make good decisions, and follow procedures correctly,* as though you are preparing a meal for everyone. In fact, the cooking metaphor is a good one...

If you imagine the lecture portion of this class, which is full of practical information about a wide variety of subjects related to thinking and behavior, as a full-course meal, then lab is designed to show you around the kitchen, let you try out a few recipes, and taste the fruits of your labor.

We do not expect you to be a professional psychologist (or chef) at the end of this semester, but we do want you to learn what it means to be a scientist by doing what scientists do, and **you can't learn by doing if you aren't doing anything. Participation is essential to your learning, and effective participation requires preparation.** About 25% of the points you earn in lab are based on your participation, including preparation, in a variety of forms. This includes scores on quizzes, which are based on the reading assignments, small oral presentations and contributions to class discussions, small group projects, and data collection.

Your lab instructor will provide additional details about how she or he will allocate these points.

PROBLEM SOLVING is a defining characteristic of science. To do well in this lab, you have to understand the logic of the research we do, answer questions about the design of our research projects, explain how changes in our methods might affect our results, and draw logical conclusions from our research. Some problems will seem too easy; others might seem like unsolvable riddles until you think long enough about them that the answer finally comes to you. This is the nature of solving problems. **If everything is easy, learning cannot happen, and the whole purpose of this lab is learning. In fact, the whole purpose of doing science is to learn, even for professional scientists.**

For most of the research projects we do, you will be completing lab records that require you to think logically and communicate clearly about the research. Written records are an important part of doing research for several reasons. First, when there are disputes about who figured out what, how and when, lab records provide documentation, which is why they are usually hand-written in pen in a bound book so that pages cannot be inserted or torn out. Another practical purpose of lab records is to keep all ideas, methods, observations, and interpretations organized in one place so that relevant decisions and details are documented. This is not just for our own records, but to allow others to understand, test, and replicate scientific observations. Nothing is ever erased or discarded, not even our mistakes. We often learn more from mistakes than from successes! But perhaps the biggest benefit of keeping complete lab records is having a good set of notes when it's time to write up formal scientific reports and presentations.

"Memory is a complicated thing, a relative to truth, but not its twin." Barbara Kingsolver's words explain why scientists keep such complete written records: We don't want an approximation or even a close facsimile of the truth. We want to report the truth as precisely as possible. That's why, with few exceptions, **we record everything we think and do in writing**: the full names of research partners, the purpose and/or hypothesis of the research, the details of our procedure (including a description of our participants or subjects, any equipment or materials we used) our predictions, all raw data (measurements for each participant/subject), how we summarized and analyzed the data, results (data summary), graphs, and conclusions/ interpretations.

Learning what to include in a lab record and how to organize all that information is a skill to which we will devote considerable time this semester. For most research projects, you will complete worksheets that ask questions that would be answered in a lab record. **Worksheets are *not* "busy work." They are designed to illustrate the standard lab record content.** By the end of the semester, you'll know what to include, so that you can confidently write up your own lab record on your final research project. The benefit of doing so cannot be overstated when it comes time to report on your research, both in writing and orally.

Lab record worksheets and other related assignments allow you to demonstrate your understanding of the research we do in lab, and your ability to solve problems and think clearly about the logic of the research and your conclusions. Your grades on these assignments should reflect your level of understanding about each research project, how accurately you apply the terminology learned in the content section of each chapter, and how well you communicate those ideas with others. They will most often be completed in groups of two to five students, and every student will be responsible for making sure everyone in their group produces high-quality work.

WRITING scientific reports is often the most challenging aspect of this course for students. The APA (American Psychological Association) publishes a style manual for the proper formatting of a scientific report. The current version is 272 pages, all devoted to how to write an APA-style report. If you major in psychology, you'll eventually have to learn how to use that style manual to write authentic APA-style reports, following every rule. At this level, however, our goal is to introduce students to the most important rules and to the detail-oriented mindset you will need in order to produce these reports in the future. In lab, you will learn how to write standardized lab reports in a style we like to call "APA-Light" (see Appendix A -- only a few pages long!). It is the same as APA style in the most important ways, like which types of content belong in each section and subsection of the report. It also follows several of the seemingly less important rules, like where to use bold text or italics and which headings should be centered. All these rules serve a purpose, and learning how to follow standardized, detailed rules for writing is a skill that is likely to be useful no matter what career path you follow.

Image © anaken/Shutterstock

While you are learning the rules, standardization may seem to complicate your writing, but in the long run, it simplifies everything. Life is easier when we use a shared system to communicate. To illustrate, try reading the following sentence out loud:

> *If difficult rather than how syntax the rules to understand anywhere wanted we, imagine would be following it each other of English we put in the verbs and nouns our sentences.*

Now read the exact same words in the proper order:

> *Imagine how difficult it would be to understand each other if we put the verbs and nouns in our sentences anywhere we wanted, rather than following the rules of English syntax.*

Like any meaningful sentence, APA reports follow certain rules of "syntax." Organized into four sections, they logically take the reader from the background and rationale for an idea (**Introduction**), to how it was tested (**Method**), to what was observed (**Results**) and finally, to the interpretations of the observations in light of the original idea (**Discussion**). Putting information in the wrong place is like messing up a carefully constructed sentence. Staying within the confines of this framework gives a natural, logical flow to the report, much like the flow of a well-written sentence. It also allows readers to find any particular type of information exactly where they expect it to be, saving scads of time. Furthermore, using consistent headings and fonts makes life much easier for those who are reviewing the writing, as it takes the guesswork out of the review process. And scientific reports are among the most heavily reviewed and carefully scrutinized bits of writing on the planet.

If you have never written a scientific report, this course will provide the information you need to write a good one. If you have written several, even to the point of being bored with the process, this course will provide the opportunity to challenge yourself and further develop your technical writing skills.

We include report writing as an essential part of this lab course because **science is a social endeavor, not an individual one.** If Albert Einstein had kept the theory of relativity to himself, it would not have been science. It is science because he publicly stated it and others were given the chance to dissect, scrutinize, and empirically test it in multiple ways. If it had not stood up to these tests, it would have been discarded. This is the social aspect of science, from which it derives nearly all its true power to separate knowledge from opinion. **Clear communication of ideas is paramount to the scientific process; without it, you're just not doing science.**

Lab bonus: Your writing skills will improve!

The hardest part of writing a good scientific report is to achieve clarity in as few words as possible. Well-written reports don't waste a moment of the reader's time. They are concise, clear, organized, and direct, with no flowery language and no unsubstantiated opinions. The most common mistake students make in writing reports is trying too hard to sound scientific. We'll talk more about this in lab, and we'll work with many examples to clarify the kind of writing that is expected. Most of your learning opportunities for science writing will come from writing workshops, rather than traditional writing of complete lab reports. By the time you are asked to write a complete report at the end of the semester, you'll have lots of experience with APA style requirements, and continued guidance as you work on meeting those requirements in your own report.

A huge portion of your lab grade is based on writing.

Why? The Psychology Department faculty at Lafayette College have decided that the ability to write about your research clearly and in APA style is a high-priority skill for *all* students who graduate with a B.S or B.A. degree in Psychology. We are in unanimous agreement that effective communication is an essential aspect of the collaborative nature of science *and* of a strong liberal arts education. Good writing starts with a lot of mistakes and gets better with each rewrite. The good news is, we don't use typewriters anymore.

Image © alphaspirit/Shutterstock

HOW TO GET THE BEST POSSIBLE GRADE
(I.E., HOW TO LEARN THE MOST)

At Lafayette College, Psychology takes its rightful place among the natural sciences. Like other natural sciences, **it requires a lot of thinking** before and after the exciting (hands-on) parts. You might not be in lab for the full 2 hours and 50 min every week, but you should expect it more often than not. There will be quizzes on reading assignments, discussions of quiz content, planning of research and the collection of data, then the compiling and interpreting of results and completion of records regarding what we did and how and what the results might mean. That's a lot to accomplish in less than three hours. Students and the instructor need to be patient with each other as we discuss our plans and review them before collecting data so that everyone knows what to do during data collection, or we risk mistakes that could render entire research projects – and all that work – way less interesting.

If you read the letter on page 1, and your emoji was far to the left, please note that even though you might not be all that interested in psychology, the rest of the class will still be counting on you to pay attention and follow directions, which is difficult to do when you feel little interest or motivation. If you find yourself struggling with this, please talk with your professor. We realize that doing research in psychology will not excite everyone (though we're still not quite sure why). We are eager to help those who are not enjoying the process to find the value in it.

Here's why: Science is all about doing things and learning from what we do. If you've seen *Finding Nemo*, you might recall Merlin's over-protective instinct to keep Nemo from "doing anything." In this lab, we'll be doing a lot, and every student in the lab, no matter what their level of interest in this subject, deserves to learn something valuable from what we do. If a few students don't pay attention because they don't care about the research, and data collection gets messed up, the whole class will simply learn that mistakes in data collection lead to an inability to interpret the results of everyone's work, and that lesson will be repeated often. As Dory brilliantly points out, that's "not much fun for little Harpo."

Another reason: Science is an ideal subject for people who love to learn. Many scientists, myself included, chose this profession because doing good science is the best way to learn more about the natural world, and that is exciting to us. Doing bad science (i.e., with no desire to learn anything) is about as much fun as stepping off a curb into the kind of puddle looks like a quarter-inch of water, but turns out to be much deeper so it gives you that sinking feeling for a moment and then your shoe and sock get soaking wet. But doing good science – the kind that flows from logical thinking, preparation, and contemplation of the results – can be very exciting because it can reveal hidden information about the world that can change the way you think.

"Science progresses best when observations force us to alter our preconceptions." ~ Vera Rubin,
American Astronomer whose work led to the discovery of dark matter

In this lab, **most of what you do will be real research, not procedural demonstrations.** Each project builds on the research skills developed in previous projects. For most of the semester, you will be doing real research, learning the skills needed to design and complete your own (capstone) research project, which you will begin working on about halfway through the semester. To ensure the success of our class's research projects and the ultimate success of your capstone research project, it is very important that you read and understand the chapters in this book and other reading assignments. Otherwise, we're all just going to be stumbling off curbs into deep, murky puddles, getting nothing out of it except for that sinking, wet-shoe feeling.

THE BIGGEST CHALLENGES IN THIS LAB

Some students find this course very difficult; others find it very easy. Your chosen emoji (from page 1) is a big factor, but not the only one. Having taught this course to nearly 2000 Lafayette College students directly and another 2500 indirectly (as coordinator for the lab), I have repeatedly observed the problems that lead some students to get lower grades than expected in this course. Even those who have taken Intro Psych at other colleges and in high school sometimes struggle, but it is almost always for one of five reasons. I'm going to list the reasons here, not to scare you, but to help you be prepared for these challenges and make an informed decision about what is best for you. I also provide suggestions to help you meet these challenges and keep them from negatively affecting your grade. My hope is that by knowing in advance what will be most difficult, you can better prepare for it.

Challenge # 1. **Terminology – not just memorization, but application!** There are about 600 words in the glossary of your lecture textbook, give or take a few. This book repeats some of those terms, but often adds technical details regarding their meanings and correct usage, and adds still more new terms that are not covered in the lecture portion of the course. Intro Psych is like a language course. You have to be able to use the words in context, not just spit back their translations, flash-card style. You'll be learning this language at a level that would be considered "fluent" in most foreign language courses, recognizing multiple examples of each term, and even providing your own examples. You will be asked to compare terms and ideas and explain fine distinctions, and to identify proper applications of the terms in situations that may seem

Image © C. Buckley (created at Wordclouds.com)

similar or ambiguous on the surface. In short, fluency requires the ability to think beyond the words, and analyze and synthesize the complex ideas they represent.

Suggestion: The solution is to give yourself *time* to think about the course content. Invest time in your own learning! A good rule of thumb for all college classes is to set aside at least two hours outside of class for every hour in class, or six hours/week for reading the textbook and studying. The average chapter is 16,000 words. The average college student reads textbooks at a rate of 240-300 words per minute, so reading a whole chapter of your lecture textbook should take about one hour. But you should not expect to absorb an entire chapter in one hour! To understand it at the level required, you must break it up into shorter sections, read each section multiple times, and think about it in contexts other than those presented in the textbook. So while you may be able to do the assigned reading in about an hour per week, you will need another four or five hours to do it properly, and think about what you have read (see Challenge #2). Most weeks, you will also need about 60 minutes outside of class to read this book and to do other reading and homework assignments for lab, plus extra time to meet with your group and your professor when you are working on your final research project and report (see Challenge # 5).

Challenge # 2: **Overcoming poor study habits**. Many students start college with poor study habits. If this does not describe you, that's great – skip to the next challenge. But if you spend most of your studying time with an open book in front of you and your mind on other things, or if you've ever read a textbook paragraph four times and still wondered what it was about, then remember this: The biggest challenge of psychology or any introductory course is to learn a LOT of material in a very short time, and *if your mind is on other things, the pace will be frustrating and insufficient to get the grades you want*. Even if your mind is on the reading, but all you do is read, and perhaps scrape a highlighter over the words and definitions that sound important, chances are good that you will not learn as much as you should in order to do well. If you plan to cram before exams, think twice: Your ability to understand and apply new information is like a muscle that takes time to develop. Athletes do not reach peak performance by cramming all their exercise and training into a 5-hour session before a competition. If you've been successful this way before, imagine how much more successful you could be if you gave your understanding some time to develop!

Suggestion: To keep yourself focused, divide your study time into 20-minute sections with 10-minute breaks. You might think that doing so would encourage distraction, but the opposite is true. By taking on smaller sections of text, you increase the amount you retain, particularly if you read each small section *actively*. What does it mean to read actively? First, prepare yourself to read by choosing a manageable section of text (usually 3 to 5 pages for a 20-minute study time). Scan or survey the section to see what it's about. Read only the headings and bold-faced words and look at the figures and their captions. Question the content and write down your questions (for example, when surveying the heading to this section, "The Biggest Challenges in this Lab," you might ask, "How many challenges are there?" "What are the biggest challenges?" and/or, "Will these things be challenging for me?"). Then read to find the answers to your questions. When you "retrieve" an answer, jot it down next to your question (for example, you might write, "There are 5 challenges." "One is that I will need to become fluent in the foreign language of psychology." Or, in answer to the personal question of how these challenges will affect you, you might say, "Lots of new terms – not a problem for me because I'm good with languages." Notice that you are not studying merely for the sake of regurgitation on an exam – you are unlikely to be asked on a quiz whether you find certain challenges particularly difficult. Rather, you are actively pursuing answers to your own questions while reading. This will help you stay focused and remember what you read, including the things you need to know for exams. And your memories will last much longer than if you had just highlighted important sentences. Lastly, before you stop reading a section of the textbook to take a break, be sure to review your questions, your answers, and any additional information you picked up from the reading. Review the content without referring to the text, unless it's necessary to clarify a point. Once clarified, be sure you can review it without the text before you close the book and take your break. This technique, called SQ3R (Survey, Question, Read, Retrieve, Review), is best applied to small sections of reading, but can be applied to whole chapters, as described in your lecture textbook (Myers & DeWall, 2018, Roman numeral pages xxx-xxxi (30-31), also pp. 18-20, 326).

Challenge # 3: **Unrealistic expectations and the myth of the introductory course.** Many students expect introductory college courses to be easier than higher level, advanced courses. But for most, the opposite is true. Unless you are an information sponge, introductory courses are generally more difficult than advanced courses because they cover a much wider variety of subjects, requiring students to switch gears often and learn many diverse topics at a surprisingly deep level. This is at least as true in psychology as it is in any other discipline. Psychology covers an incredibly wide variety of subjects. Introductory courses in college are designed to prepare students for higher-level classes. This means that you must learn about all the topics as though you were going to go on in psychology, even if you never plan to take another course in this field.

Suggestion: There is nothing for this but to change your expectations. That will be easier if you understand that the Psychology Department offers this course as a proper introduction to the field for students who plan to go on in psychology and/or neuroscience. Teaching it any other way would be unfair to those students. If you are majoring in economics, government and law, or some other field, and you are hoping for a light introduction to psychology as a natural science, imagine the introductory course in your major being watered down to make it easier for non-majors to get through it. Is that how you would want to prepare for your major? Whatever your reason for choosing a liberal arts education, embrace that choice and make the most of it. Step outside your comfort zone, and learn to the best of your ability. If you do, you will undoubtedly learn something of value. In keeping with the liberal arts philosophy, we hope one of the things you will learn is that widening your horizons can be a richly rewarding experience.

Challenge # 4: **Unlearning the stuff you thought you knew.** Psychology is a popular topic, often talked about in the media. Although thousands of popular books have been published that are categorized as "psychology," the appropriateness of that categorization is sometimes questionable. In spite of its popularity (or perhaps because of it), psychology is often misrepresented and misunderstood. People see it as a "soft science," implying that the rules of scientific thinking still apply, but that they are more flexible and break more often than they do in physics or chemistry. This is just one of the many misconceptions about psychology. Misinformation makes it difficult to learn new content, since you have to actually let go of things you thought you knew. Your lecture professor will spend some time on this topic, so we won't belabor the point here. Suffice to say, learning is difficult enough without having to unlearn first.

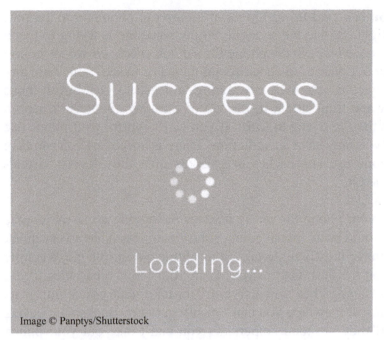

Image © Panptys/Shutterstock

Suggestion: Question everything. Practice the scientific attitude presented in Chapter 1 of this book. In this course, you will usually find evidence (citations) for the information presented in the lecture and lab textbook, and you can always obtain the original research articles from our campus library or through interlibrary loan (super easy). In today's world of social and news media, finding evidence behind the information is a lot harder. In many cases, the evidence simply doesn't exist. Some of the things you think you know are probably not true! Science education is not just about learning facts. It is about learning how to determine the "truth" about the natural world through systematic analysis, attention and observation, while realizing that scientific truth is a dynamic construct. The only logical way to deal with this is to question everything and examine the evidence. Let go of that inner expert who keeps telling you that your knowledge is made up of facts, or even that your textbook is full of facts, and instead ask yourself "What's the evidence?" and, "What's the source of that evidence?" If you practice this way of thinking, you will soon find that old ideas are easier to replace.

Challenge # 5: **Lab reports take time to write.** Writing clearly is not as easy as people think. Perhaps the number one reason why grades suffer in Intro Psych is that students do not have the time (or, in some cases, must develop the skill) to proofread and revise their writing for clarity, and clarity is usually what distinguishes a grade of A from a B (or C) when it comes to lab reports.

Suggestion: If you want to improve your writing skills and earn an A, you will most likely need to be more careful than you already are about how you write. You'll need to get into the habit of reading every sentence you write multiple times, preferably out loud, making sure each sentence has the exact meaning you intend to convey, and no other meaning. This is particularly important when it comes to your lab report on your final project, but practicing it throughout the semester on lab records and other homework assignments will help your grades and improve your writing. The first draft of your lab report should be written well before it is due so that you can spend as much time as possible looking for ways to improve the clarity. One main goal of this course is to teach students how to write clearly and concisely, following the rules of structure and organization accepted by the scientific community. The only way to do that is through practice. If you struggle with this, remember that you have an instructor and a PLA to help you. And if it helps, try to keep in mind that struggling is indicative of a high level of learning. If it were easy, you wouldn't be learning anything.

A Bonus Challenge: **Phone addiction is a real thing.** Most of us use our phone more than we realize. We hear it buzz or we see it light up, and we suddenly know someone is trying to reach us. That information is hard to ignore, so we take out the phone for a quick check. Or we're feeling bored, so we instinctively look take out our phones to check social media or to see if there are any messages. Taking out your phone in class is extremely distracting, not just to you, but to those around you who notice your behavior and think about it, instead of thinking about the research they are attempting do or the concepts they're trying to learn. If you can't control your phone use in situations where it is inappropriate, you may have an addiction. There is a free test you can take online to determine whether your phone use approaches or exceeds unhealthy levels: virtual-addiction.com/smartphone-compulsion-test.

Suggestion: Because you might need your phone for taking quizzes or logging on to our course Moodle page during lab, turning it off would be an inconvenient solution, unless it has a very quick startup time. The next best thing is to make it difficult to take your phone out during lab. Keeping your phone in an easy-access pocket, on the desk next to you, or in your lap is a bad idea if you want to avoid being distracted by it. Instead, when you arrive in lab, take your phone out of its usual, easy-to-retrieve location and put it somewhere you can't easily get at it. Backpack pockets with zippers work well, particularly if they are loud zippers, so you can't take out your phone without everyone in lab knowing about it. If you don't have a loud-zippered pocket, you can always leave your phone in the front of the room with your professor, or in the storage space on the wall. Someday, you're going to be glad you trained yourself to get through meetings without it.

"Yoohoo, the meeting's over here."

CHAPTER 1
THE PHILOSOPHY AND PRACTICE OF PSYCHOLOGICAL SCIENCE

CONCEPTS

APPLICATION

GLOSSARY OF TERMS AND EXAMPLES

CHART 1 - CONCEPT LEARNING OBJECTIVES

People come into this course with a wide variety of previous experience in the field. Some have barely heard of psychology as a science, while others have already done research in this field. To help you focus on the knowledge and skills you don't already have, each chapter of this manual will include charts like the one below for the Concept section and for each Application. **Whenever you see a new chart, take a few minutes before reading the next section to consider the learning objectives. Check the boxes on the gray side of the chart that reflect how much you already know about each objective.** While you read, focus your attention on the content and skills (objectives) where you checked less than "4" on the chart. To make sure you learned the important information, **re-assess your knowledge of the objectives by completing the white side of the chart after reading that section and/or doing the research**. If you thought you knew something, but found while reading that you were wrong, you should correct your answers on the gray side of the chart before you complete the white side. These charts might be collected (anonymously) during the semester to help improve the course and the lab manual.

Chapter 1 Concepts / Objectives	START HERE ▼ BEFORE READING THE NEXT SECTION Check how well you feel you can accomplish each objective.				FINISH HERE ▼ AFTER YOU HAVE READ UP TO THE NEXT CHART Check how well you feel you can accomplish each objective, and fix any inaccurate answers on the left.			
	I don't know how **1**	I know a little about this **2**	I know enough about this to guess correctly **3**	I know how to do this and/or have already done it. **4**	I don't know how **1**	I know a little about this **2**	I know enough about this to guess correctly **3**	I know how to do this and/or have already done it. **4**
1 Define science.								
2 Recognize three myths about the scientific method.								
3 Explain the difference between the scientific method and a "scientific attitude."								
4 Can one do science without reporting it? Why or why not?								
5 Explain the similarities and differences in the goals of science as described by Karl Popper and Thomas Kuhn.								
6 Do psychologists seek to verify ideas or falsify them? Explain.								

		I don't know how 1	I know a little about this 2	I know enough about this to guess correctly 3	I know how to do this and/or have already done it. 4		I don't know how 1	I know a little about this 2	I know enough about this to guess correctly 3	I know how to do this and/or have already done it. 4
7	Define confirmation bias and explain how it can affect scientific progress.									
8	Compare essentialist and operationist philosophies and tell why psychologists are operationists.									
9	Explain why scientists call the things they study "variables" and why it is necessary to "operationally define" variables.									
10	List and briefly describe five basic types of research that psychologists do.									
11	Explain differences in the conclusions that can be drawn from each type of research.									

After you complete this half of the chart, read pages 21-29. Then return to page 19 and complete the white half of this chart.

After you complete this half of the chart, go to page 33 and complete the gray half of Chart 1A. Then read pages 35-37 to prepare for the research you'll do in lab.

SCIENTIFIC ATTITUDE AND THE SCIENTIFIC METHOD

"Science is more a way of thinking

than it is a body of knowledge."   ~ Carl Sagan

Psychologists rely on **a "scientific attitude"** as they search for explanations related to behavior and cognition. A scientific *attitude* is a much broader concept than the scientific *method*. The *scientific method* is a set of steps used for certain kinds of science, and an important framework for objective decision making. Your lecture textbook (Myers & De Wall, 2018, pp. 1-3, 24, 630) introduces the term *scientific attitude* to describe a general way of thinking, necessary for doing any kind of science. Here we expand on their discussion of what this attitude requires. We offer six keys to doing science. With the exception of #6, they are all about the way you think, rather than about what you know or what you do:

1. **Let go of your inner expert.** The typical notion of an expert is one who knows a lot more than others about something. Experts generally do not seem as curious as we are about their field of expertise, but natural curiosity is the driving force behind scientific thinking at *any* level of expertise. Letting go of your inner expert, regardless of your current level of knowledge, implies *a constant desire to learn more.* In the words of one highly accomplished cell biologist, "the desire to learn more is my reason for getting up in the morning." But letting go of our inner expert is not easy. Humans enjoy feeling knowledgeable, especially when it comes to interpreting the behavior of others. For example, most drivers, when they see another driver make a mistake, believe themselves to be better drivers, and are quick to label the other driver with certain... unmentionable adjectives and descriptive nouns. Research shows roughly 80-90% of drivers believe themselves to be better than average at driving (Roy & Liersch, 2014), which is, of course, a mathematical impossibility. As you will learn in the lecture portion of this course, the human mind is very good at convincing itself that it knows more than it actually does. In truth, we are easily fooled. The other driver's mistake might be her only mistake in 10 years; your own average number of mistakes might be much higher. Having a scientific attitude means humbly *accepting the possibility that you could be wrong about things*. You probably know some people who refuse to admit when they are wrong, despite the evidence before them. A good scientific attitude leaves no room for that kind of hubris. For professional scientists, questioning the accuracy of their own ideas is a vital part of their job description.

The first principle is that you must not fool yourself and you are the easiest person to fool. ~Richard Feynman, Physicist

2. **Be a persistent skeptic.** Skepticism is often confused with cynicism, but is in fact quite different. A cynic may stop at nothing to reveal unpleasantness, including selective attention to only those ideas that confirm the belief that unpleasantness exists. A skeptic (ideally) will

stop at nothing to reveal the *truth* by searching for all available evidence with respect to a particular claim or idea. The pleasantness (or lack of it) associated with an idea has no bearing on the skeptic's examination of it. Contrary to popular opinion, then, skeptics are not "negative" people; they are truth-seekers. They don't accept ideas (even their own) without observable evidence, gathered systematically. For most of us, it is easy to be skeptical about things that don't fit in with our own view of the world. A scientific attitude also requires skepticism about things that do.

3. Be a careful, systematic observer. Systematic observation is much more than simply opening one's eyes. It also requires careful attention to details and logic, past ideas, how they were tested, and the results of those tests. Being systematic means building new knowledge upon a solid framework of logic and observation, being aware of potential biases in one's observations, and finding ways to minimize or eliminate those biases. For example, one might casually observe a child playing, but a **systematic observation** would involve awareness and observation of the relevant factors that might affect either the child's behavior or one's own observations, like the time of day, or the observer's knowledge of any medications the child may be taking, and even any medications the observer may be taking. Systematic observations produce descriptions of behavior that can be understood and replicated by others. Good record-keeping is part of this process, but so are careful reading and critical thinking.

4. Be a critical thinker. All evidence is *not* created equally. Certain sources of scientific information (e.g., peer-reviewed journals) present stronger or better evidence than others because the work has been scrutinized by other scientists even before publication. Critical thinkers are aware of the sources of evidence and upon what foundations and assumptions those sources are built. Some studies are funded by organizations with an interest in certain outcomes. Sometimes innocent biases and assumptions are built into the way a study is done, and may influence the results. Thinking critically means learning to assess the quality of evidence. Learn to recognize your own biases and assumptions, and to recognize and verify the characteristics of evidence that make it trustworthy. Regardless of where you stand right now, this is a skill you will continue to develop in this course, and one that will serve you well in life.

5. Think logically, but with an awareness of emotions. Without question, a good scientific attitude relies heavily on logic. For example, if we take multiple measurements of two things called A and B, and observe that every time the value of A is high, B is also high, and when A is low, B is also low, then it is logical to conclude that we can simply measure A to predict the value of B, and vice versa. Another example: Imagine a closed system with two movable objects called X and Y. You can move (manipulate) X any way you want and then observe the effects on Y. If Y moves in some predictable way whenever you whenever you move X, you can logically conclude that X affects Y. Such is the simple logic of scientific reasoning. All this talk of logic might give the impression that scientists do not allow emotion or intuition to affect their judgment. Years ago, this might have been the goal, but happily, we have learned (through research in psychology!) that emotion can play an important role in good decision making (for example, see Kidwell, Hardesty and Childers, 2008). If you're a fan of vintage *Star Trek*, you might recall how Captain Kirk repeatedly demonstrated to his (Vulcan) First Officer Spock that making the best decision often requires accepting an emotional component to your assessment, particularly when evidence is sparse or unobtainable.

6. Communicate your ideas and observations clearly and publicly. This is one of the most important aspects of ALL science, whether or not the scientific method is used. Clear and accurate presentation of ideas and observations is crucial to the success of science because **science is a collective endeavor.** Scientific knowledge grows as a collection of ideas that are publicly available for scrutiny. Without clear and accurate communication of the ideas and the evidence for or against them, we do not give others the opportunity to consider the logic of our research or the validity of our conclusions. In short, **we are not doing science unless we publicly share our ideas and observations**. In general, contrary to the practice of some popular media, a scientific result should not be trusted until it has been properly reviewed, reported and scrutinized by other scientists.

All scientists must communicate their work, for what is the point of learning new things about how the world works if you don't tell anyone about them? ~Jim Al-Khalili, Physicist, Author, Broadcaster

THREE MYTHS ABOUT THE SCIENTIFIC METHOD

The *scientific method* is just one of the ways in which the scientific attitude can be applied. It is defined by the same old five steps you've probably learned repeatedly since grade school (in case you need a refresher, they are listed in the gray box on page 24). It is a useful framework for making objective decisions about reality, and we will refer to it and use it often in this lab. But before we do, there are **three common myths about the scientific method** that we must immediately dispel.

Myth #1: That the scientific method is only for scientists. Not true, any more than creative thinking is only for artists. Any time a person thinks about a problem and takes a guess at an answer, tests out the answer by making direct observations, draws conclusions and talks to others about it, the scientific method is essentially in use, whether or not that person is a scientist.

Myth #2: That the scientific method is completely objective and unbiased. The scientific method is a logical way to maximize objectivity and minimize bias as we try to figure out how things work in the world, and it is a powerful tool for everyone who uses it properly. But even when it is perfectly applied, there is no such thing as perfect objectivity. You will learn more about bias as you study human cognition in the lecture portion of this class, hopefully while keeping in mind that scientists are human!

Myth #3: That the scientific method is the only way that scientists gather evidence. In many books, even some textbooks, science is presented as virtually synonymous with the scientific method, leading to misconceptions about the practice and philosophy of science. This lab course is designed to teach the philosophy of science while you practice the techniques governed by that philosophy. Thus, it encompasses much more than just the scientific method. You will learn about five basic types of scientific research: *exploratory, descriptive, correlational, quasi-experimental,* **and** *experimental*. These will be defined in more detail as we examine each one, but for now it is sufficient to point out that at least two of them (exploratory and descriptive studies) do not follow the five steps of the scientific method shown in the gray box below. However, in order to be effective, **all of these types of research require the scientific attitude you just read about, which is summarized in the white box**.

HOW TO HAVE A SCIENTIFIC ATTITUDE

1: Let go of your inner expert (aspire to learn and be willing to accept that you could be wrong).

2: Be a persistent skeptic.

3: Be a careful, systematic observer.

4: Be a critical thinker, aware of sources, biases and assumptions.

5: Think logically, with an awareness of emotions.

6: Clearly communicate and publicly share ideas and observations because...

SCIENCE PROGRESSES COLLECTIVELY!

STEPS IN THE SCIENTIFIC METHOD

Step 1: Identify a question, gather background information, and **think** about it.

Step 2: Generate a testable hypothesis (an explanation or answer to the question that logically leads to certain testable predictions).

Step 3: Empirically test the idea (make observations with or without manipulations).

Step 4: Analyze data and draw conclusions regarding observed outcomes compared to predicted outcomes.

Step 5: Clearly present the information from steps 1-4 to be scrutinized by other scientists. Note that doing this step well provides the "background information" (Step 1) for other scientists to test the same or a new hypothesis, because...

SCIENCE PROGRESSES COLLECTIVELY!

THE PHILOSOPHY AND PRACTICE OF SCIENCE

What distinguishes science from pseudoscience? This question is particularly important for those who study psychology because it is a relatively young science, compared to physics, chemistry, or biology. The first psychology experiments were recorded about 150 years ago, but even today, there are those who will say that psychology is "not a real science." They could not be more wrong.

It is possible that the confusion comes from not knowing what a science is. This is understandable, because even philosophers of science are in some disagreement on that point. You have just read that not all science uses the scientific method, and that a scientific attitude can be used even when you're not doing science. So how does anyone know who is "doing science" and who's not? This question is harder to answer than you might think.

For the vast majority of modern history, scientists have tried to describe and understand the natural world by verifying or confirming their explanations through logic and observation. That was science. However, during the 20th century, largely due to the writings of the philosopher, Karl Popper, many scientists began to reconsider how they went about doing science.

Popper wrote extensively about the difference between **verifiability** and **falsifiability**. He argued that verification— confirming that one's ideas are correct through observation— is not the best way to do science. Indeed, he saw verification as scientifically impossible! Any observation that seems to verify an idea might be limited to the instance in which the idea was tested. For example, we might observe the scales on a fish and propose that all fish have scales. To test our rule about the nature of fish through verification, that is, to confirm it, we would have to check every fish, even those we have not yet discovered! (There are more than 33,000 known species of fish, and that number is growing!) According to Popper, falsification— testing one's ideas with the intent to show that they are wrong—is the way to do science. Logically, it takes far fewer observations to show that an idea is wrong (to find one fish with no scales). Therefore, to improve our understanding of the natural world, falsification is decidedly a more practical approach. Furthermore, Popper argued that research and observations designed to verify ideas are inherently biased. In the 1960s, experimental research in psychology showed that humans are highly susceptible to **confirmation bias**, a tendency to only pay attention to observations that support their own ideas, while ignoring observations that contradict their ideas. By designing our research to show that an idea is true (rather than setting out to show it is false), Popper said that we are quite

Image © Keystone/Staff/Getty

Good tests kill flawed theories; we remain alive to guess again.

~Karl Popper (1902-1994)

Figure 1.1 - Fish or not? If seeking to *verify* the idea that all fish have scales, this zebra clingfish might be ignored due to *confirmation bias*. In fact, it is a fish, and its discovery *falsifies* the idea that all fish have scales.

Image © Levent Konuk, 2013/
Shutterstock, Inc.

likely to fall prey to confirmation bias, and miss instances in which the idea turns out to be wrong. We could spend 20 years confirming repeatedly that each species of fish we find has scales. Anything that looks like a fish but has no scales would be likely to be ignored, including the poor little zebra clingfish, which has no scales, but is definitely a fish (Figure 1.1).

For many scientists, ideas that cannot be tested for falseness are not considered science, and in practice, all good science should seek to find the flaws in our current understanding, and not set out to verify the scientists' ideas. The quote under Popper's photograph illustrates his point of view quite nicely. This is the general approach we will accept for this course. However, it should be noted that falsifiability as the acid test of what makes any endeavor scientific is not embraced by all scientists.

Thomas Kuhn, an MIT physicist and philosopher, argued that Popper's definition only applies to one kind of science, and the relatively rare kind, at that. Kuhn called this rare science "revolutionary" because it results in the overthrow of established ideas. The rest of science he

Image © Bill Pierce/Contributor/Getty

called "normal science." On a day-to-day basis, he said, the vast majority of scientists do not try to show that previously suggested scientific ideas are wrong. Instead, we take what we currently know about an area of study, the established ideas, and test our understanding of those ideas by designing research that we hope will produce the predicted results. Thus, Kuhn argued that normal science is more like "puzzle solving," and is not practiced according to Popper's strict criterion of falsifiability, but it remains science, nonetheless.

Under normal conditions the research scientist is not an innovator but a solver of puzzles, and the puzzles upon which he concentrates are just those which he believes can be both stated and solved within the existing scientific tradition.   ~Thomas Kuhn (1922-1996)

Importantly, Kuhn was also concerned about confirmation bias, but saw it as just as likely to occur, whether one is attempting to falsify an idea or to solve a puzzle. Kuhn argued that defining science as the falsification of ideas requires that we discard ideas after they are falsified, and this is not common practice. In normal science, when an experiment fails to support an idea, research methods, experimenter errors, or faulty equipment are more likely to be blamed for the negative results than an incorrect idea, particularly if that idea is largely accepted by the scientific community. Scientific ideas are more often retested than rejected after a failure to gain support, and confirmation bias is therefore not eliminated.

Kuhn's argument has merit. It would be expensive and time-consuming to toss out every idea the moment evidence against it arises, without any attempts to improve the quality of the evidence, if it can be improved. So part of doing science is figuring out the most likely reason why our observations did not match our predicted results, and scientists spend more time doing that than strictly trying to falsify ideas. However, if several experiments or experimental modifications continue to falsify an idea, most scientists will eventually revise that idea, or reject it and move on to test other ideas. Just as the evidence from one scientific study showing support should not be taken as proof that an idea is absolutely true (more on this in other chapters), one study that refutes an idea is not a good reason to trash the idea. Instead, our scientific understanding of nature progresses slowly, through the combined effort of many scientists and many observations. Shortly after the death of Thomas Kuhn, Vice President Al Gore summarized this point nicely in his MIT commencement address: "[Kuhn] showed how well-established theories collapse under the weight of new facts and observations which cannot be explained and then accumulate to the point where the once useful theory is clearly obsolete."

In conclusion, most scientists, including those who study psychology, agree that the goal of science is to better understand the natural world, both by putting our explanations to the test and by working out the details of those explanations through puzzle solving. We agree that each explanation of any behavior or phenomenon must be communicated clearly so that it can be scrutinized by others. And we all agree that as evidence is gathered and recognized by the community of researchers in any particular field of science, the best ideas within that field may change with growing evidence for or against them.

In contrast, pseudoscientific ideas do not change, despite logic and evidence against them. Astrology is a good example. Because it is based on astronomical observations, some people consider astrology to be scientific, and believe that the position of stars in the sky relative to our sun on a person's birthday can impact that person's personality. A professional astrologer claimed that Jennifer Garner, announcing her divorce from Ben Affleck, is, "like most Aries...courageous and hides her pain and just gets on with things so well."[1] However, in the centuries since early astrologers made their claims, the position of the  sun relative to the constellations of the zodiac has changed. The International Astronomical Union redefined the constellation boundaries for the zodiac in 1930. (You might have been born under a different sign than you think!) Based on her birth date of April 17, Ms. Garner was actually born while the sun was in Pisces, and the same astrologer says of Pisces, ". . . being loved is vital to

---

[1] Perezhilton.com/2015-07-03-terry-nazon-ben-affleck-jennifer-garner/?from=post

their well-being."[2] How different from the Aries, who "just gets on with things so well" at the end of a 10-year marriage. Still, astrology is held by many to be true, no matter what logic or observations refute it. To believe things that have no logical or observational support may be human nature, and people may find it comforting or helpful, but it is important to realize that ideas and beliefs that do not change when evidence piles up against them do not qualify as science.

Another notion that does not mix well with the philosophy of science is **essentialism**, which holds that the ultimate truth of reality can be discovered by capturing its "essence" with proper definitions. Essentialists also seek to explain the natural world, but their goal is to discover the ultimate, unchanging truth. Many people want to know: What is the meaning of life? What is our purpose on this planet or in the universe? What is true love? These questions are not the stuff of science. Unfortunately, perhaps because psychologists study emotions and other topics about which essentialist questions are often asked, people commonly complain that despite years of research, psychology has never come up with a satisfactory answers to questions like, "What is love?" and "What is the purpose of human life?" Because psychology is a science, we do not seek essentialist answers to our questions. Instead, we seek better understanding. Among other things, we study the biology of love, factors that influence the feeling called love, and the ways in which being "in love" changes thoughts and behaviors. We also study how people find and define their own purpose in life, how society influences those definitions, and how belief in a purpose influences behavior. But finding one essential definition of that will reflect an unchanging truth about our purpose as human beings is not a goal for any science, including psychology.

The Birth of Science

[2] terrynazon.com/12suns_pisces.php

Rather than essentialism, science uses an operationist approach. ***Operationism*** (also known as, ***operationalism***) also seeks the truth about reality, but recognizes that the truth can change. The history of science tells us that what we currently recognize as "true" could be wrong. Rather than seeking essential definitions, operationists use ***operational definitions*** (accurate, functional, and reliable ways to identify or measure things). The things we measure or identify, we call ***variables*** because they all vary in one way or another. When you stop and think about it, there is almost nothing in the known universe that does not vary (with a few notable exceptions, conveniently called "constants," like π, τ, λ, and the speed of light, but we don't use these very often in psychology[3]). Psychologists and other operationists put great effort into clearly communicating the operational definitions of the variables we study. This facilitates the collective process of science by allowing others to unambiguously check our findings. You'll read much more about variables and operational definitions in Chapter 2.

In psychology lab, as in any other sciences, our philosophy will be operationist. We will attempt to solve puzzles and test hypotheses, and we'll do this several different ways. That is, we'll use five different types of research.

TYPES OF RESEARCH

In science, as in life, one's choice of words matters. Although most people refer to any kind of scientific study as an experiment, psychologists reserve the word "experiment" for a specific type of research (one that tests the idea than one variable directly affects another). Other types of research have different names, and although they might test ideas, they are not properly called "experiments" unless they have certain characteristics. It is important to distinguish among the different types of research because the conclusions they allow are different. Big mistakes in critical thinking often involve claiming evidence for an idea by drawing a conclusion that is inappropriate for the type of research used to test the idea. General descriptions of the five types of research we will introduce in this course are described below and visualized in Figure 1.2.

Exploratory research has no specific goal or question, but seeks to explore the vast unknown, symbolized by the wavy line in Figure 1.2. There is no specific problem being addressed, except a desire to know more about some unknown subject. We take a systematic approach, in that we have a generally have a plan for exploring and take careful notes on our observations, but the point of exploratory research is to jump into the unknown. There is no purposeful manipulation or specific prediction, and no particular expectation of differences or relationships to be observed. The conclusions that can be drawn from exploratory research are generally simple descriptions of what was observed.

Out of all the variables in our universe that we can explore, including human behavior, when we choose something specific, we often start with a descriptive study. In ***descriptive research***, some variable is identified before we begin to study it. We carefully define it, then observe and describe it. Our definitions may change as we observe and learn more, but unlike exploratory research, we

---

[3] τ and λ are actually used in neuroscience, where they refer to the time constant and the space (or length) constant, respectively. These values affect action potential velocities, or, in plain language, how fast neurons can transmit information.

know what we are looking for. Again, there are no manipulations or specific predictions. Instead, events or behaviors are systematically observed and described quantitatively. The variable (symbolized by X or Y in Figure 1.2) can be anything at all of interest (e.g., football stats, or the average number of flowers purchased for weddings, or how much time college students spend studying per week). The purpose of descriptive research is to clearly describe the variable (typically, to describe how it varies) and to report on it using the appropriate data summaries. For both exploratory and descriptive studies, all that can be concluded is exactly what has been observed – no more, no less. No conclusions can be drawn about relationships between the observations. No predictable relationship has been tested, so no predictable relationship can be claimed to exist. Likewise, no cause for the observations can be inferred.

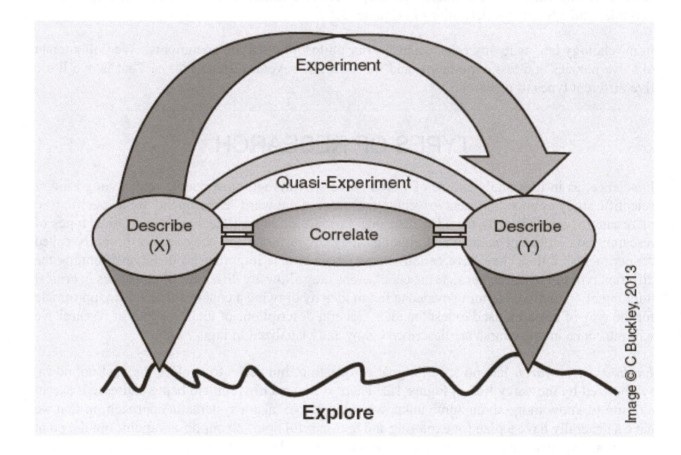

Figure 1.2 Types of research. It may help to visualize the types of research as different ways of investigating a vast ocean of information that varies over time and space. Exploratory research (simulated by Application 1A) explores the unknown in this "ocean." Descriptive research (Chapter 2) isolates one or more specific things from this ocean to study up close and describe in detail. Correlational research (Chapter 4) examines changes in two or more things to test whether they appear to be linked to each other in some predictable way. Experimental research (Chapters 5, 6 & 8) tests whether manipulating one thing affects another, and quasi-experimental research (Chapter 7) attempts to examine the same question, but in a more natural way, usually because we have no ethical or practical way doing a true experiment. Note that the arrow connecting cause-and-effect in experimental research disappears with quasi-experimental research, because only true experiments can provide good evidence for a cause-and-effect relationship. In this course, you will get a chance to try each type of research.

In *correlational research* (symbolized by the link between X and Y in Figure 1.2), at least two variables are systematically observed and described in order to test an *a priori* prediction that changes in one will be associated with changes in another. Again, nothing is manipulated; only observed (measured). But with correlational research, we do have a specific prediction: that there is some kind of observable relationship between the two variables. When the measured value of one behavior or event changes, if the other also changes in the predicted direction, then we can conclude that knowing the value of one will give us some confidence in predicting the value for the other. For example, we might measure attendance at football games and a quarterback's passing yards at those games to test the idea that the quarterback's performance (X) is correlated with the number of people watching (Y). Note that if X does correlate with Y in some predictable way (e.g., if our quarterback passes for more yards when there are more people in the stands), we *cannot* conclude that being watched by more people *causes* the quarterback to pass more successfully. It could be that more people attend games when our team plays weaker teams, so that both passing yardage and attendance at the game increase because of the weak opponent. Or there might be some other explanation. However, if the relationship appears to exist as predicted, regardless of what is causing what, we should still be able predict with some confidence the future success of the quarterback from the number of tickets sold.

In *experimental research*, scientists test whether there is a cause-and-effect relationship between two variables. They do this by manipulating the cause and measuring the effect. For example, we might state that a particular type of training improves job satisfaction. To test that idea, we would manipulate the type of training provided (the cause, symbolized by X in Figure 1.2). One group of workers would receive this type of training, while another group would not. Later, we would measure job satisfaction (the effect, symbolized by Y), perhaps by asking the workers in both groups how satisfied they feel with their jobs. The idea we're testing is that manipulation of variable X will have some influence on the value of Y (symbolized by the arrow from X to Y). For a true experiment, the workers should be randomly assigned to either receive or not receive the training. If, instead, those who got training worked in a different building than those who did not, any differences in job satisfaction could be due to other factors, such as different bosses or different air quality in the two buildings. Randomly assigning individuals to either receive or not receive training would be the best way to assure that the only difference between these groups was the training. If the groups then differ in job satisfaction, we can conclude that the training probably improves job satisfaction (more on random assignment in Chapters 5, 6, 7, and 8).

In *quasi-experimental research*, a cause-and-effect relationship is also stated, but for a variety of reasons, randomly assigning individuals to different groups is not possible. Imagine, for example, that to comply with training regulations, we can only require workers with less than one year of experience to attend our training session, while workers who have seniority must be placed in the no-training group. We would still have an experiment of sorts, in that we would be attempting to examine a cause-and effect relationship. As with our experiment, we would manipulate training by providing it to one group and not providing it to the other, and we would measure job satisfaction in both groups and predict higher satisfaction in the group that was trained. However, this is cannot be called an "experiment" because workers are not randomly placed into the two groups. Instead, they are assigned to each group based on some trait they possess (in this case, the number of years they have worked for the company). Differences in this trait could cause these two groups of people to differ in other important ways, like age, experience, and level of job responsibility. This means that if we observe any differences in job satisfaction, we can no longer be confident that they are due to the training. They could instead be due to different ages, experience levels, or job responsibilities. Therefore, we can only conclude that a difference in job satisfaction exists between a group that was trained and a group that was not; we *cannot* determine whether that difference was *caused* by the training. As the name implies, quasi-experiments are like experiments, but lack important characteristics (most notably, control over other variables) and therefore do not allow the researcher to draw a cause-and-effect conclusion. Figure 1.2 shows a link between X and Y, but no arrow because a quasi-experiment allows us to conclude a link between X and Y (like correlational research), but we cannot conclude that X directly affects Y.

You've just completed the "Concepts" Section of Chapter 1. Before you read on, do the following three things:

☐ 1. Go back to pages 19 & 20 and complete the white side of Chart 1.

☐ 2. Come back to page 33 and complete the gray side of Chart 1A.

☐ 3. Read pages 35 to 36. Do not complete the white side of Chart 1A until your lab instructor asks you to in class.

CHART 1A - APPLICATION LEARNING OBJECTIVES

You will now begin your first research application: an exploration of the diversity of research methods that led to the information in your lecture textbook. The chart below lists what you are expected to learn by reading the background information **and** completing this project in lab. Complete the gray half of this chart first to see how well you already know these skills. As you read the next section and do the exploration in lab, pay closer attention to the skills you rated less than "4" on the chart. **Do not complete the white half of this chart until asked to do so in lab**.

Study 1A Recognizing Types of Research Objectives	START HERE ▼ BEFORE READING THE NEXT SECTION AND DOING THIS RESEARCH Check how well you feel you can accomplish each objective.				FINISH HERE ▼ YOUR LAB PROFESSOR WILL TELL YOU WHEN TO COMPLETE THESE COLUMNS (IN LAB)			
	I don't know how **1**	I know a little about this **2**	I know enough about this to guess correctly **3**	I know how to do this and/or have already done it. **4**	I don't know how **1**	I know a little about this **2**	I know enough about this to guess correctly **3**	I know how to do this and/or have already done it. **4**
1 Recognize citations of original research on at least two different topics in your textbook.								
2 Explain the relevant details of the original research you found.								
3 Recognize the types of research used in those studies and explain how or why they exemplify each research type.								
4 Describe at least one limitation of each study you found.								

▼

After you complete this half of the chart, read pages 35-36. Do not complete the white half until asked to do so in lab.

STUDY 1A
A SIMULATION OF EXPLORATORY RESEARCH: RECOGNIZING TYPES OF RESEARCH

Exploratory research generally means that you are examining the unknown, without any specific expectations about what you will find. For this project, you will explore the world of psychology, as presented in your lecture textbook. You'll browse through the chapters, looking for research on topics that interest you. The project has four important goals: First, you'll get a little practical experience with the first step of any research project (thinking about previous research on a topic of interest); second, you'll learn the distinguishing characteristics of each type of research and gain practical experience recognizing them; third, you'll get a sense of the breadth of psychology as a field of study; and fourth, you'll practice thinking critically about the kinds of conclusions you can (and cannot) draw from each type of research.

As an example, let's use the famous "prison study" conducted by Philip Zimbardo at Stanford University (read more about it in Myers & DeWall, 2018, pp. 481-482). Zimbardo observed how ordinary people reacted when placed in positions of power or subordination to test the idea that social situations strongly influence human behavior. Student volunteers were randomly assigned to become guards or prisoners in a simulated prison environment. Once assigned to these roles, their behavior was observed for several days, and the results were drastic. Guards abused their power, degrading the prisoners and taunting them, while prisoners became weak and submissive. Recall that all participants were ordinary students, randomly assigned to become guards or prisoners for this research only. The study had been planned with a two-week observation period, but had to be discontinued after just six days due to the dramatic (thankfully temporary) effects on behavior. Was the Zimbardo study exploratory, descriptive, correlational, quasi-experimental, or experimental research? Use the descriptions on pages 29 through 32 and the glossary of this chapter to help you decide.

Answer: Zimbardo was testing the power of situations to influence human behavior. This is an example of a cause-and-effect relationship, where the *cause* is the situation, and the *effect* is the observed behavior. Zimbardo manipulated the situation by *randomly* assigning student volunteers to be guards or prisoners and observed the behavior of the students in those situations. If personalities or common life experiences affect behavior more than the situation itself, the prisoners and guards might have just talked with one

© LightField Studios /Shutterstock.com

another, or maybe studied together until the research was over, unaffected by their strange situation. Zimbardo's cause-and-effect hypothesis would have been falsified. Instead, he observed big differences in behavior between students who were assigned to each role, with guards using their time to bully and abuse prisoners, and prisoners becoming docile, weak, and subservient. This lends support to the conclusion that situations can have powerful impacts on behavior. This study was a true experiment because the researchers used random assignment to test a cause and effect relationship. Evidence from true experiments supports the conclusion that one thing directly affects something else.

For this exploratory project, you will be looking through your lecture textbook for examples of research in psychology and trying to determine what types of research they best represent, just as we did with the Zimbardo study above.

Here's some advice on how to find usable original research in your Myers and DeWall textbook:

1. Look for graphs and read the figure captions. If you see names in parentheses at the end of the description like this: (Federer & Nadal, 2008), then you have probably found a citation of original research (though it is unlikely to be as thrilling as that tennis match was). The critical thinking sections are another good place to look.
2. Skim the text for citations (names in parentheses with a date, or just a date in parentheses). When you find a citation, read the text around it and see whether it contains a theory or general information. If so, you probably won't be able to identify the type of research[4], so keep looking.
3. Look for key phrases associated with citations, like "performed an experiment," "studied," "examined," "investigated," or "reported." But be aware that sometimes Myers and DeWall are not careful about their use of the word "experiment." They might be describing a correlational study or a quasi-experimental study and calling it an experiment! (If you're in Professor Buckley's lab and you see a correlational study that they call an experiment, please let her know! You'll get to see her grumpy face.)

Use the lab record worksheet on pages 37 and 38 to record the studies you select and answer the questions about them in groups (everyone should use the same two studies to complete the worksheet; one copy will be collected per group). Each group should find two different types of research, and there will be a time limit. After all groups are finished with page 37, groups will swap worksheets and a different group will complete page 38, noting whether they agree or disagree with your answers. We will return to these worksheets throughout the semester as we discuss each type of research, and your professor will use the studies you choose here as examples of published research in psychology. So please choose studies that you find interesting!

---

[4] An example of a citation for a theory is shown on page 428: "Stanley Schachter and Jerome Singer (1962) demonstrated that how we appraise our experiences also matters." In this case, there is certainly original research behind that statement, but there is not nearly enough information for you to identify the type of research used because the rest of the paragraph goes on to talk about a general theory of emotion. An example of a citation for a general idea can be found on page 200: "In prosperous communities, the time from 18 to the mid-twenties is an increasingly not-yet-settled phase of life, now often called 'emerging adulthood' (Arnett, 2006...)". The textbook authors are providing a definition of a term that may have been coined by Arnett's 2006 publication. Again, the publication may be about original research, but you are not given enough information to identify the type of research used.

LAB RECORD FOR STUDY 1A
RECOGNIZING TYPES OF RESEARCH

Group Members' Names: _____

First Study   Brief Topic: _____

Page # _____ (in Myers & DeWall)   Figure Caption?   Yes   No

Researchers' Last Names: _____

Year of Publication: _____

Brief Description of Research: _____

_____

_____

Type of Research (Circle one):

Exploratory   Descriptive   Correlational   Experimental   Quasi-Experimental

Explain WHY you think this study fits that type of research: _____

_____

_____

- -

Second Study   Brief Topic: _____

Page # _____(in Myers & DeWall)   Figure Caption?   Yes   No

Researchers' Last Names: _____

Year of Publication: _____

Brief Description of Research: _____

_____

_____

Type of Research (Circle one):

Exploratory   Descriptive   Correlational   Experimental   Quasi-Experimental

Explain WHY you think this study fits that type of research: _____

_____

_____

REVIEWING GROUP: CHOOSE 1 OR 2 OF THE ANSWERS ON THE BACK OF THIS PAGE TO EVALUATE BELOW.

Reviewing Group's Names: _____

Which answer are you reviewing? (Circle one)   First Study   Second Study

Brief Topic: _____

Find the page where the study is described in Myers & DeWall.

Read about the research and consider the other group's answer.

Does your group agree or disagree with the research type that the other group circled?

               We Agree   We Disagree

If you agree, give another reason why this research type was correctly identified:

_____

_____

If you disagree, then what type of research do you think best describes the study? (Circle one)

Exploratory   Descriptive   Correlational   Experimental   Quasi-Experimental

Explain WHY you think this study fits that type of research: _____

_____

_____

What type of conclusion was drawn in this research? (Check the one that fits best)

☐ Description of one variable

☐ Predictable link between two variables

☐ Cause and effect: One variable directly affects another

Was that an appropriate conclusion, as far as you can tell?   Yes   No   Not Sure

Explain your answer: _____

_____

GLOSSARY OF TERMS AND EXAMPLES

Where to find these terms: EP = *Experience Psychology!* (this book),
MD = Myers & DeWall, 2018 (lecture textbook). Figures are in EP.

Confirmation Bias: The tendency to focus on evidence that supports our ideas while ignoring evidence against our ideas.

> ***Example:*** Politically biased reporting
> ***Where to find this term:*** EP 25, 27, Fig 1.1, MD 331-332, 341, 343, 626

Correlational Research: A study that measures two or more things that vary (variables) with the goal of testing a predictable relationship between them.

> ***Example:*** Many of the studies on love and marriage (MD 515-516)
> ***Where to find this term:*** EP 23, 31, 32, 35, 36, Fig 1.2, also Chapter 4; MD 29-32

Descriptive Research: A study that measures or identifies one or more things that vary (variables) with the goal of describing it (them) in some useful way.

> ***Examples:*** Studies that describe the characteristics of love (see MD, p 515-516)
> ***Where to find this term:*** EP 23, 24, 26, 29, Fig 1.2, also Chapter 2; MD 26-29, 37

Essentialism: The philosophy that holds that the goal of research should be to understand the essential meaning of concepts.

> ***Example:*** If we were to attempt to explain the one true meaning of a conceptual variable, such as "communication," and could not settle for definitions that capture parts of what communication is about, we would be taking an essentialist approach. This would be extremely difficult to do, since communication can include many diverse behaviors (e.g., billboards, bird plumage, babies crying, sky-writing, sign language, skunks spraying, facial expressions... even the way furniture is set up in an office can communicate information about the executive).
> ***Where to find this term:*** EP 28, 29

Experimental Research: A study designed to test a cause-and-effect relationship between two things that vary (variables).

> ***Example:*** A study about how the contexts for encoding and retrieving information affect memory performance in scuba divers (MD 312). The conceptual variables are "similarity of context" (which is the cause, and has two levels, same context and different context), and "memory performance" (which is the effect, and is measured by percent of words recalled).
> ***Where to find this term:*** EP 25, 31, Fig 1.2, also Chapters 5, 6 & 8; MD 25, 32-37

Exploratory Research: A study designed to explore, generally without specific goals or predictions.

> ***Examples:*** Early studies of the brains of humans and animals, and some current studies of the living brains of humans, especially "diffusion spectrum imaging" (MD, 67).
> ***Where to find this term:*** 29, 35, Fig 1.2

Falsifiability: The qualifying characteristic of any scientific idea. Every scientific idea must be falsifiable, meaning that it can be subjected to tests designed to show that it is wrong (whether or not the technology is available to do so). The more of these kinds of studies (tests) the idea withstands without being shown wrong, the more confidence we can have that the idea is right.

> ***Example:*** The idea that Santa Claus exists "in spirit" is not falsifiable. It cannot be tested and shown to be wrong, because any study designed to show that the "spirit" of Santa is not real could be dismissed by saying that the scientist "misbehaved," and therefore did not deserved to witness the spirit of Santa. The idea that one's father is dressed up as Santa Claus is falsifiable (if Dad and Santa are in the room at the same time, the idea is falsified).
> ***Where to find this term:*** EP 25, 26, Fig 1.1,

Operational Definition: See Chapter 2 Glossary

Operationism (Operationalism): The philosophy that holds that the goal of research should be to improve our understanding of reality by careful definition and observation of concepts and the relationships between them, while recognizing that this endeavor is imperfect and that the "truth" as we understand it changes with new information.

> ***Example:*** Every scientific study described in the lecture textbook takes an operationist approach (MD, 1-644 ☺)
> ***Where to find this term:*** EP 29

Quasi-Experimental Research: A study that, like an experiment, manipulates something that is expected to change something else, but does not randomly assign subjects or participants to different treatment groups, so that those groups might differ in some way other than the purposeful manipulation of differences.

> ***Example:*** Storms (1983) has compiled the results of many quasi-experimental studies on environmental factors that have been suggested to "cause" homosexual orientation. No evidence for any relationship between environmental factors such as parenting, sexual orientation of parents, or childhood experiences and adult sexual orientation was found. (MD, 411).
> ***Where to find this term:*** EP 31, Fig. 1.2, also Chapter 7

Scientific Attitude: To be curious, unassuming, and eager to learn; to actively seek verifiable means of learning more; to be aware of our own and others' built-in assumptions and biases; and to reason logically, with an awareness of the impact of our emotions, and share ideas publicly.

> ***Examples:*** Lafayette Students! ☺
> ***Where to find this term:*** EP 21-23, 24, 25; MD 1-3, 24, 630

Scientific Method: One of several ways of doing science, this is a five-step way of answering questions about the natural world. Key steps are the formulation of a hypothesis which leads to predictions about what will be observed and observations that test those predictions.

> ***Example:*** A scientist hypothesizes that a pathogen in her water supply is killing her plants. She tests this by randomly separating her plants into two groups. She continues giving one group the same water, and gets a purified water supply for the second group. She predicts that the second group of plants will have fewer dead leaves, counts dead leaves on all plants after one week, and observes the same number of dead leaves in both groups. She shares this information with a friend, who suggests that the pathogen might be living on the plants, rather than in the water supply.

> ***Where to find this term:*** EP 21-24, 25, MD 21, but be careful about fuzzy explanations of theories and hypotheses in MD. We are MUCH more specific in lab when we use these terms.

Systematic Observation: Observation with a clearly defined plan or system for gathering information.

> ***Examples (systematic):*** Exploration of solar storms by observing the sun at regular intervals and measuring size and temperature of sunspots. Description of parent-child attachments by observing specifically defined behaviors indicating attachment or lack of attachment. Correlation of GPA from college records with number of high school math classes taken, from high school transcripts. Experimental study of the effects of money on ratings of happiness by giving precise amounts of money and surveying mood.

> ***Examples (NOT systematic):*** Taking a piece of paper and a pencil out onto the quad, intending to write down the ways that college students behave while on the quad.

> ***Where to find this term:*** EP 22

Variable: See Chapter 2 Glossary

Verifiability: Refers to whether or not an idea can be shown to be correct. Although the term is often used loosely, this quality is no longer stressed in scientific research, since the real test of the truth of an idea is whether it is falsifiable, meaning that it can be subjected to tests designed to show that it is wrong. This is because it is infinitely more difficult to convincingly verify an idea than it is to convincingly falsify it.

> ***Example:*** In order to verify that a person (e.g., Abe Lincoln) is always honest, one would have to watch Abe in hundreds of different situations and verify that he is honest in each of them. To falsify the idea that Abe is always honest, one could set up just a few situations in which most people would be dishonest, and see whether Abe is honest in those situations. Putting the idea to the test (falsifying) means actively *trying* to show it is wrong, rather than looking for all the instances in which it is right (verifying).

> ***Where to find this term:*** EP 25, Fig 1.1

The limits of my language mean the limits of my world.

~Ludwig Wittgenstein (1889-1951), Philosopher, Cambridge Professor

CHAPTER 2
DESCRIPTIVE RESEARCH

CONCEPTS

APPLICATIONS

GLOSSARY OF TERMS AND EXAMPLES

CHART 2 – CONCEPT LEARNING OBJECTIVES

Chapter 2 Concepts / Objectives	START HERE — BEFORE READING THE NEXT SECTION: Check how well you feel you can accomplish each objective.				FINISH HERE — AFTER YOU HAVE READ UP TO THE NEXT CHART: Check how well you feel you can accomplish each objective, and fix any inaccurate answers on the left.			
	I don't know how **1**	I know a little about this **2**	I know enough about this to guess correctly **3**	I know how to do this and/or have already done it. **4**	I don't know how **1**	I know a little about this **2**	I know enough about this to guess correctly **3**	I know how to do this and/or have already done it. **4**
1 Provide at least two examples showing the value of descriptive research.								
2 List and describe three subtypes of descriptive research.								
3 List and describe two subtypes of observational research.								
4 Explain the difference between a conceptual variable and its operational definition.								
5 Distinguish between validity and reliability of operational definitions and explain how to improve each of these qualities in any operational definition.								

After you complete this half of the chart, read pages 47-53. Then return to page 45 and complete the white half of this chart.

After you complete this half of the chart, go to your assigned application chart(s) and complete the gray half. Then read about that study to prepare for the research you'll do in lab.

DESCRIPTIVE RESEARCH:
MORE SCIENCE WITHOUT THE SCIENTIFIC METHOD

The main goal of ***descriptive research*** is to identify and provide a systematic description of a known behavior or phenomenon. This type of research is similar to exploratory research in that both are idea-generators, not idea-testers. They do not fit neatly into the five steps of the scientific method, and they are not designed to test correlational or cause-and-effect relationships. Descriptive studies are more goal-directed and structured than exploratory studies. In a descriptive study, some behavior, event, or characteristic is clearly defined, and the goal is to measure and describe it in some useful way. Exploratory and descriptive studies are not mutually exclusive, and what starts as one often leads to the other.

Are these types of research real science? With no predictions, no ideas being put to the test, nothing being falsified... don't they violate the philosophy of science that you just read about in Chapter 1? ***Falsifiability*** is a central tenet of science, and these types of research do not seek to falsify ideas. However, the defining characteristic of science (that ideas are falsifiable) is not the same as the requirement of the scientific *method* (that we attempt to do the falsifying). As previously noted, not all science must follow the five-step scientific method. Producing a logical, falsifiable idea based on systematic observations (your own or reported observations) and then publicly sharing that idea is doing science. And if the idea stands up to multiple attempts to falsify it, it can become a major contribution to science (just ask Einstein!)[1].

One more philosophical question: Didn't we also define science as an approach to solving problems? If exploratory research often has no specific problem in mind, and descriptive research seeks only to describe, what problem is being solved? The problem is a general one: *What knowable information is out there, waiting to be discovered?* Certainly, there is much to explore and describe. And when we produce falsifiable ideas related to the things we explore and describe, and we share those ideas with the public, we are contributing in important ways to our understanding of the natural world. In short, we are doing science.

USEFULNESS AND EXAMPLES
OF DESCRIPTIVE RESEARCH

When most people think of important research, they typically think of experimental rather than descriptive research. You don't often hear the phrase "ground-breaking description." However, descriptive research has contributed much to the breaking of new ground in psychology.

For ease of discussion, we should first clarify the meaning of a word introduced in Chapter 1 that is commonly used in all types of psychology research and in all other sciences. A ***variable*** is anything that changes or can be made to change. All of the thoughts, behaviors, events and

---

[1] Indeed, all that is needed to try to falsify Einstein's Theory of General Relativity is a solar eclipse, like the one you might have seen during the summer of 2017: https://eclipse2017.nasa.gov/testing-general-relativity. If you missed it, mark your calendar for the next one to pass through the United States: April 8, 2024.

characteristics that are the subjects of psychological science are variables. As noted in Chapter 1, there is very little in the natural world that does not change in some way, or cannot be made to change, whether the change occurs over time, across or within individuals, from one location to another, or in any other way. You might say, "My friend's name is Patrick, and that will never change. It will always be his name." However, it can be made to change. He could be called "Pat," "Buddy," "Mr. Star," or "P-Star7." Names are actually an interesting variable to study, particularly for descriptive research. They certainly change within a culture over time. Eighteen years ago, the most popular baby names in the US were Emily and Jacob. In 2018, they were Emma and Liam. The Social Security website is a great source for descriptive data on baby names. At ssa.gov/oact/babynames, you can enter any name to find out how it has changed in popularity over the past 100 years.

Researchers often use descriptive approaches to begin the investigation of a variable, though not always. In descriptive research, there is no attempt to determine the cause of the variable, nor to predict its relationship to anything else. We only seek to describe it in some useful way. Why is this so useful?

Descriptive studies give us high-resolution snapshots of the world around us, as though we are taking apart our surroundings to see the different pieces from previously unexamined angles, with the simple goal of describing reality in clear, meaningful, objective ways. Often, descriptive research leads to falsifiable ideas that would not have occurred to us without this intense level of study, such as "A name jumps in popularity whenever a female celebrity chooses it for her baby."

Descriptive research is not just for psychologists. Astrophysicists' descriptions of the properties of the stars, planets, and galaxies have led to testable ideas about gravitational effects on satellite systems and predictions of meteor trajectories. Geneticists' descriptions of the human genome have led to advances in the identification and treatment of disease. The United States Census is a good example of large-scale descriptive research with important social, political, and economic applications (to see uses of US Census data, go to: census.gov/about/what.html).

Figure 2.1. Descriptive research by Jean Piaget. One of many questions Piaget asked of children: Two identical glasses containing the same amount of liquid were placed in front of each child (top image). A child watched as the liquid was poured from one of the two shorter glasses into the taller, narrower glass. In the bottom image, the child points to the glass that has "more liquid." Piaget described this level of reasoning as preoperational, because children were not yet able to perform "mental operations" on the objects in front of them. They did not mentally reverse the pouring of the liquid back in to the wider container, and did not yet understand that a given quantity of liquid does not change with the shape of its container.

Two excellent examples of ground-breaking descriptive research in psychology can be seen in human development research by Jean Piaget and animal behavior research by Jane Goodall.

Piaget observed children's responses to a variety of questions and problems like the one shown in Figure 2.1, and described identifiable stages in the development of human reasoning. As you will see in the lecture portion of this class, an awareness of these stages (see Myers & DeWall, 2018, pp 174-179) has been critical to the development of more effective teaching strategies in early childhood education, and has formed the basis for a good deal of research in developmental psychology for over 75 years.

For many years, human hubris led us to believe that we were the only species on earth to use tools. Zoologist Jane Goodall changed all that with her descriptive studies of chimpanzee behavior, and was the first to report non-human animals using tools. She watched in amazement as chimps placed twigs and blades of grass into otherwise inaccessible spaces, waited patiently for insects to climb aboard, then carefully lifted the makeshift spoon to their lips and nibbled on the insects (Figure 2.2). Her descriptive research shattered the illusion that the human ability to use objects to achieve our goals makes us special. Documented evidence now exists for tool use by many animals, from apes to insects. Perhaps the most entertaining example can be seen on video at youtube.com/watch?v=pvzOAnfzR90. Watch the whole 40 seconds of video to see why that animal is carrying two halves of a coconut shell.

Image © Kjersti Joergensen/Shutterstock

Figure 2.2. Because of descriptive research of Jane Goodall, we have long known that humans are not the only species to use tools to achieve goals.

These exciting observations have helped us more fully appreciate the complexity of animal behavior and better understand our own evolutionary history.

Doing quality descriptive research is not as easy as it seems. The goal is not merely to describe, but to provide *systematic* descriptions of events or behaviors of interest. To be systematic, we must set out to observe with a plan.

There are basically three ways in which descriptive data can be collected (Figure 2.3). They can be thought of as three subtypes of descriptive research: (1) *Observational descriptive studies* involve watching people or other animals, either in a natural setting or in a contrived environment. Note that data are recorded from the point of view of the observer. (2) A *case study* is a detailed, in-depth description of one individual with unusual or interesting behaviors, symptoms, or circumstances, also from the point of view of the observer. (3) *Surveys* provide data from the point of view of the participant (often called "self-report" data), but the questions asked can sometimes influence the answers given (more on this in Application 2C). Surveys can be administered online, on paper, over the phone, or in face-to-face interviews.

Observational descriptive studies can be categorized in two basic ways. The first is *analog observation,* which occurs when humans or non-human animals are observed in a contrived, laboratory environment. We create a situation in the lab that simulates a natural event or environment, so that behavior can be observed with fewer outside influences. In doing so, the behaviors we observe may lose some of their real-world similitude, but we gain confidence in the accuracy of our measurements, as there are fewer outside factors that could impact the behaviors we're observing, and that, in turn, decreases the variability in our measurements.

In *naturalistic observation*, our goal is to describe behavior as it occurs in nature. No interference or intrusion is allowed. Multiple hidden variables, such as moods, prior experiences, lighting, and even un-noticed breezes or scents on the air could influence the behavior or our observations of it. A behavior observed naturalistically is generally more varied than analog observations would suggest, and it might be harder to describe systematically, but doing so can provide valuable information that might never be exposed in a laboratory environment. Both naturalistic observations and analog observations have made valuable contributions to our understanding of behavior. Figure 2.3 places these terms into a meaningful context with the types of research presented in Chapter 1.

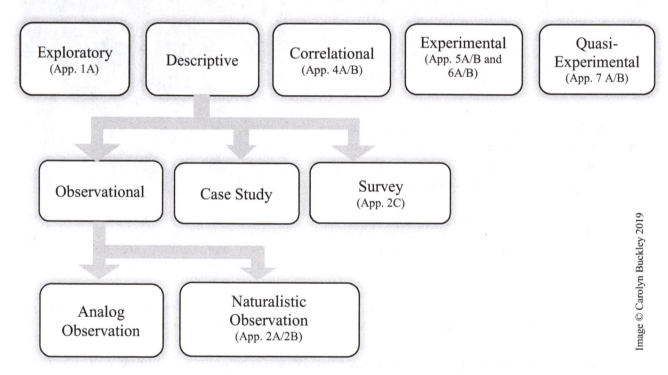

Image © Carolyn Buckley 2019

Figure 2.3. A summary of the types and subtypes of research. The top row shows the five main types of research. The middle row shows subtypes of descriptive research, and the third row shows the subtypes of observational descriptive research. The research applications in this book are also shown in order to clarify which types of research we do in this lab (you've already completed App. 1A).

CONCEPT CHECK (Answers in Appendix B):

Piaget's research was _____, while Goodall's research was _____.
　　　　　　　　　　　　(naturalistic or analog?)　　　　　　　　　　　　　　　　　　　　　(naturalistic or analog?)

CONCEPTUAL VARIABLES
AND OPERATIONAL DEFINTIONS

The decision to use naturalistic or analog observation determines where we will do our research (where the behavior naturally occurs, or in a lab or other contrived environment). The decision regarding *what* to study determines our ***conceptual variable.*** This term can be applied to *any* variable. The fact that we decide to study it makes it our concept of interest, i.e., our conceptual variable. It can be a behavior (for example, dolphins "walking" on their tails), a characteristic (e.g., employee hygiene), or an event (a rock concert), but must always be a noun or noun-phrase, and must have variable qualities. These qualities are sampled over time, people, or situations to produce numbers (data) that are used to describe the behavior, characteristic, or event.

A single conceptual variable can be measured to produce data in several ways. Note that the word "data" in this context is a synonym for "numbers" and is therefore plural.[1] Typical data from descriptive studies include ***prevalence*** (proportion of times something actually happens out of the total number of times it *could* happen), ***frequency*** (the number of times something happens in a given period of time), or ***duration*** (how long something lasts). For example, we can measure the proportion of all concerts at a given venue that feature rock music (prevalence), or the total number of rock concerts in a single summer (frequency), or the average length of each rock concert (duration). Another example: We can describe the conceptual variable of employee hygiene by observing all the employees at a restaurant who wash their hands after using the restroom out of all those who use the restroom (prevalence). Or we can count the number of times hand-washing occurs within a given period of time (frequency), or the average length of time employees spend washing their hands (duration). To practice applying these terms, match the following descriptions of the conceptual variable, "dolphins tailwalking," with the type of data being used to describe it.

CONCEPT CHECK: Draw lines to match descriptions with the types of data they describe.   Answers are in Appendix B.

Tailwalks lasted an average of 7.1 seconds, from the point when the dorsal fin left the water until it was submerged again.	Frequency Data
Roughly 10 percent of dolphins engage in tailwalking behavior.	Duration Data
We observed an average of 2.3 instances of tailwalking per 10-minute play period.	Prevalence Data

---

[1] One number would be called a "datum" or "data point."

Whether we are reporting prevalence or frequency by counting, or using a stopwatch to measure duration, we must clearly and precisely define *what* we are counting or timing. As noted in Chapter 1, an ***operational definition*** is an accurate, functional way of identifying or measuring a conceptual variable. Writing good operational definitions is difficult, but is absolutely necessary. The collaborative and social nature of science demands that we clearly explain precisely what was observed and *how*. Otherwise, there can be no assessment of the quality of the data obtained. So what constitutes a good operational definition? Let's first consider an example.

Imagine you are traveling to outer space, and you've been severely warned to avoid the aliens when they are angry. Happy aliens are great, but you can be killed instantly by an angry alien. Naturally, you want to study alien anger before you go, so alien anger is your conceptual variable. You need know it when you see it and know how to measure it. In other words, you need an operational definition of alien anger. Assuming you can only use one of the two operational definitions below, which would you prefer?

An angry alien will have a somewhat sad posture, but a pleased-looking mouth, with alert, suspicious eyes and curious ears. It will also make some loud sounds, almost like an excited donkey or a European ambulance.

An angry alien will have a rounded, protruding backbone with drooping shoulders. Both corners of its mouth will turn up; the eyes will move left and right, and the ears will point straight up. It will make a two-syllable, "ee-aw" noise.

Image © Scott Maxwell/LuMaxArt/Shutterstock

Let's first consider applying the definition on the left. What do a "sad posture," "a pleased-looking mouth," and "curious ears" look like? How does an "excited donkey" sound, and how is that like a European ambulance? What if you've never seen an excited donkey or been to Europe? These descriptions depend heavily on experience and are likely to have different meanings for different people. The definition on the right is more precise. It relies only on *directly observable traits*. It would take a split second to spot a protruding backbone and ears pointing straight up, but you might be dead before you could figure out whether the alien's posture was "somewhat sad" or its eyes were "suspicious." If we wish to identify the conceptual variable of alien anger, the box on the right has a much better operational definition.

GOOD OPERATIONAL DEFINITIONS ARE BOTH VALID AND RELIABLE

Validity refers to the accuracy with which the operational definition captures the true meaning of the conceptual variable. Like an arrow fired by an expert archer, a valid operational definition hits the center of the target. It must be based on careful and comprehensive observation (often achieved through exploratory research). Hence, to know for sure whether our definition of alien anger is valid, someone would have to irritate many aliens! Thankfully, most operational definitions in psychology can be validated without risking our lives.

Reliability is about consistency. It is the steadfastness with which an operational definition measures or identifies something (ideally, that something is the conceptual variable). Repeatedly, even with different observers, a reliable operational definition produces the same result when used to measure or identify the same thing. An operational definition can be *reliable* without being *valid*. A practiced archer, given an unbalanced bow, might repeatedly hit the target three inches above center. She is very reliable (always hitting the same area), but not very accurate (that area is not the center of the target). Can an operational definition be *valid* without being *reliable*? Consider an inexperienced archer; if her arrows land in no predictable, consistent way, there can be no practical accuracy. The more unreliable the definition, the more measurements one would need to achieve any validity. It could take thousands of unreliable arrows aimed at the target to produce a trustworthy, valid (bullseye) average.

To improve validity, we need to match the conceptual variable (what is being studied) with its operational definition (how it is being identified or measured). To improve reliability, all ambiguity should be removed from the operational definition. The definition of alien anger on the right is less ambiguous and therefore more reliable than the one on the left. The fewer different ways in which a definition can be interpreted, the more reliable it will be. Leaving definitions open to interpretation or having them rely too much on the personal experience of the observer (e.g., familiarity with donkeys) means leaving room for error, and as error increases, reliability decreases.

Table 2.1 shows some more examples of conceptual variables and possible operational definitions. Check the boxes that match your own opinion of each definition. Then think about how you could make each definition more valid or more reliable. This will be excellent practice for research Applications 2A or 2B.

Table 2.1. Some Examples of Conceptual Variables and Possible Operational Definitions.

Conceptual Variable	Operational Definition	How **valid** is this definition?				How **reliable** is this definition?				Suggested Improvement to Operational Definition
		not at all	a little	moderately	perfectly	not at all	a little	moderately	perfectly	
Surfing Ability	Average duration of each ride over five rides									
Thrill-Seeking Behavior	Number of roller coaster rides over summer vacation									
Smoking Addiction	Number of cigarettes smoked in one day									
Consumerism	Average number of nonfood items bought per day									

CHART 2A - APPLICATION LEARNING OBJECTIVES

As with Application 1A (and all applications for the rest of this book), complete the gray half of this chart before reading about the project and coming to lab. As you read the next section and do the research in lab, pay particular attention to the skills you rated less than "4" on the chart. **Do not complete the white half of Application charts (those with letters after the number) until asked to do so in lab** (after we've finished all work related to the research project).

2A Naturalistic Observation Objectives	**START HERE** ▼ BEFORE READING THE NEXT SECTION AND DOING THIS RESEARCH Check how well you feel you can accomplish each objective.					**FINISH HERE** ▼ YOUR LAB PROFESSOR WILL TELL YOU WHEN TO COMPLETE THESE COLUMNS (IN LAB)			
	I don't know how **1**	I know a little about this **2**	I know enough about this to guess correctly **3**	I know how to do this and/or have already done it. **4**		I don't know how **1**	I know a little about this **2**	I know enough about this to guess correctly **3**	I know how to do this and/or have already done it. **4**
1 Choose a conceptual variable related to the behavior of college students and write a good operational definition for it.									
2 Create a logical, systematic, clear data collection sheet.									
3 Apply your operational definition to systematically observe behavior.									
4 Express the results of systematic observations in terms of raw data, data handling, and data summaries, applying these terms appropriately.									
5 Define reliability and validity and apply these terms to assess and improve your operational definition.									

		I don't know how 1	I know a little about this 2	I know enough about this to guess correctly 3	I know how to do this and/or have already done it. 4		I don't know how 1	I know a little about this 2	I know enough about this to guess correctly 3	I know how to do this and/or have already done it. 4
6	Explain how validity and reliability of operational definitions and the way data are collected affect the meaning of the results.									
7	Identify and clearly express the relevant details of your research methods, including participants, materials, and procedures.									

↓

After you complete this half of the chart, read pages 57-60. Do not complete the white half until asked to do so in lab.

STUDY 2A:
NATURALISTIC OBSERVATION
OF COLLEGE STUDENTS

Image © Yuriy Rudyy/Shutterstock.com

For this research project, you and a partner will decide on a **conceptual variable** that can be identified and measured on campus. You will write two **operational definitions** of the variable, decide on one, and figure out how to apply it and how you will summarize the data collected. You'll design a data collection sheet and use it to measure the conceptual variable. Back in the lab, you'll summarize your data and report them to others in your lab for discussion. Having had experience with the conceptual variable you tried to measure, you will attempt to improve the **validity** and/or **reliability** of your definition. When this research is done, we can use the data you collect to generate testable ideas (hypotheses) that explain your observations or relate them to other observations. Chapter 3 will provide more information on summarizing data and generating hypotheses.

ADVICE FOR CHOOSING A CONCEPTUAL VARIABLE AND OPERATIONALLY DEFINING IT

A conceptual variable must be a noun or noun-phrase. It can be any behavior, characteristic, or event that can vary across individuals, over time, or in different places, and the variability must be identifiable or measureable. **You must also consider the ethics of your observations** and be sure to adhere to strict ethical guidelines, which require that we do not cause potential stress to others without the consent of the person being observed. Asking a person for permission to be watched would obviously affect his or her behavior, so your study would not be naturalistic if you have to ask for consent. It is therefore your responsibility as a researcher to make sure you do not cause any stress to the people you observe. This means you may not observe behaviors that are personal (like bathroom behavior), or stress people out by noticeably watching them for any longer than about 5 to 10 sec, depending on the situation and whether or not your own behavior, as an observer, is noticeable. To decide on a conceptual variable (CV), it might help to brainstorm (with your research partner) a list of common behaviors for this time of day, then choose something from the list. Your CV can also be some characteristic of a more general behavior. For example, you might have "eating behavior" on your list, but if you think a little deeper, there are several aspects of eating that can be described separately, like hunger, haste, nutritional awareness, or social interaction while eating. These can be operationally defined by the amount eaten or purchased, the number of chew cycles per bite, the proportion of healthy foods on the plate, or the amount of time spent talking versus eating, respectively.

Writing an operational definition for your CV is more challenging. Three pieces of advice:

1) Make sure it is something that can be directly observed, not inferred. For example, an operational definition of studiousness might be the number of books a person brings into the library, or number of times one looks away from a book during a 10-sec period (people who are studying can be watched for a little longer than others, as they are less likely to notice). While it may seem more valid to measure the amount of mental focus or the amount being learned, these aspects of studiousness are unobservable and are therefore not good operational definitions.

2) The observations you plan to make must be stated in quantifiable terms. Note the difference between "looking away from work" and "the average number of times people look away from their work." Or compare "people looking away from work" to "the number of people who look away from work." Which definitions give the reader the clearest indication of what you would observe, count and record? Also consider which is the better indicator of any particular behavioral characteristic of individuals: Measuring the characteristic itself in multiple individuals, or counting the number of people who show the characteristic? When the behavior of interest can be directly measured, it is preferable to do that, rather than counting people, as each person may display any level of the behavior.

3) Note that no operational definition will be perfect. It must match, as well as possible, the conceptual variable, but there will inevitably be complications. There may be aspects of the CV that are not captured by your definition. For example, sometimes studiousness does not involve books. But if you expand your definition to include those studying on

computers, it might become difficult to determine whether students are studying or web-surfing. Your definition should be like a net that captures as much as you can of the meaning of the conceptual variable, without catching a lot of other stuff that has nothing to do with your CV.

Important: You *should not make predictions* about what you will observe. You can (and should) record other data that are of interest to you and might be related to your conceptual variable, like the apparent gender identity of each person you observe, or whether people were in groups while being observed, but you are not setting out to test these relationships, so you should not even predict that such relationships exist. The goal of descriptive research is to describe as objectively as possible. Having a specific prediction may bias the way you observe (more on that in later chapters).

PROCEDURE 2A
(more information will be provided by your lab instructor)

This will be a ***naturalistic observation*** of people in the Lafayette College area (most likely college students).

1) You and a partner will agree upon a conceptual variable of interest, and each of you will independently write an operational definition for that variable.
2) Get together and discuss your operational definitions, decide on your best, and revise as needed using the advice described on the previous page. Remember that you can NOT interact in any way with the people you observe (e.g., smiling or saying hello to see how friendly they are would not be *naturalistic* observation).
3) Discuss where and how the conceptual variable can be measured using your definition. You should have answers to these questions before you seek approval of your project:
    -   Location for your observations? (Be precise – where will you stand/sit?)
    -   Participants? (How will you decide who should be included and excluded?)
    -   How will you avoid being noticed while observing and/or recording?
4) Design a data collection sheet, being sure to include these important elements: 1) Date and Time of Day, 2) Location, 3) Names of Observers, 4) Conceptual Variable, 5) Operational Definition, 6) A table for checking off or writing down *quick symbols* to record your observations, and 7) (if you use symbols that are not obvious) include a key somewhere on the datasheet. **Sample data sheets are shown on page 60.**
5) Upon approval of your data sheet by your instructor, leave the classroom to make your observations as a pair. Pay close attention to your assigned return time and make sure you are back in lab on time. You may travel anywhere within a 5-minute walking radius. The total length of time for your observations will be given to you when your work is approved (usually about 25-30 min).
6) When you return from your observations, complete the first part of your lab record, up to the dotted line. Fill in all relevant details of your data collection procedure, as indicated on the lab record worksheet (page 65).
7) For homework, after reading Chapter 3 on how to summarize data, you will summarize your data for an informal report to the rest of the class and complete the rest of your lab record.

SAMPLE DATA SHEETS

A

Time: 3:15 pm to 3:45pm   Date: Sept. 4, 2017
Observer Names: Shelly Scientist, Robin Researcher
Location: Lafayette College "Quad" (in front of Farinon)
Conceptual Variable: Extroversion
Defined as: For people who are walking alone, the number and type of social interactions they have with other people who walk within sight and within 10 feet from them (other pedestrians).

Subject #	Apparent Gender		Behavior (✓ = Yes)				
	Subject	Pedestrian	Smile	Wave	Words	Contact	None
1	m	m		✓			
2	F	F	✓		✓		
3	F	F					✓
4	F	m	✓				
5	m	m				✓	
6	m	F			✓		
:	:	:					
:	:	:					
∨	∨	∨					

B

Time: 3:10 to 3:40pm   Date: Jan 30, 2018
Observer Names: Steve Scientist, Rick Researcher
            (no relation to Shelly or Robin)
Location: Lafayette College Early Learning Center
Conceptual variable: Parental Affection
Defined as: Duration of parent-child hugs, hand-holds, or hand-resting-on-child contact over 10-second observation periods.

Parent-child Pair #	Apparent Gender		Seconds of Contact (out of 10 sec.)			
	Parent	Child	Hug	Hand-Hold	Hand-Resting	None
1	F	F	8			2
2	F	m		6	2	2
3	m	m	6			4
4	F	m			3	7
5	F	m			5	5
6	M	F				10
7	m	m	3	2		5
:	:	:				
:	:	:				
∨	∨	∨				

CHART 2B - APPLICATION LEARNING OBJECTIVES

2B Applying and Refining Operational Definitions Objectives	START HERE ▼ BEFORE READING THE NEXT SECTION AND DOING THIS RESEARCH Check how well you feel you can accomplish each objective.					FINISH HERE ▼ YOUR LAB PROFESSOR WILL TELL YOU WHEN TO COMPLETE THESE COLUMNS (IN LAB)			
	I don't know how 1	I know a little about this 2	I know enough about this to guess correctly 3	I know how to do this and/or have already done it. 4		I don't know how 1	I know a little about this 2	I know enough about this to guess correctly 3	I know how to do this and/or have already done it. 4
1 Gain experience applying an operational definition to collect data that describe human behavior.									
2 Create a logical, systematic, clear data collection sheet.									
3 Identify and clearly express the relevant details of your research methods.									
4 Express the results of systematic observations in terms of raw data, data handling, and data summaries, applying these terms appropriately.									
5 Define reliability and validity and apply these terms to assess and improve your operational definition.									

After you complete this half of the chart, read pages 63-64. Then go to lab and wait until the instructor tells you to complete the white half of this chart.

STUDY 2B -- APPLYING AND REFINING OPERATIONAL DEFINITIONS

Writing a good operational definition takes time, particularly if you've never done it before. A good way to decrease that first-time stress is to try applying someone else's operational definition and then try to improve that definition based on your experience using it. For this application, your instructor will provide a conceptual variable along with a few operational definitions. As a pair, you will choose one, then go out on campus for 25-30 min to measure your conceptual variable using your chosen definition. When you return, you'll reflect on how to improve its validity.

Before you leave, you will have to think about how to apply your operational definition. What location will you use? If you'll be measuring the duration of some behavior, you will need at least one stopwatch or timer. **The total observation time should be exactly the same for each participant**. If you're counting the number of times someone touches their own face while studying, you'll need to watch each person for the exact same amount of time. Watching one person for 5 seconds and another person for 8 seconds introduces unnecessary variability into your data. We'll explain why that's bad in Chapter 3, but for now, let's just agree that it's bad and try to avoid it by using a stopwatch or timer when necessary.

Your instructor will provide more details on this research project. Any changes you want to make to your chosen operational definition must be approved by your instructor. You may not extend the observation times; **observations of any one person or group of people should never exceed 10 sec.** People *do* notice when they are being watched, and it can produce an uncomfortable or "creepy" feeling that is not only unethical for this research project, but will also produce changes in behavior, negating the naturalistic component of your naturalistic observation. In most cases where more than a quick glance is needed, a 10-sec period is sufficient to collect the necessary data. When observing for more than a brief glance, it is important to use a timer so that every participant is watched for precisely the same length of time, as noted above. That is part of what it means to do "systematic observations" (see Chapter 1 glossary, p. 41).

You will also create a data sheet on blank paper so that you can collect data quickly and easily, with minimal time taking your eyes away from your observations. Sample data sheets are shown on page 60. Be sure to include all the important elements: observer name(s), location, date, time of day, CV, and operational definition. Set up a separate row for each participant or event (or group) you observe. It's usually good, if possible, to record the apparent gender identities of participants (use M and F), even when they are observed in groups, provided this does not take too much time away from observations of your behavior of interest.

Important: You should *not* make predictions about what you will observe. You can (and should) record other data that are of interest to you and might be related to your CV, like the apparent gender identity of each person you observe, or whether they have a phone out, but you are not setting out to test relationships, so you should not predict that any relationships exist. The goal of descriptive research is to describe as objectively as possible. Having a specific prediction could bias the way you observe (more on that in later chapters). When you return, you will summarize

PROCEDURE 2B

(more information will be provided by your lab instructor)

This will be a *naturalistic observation* of people on campus (most likely, college students).

1) Your instructor will assign a conceptual variable and a few operational definitions to choose from. As a pair, choose one of the definitions to use.

2) Discuss where and how the conceptual variable will be measured using your definition. You should have answers to these questions before you seek approval of your project:
   - Location for your observations? (Be precise—where will you stand/sit?)
   - Participants? (Include how will you decide who should be included and/or excluded)
   - How will you avoid being noticed while observing and/or recording?
   - What, precisely, will you record and how?
   You can fill in remaining details of your procedure after you collect data.

3) Design a data collection sheet, being sure to include these important elements: 1) Date and Time of Day, 2) Location, 3) Names of Observers, 4) Conceptual Variable, 5) Operational Definition, 6) A table for checking off or writing down *quick symbols* to record your observations, and 7) (if you use symbols that are not obvious) include a key somewhere on the datasheet. **Sample data sheets are shown on page 60.**

4) Upon approval of your data sheet by your instructor, leave the classroom to make your observations as a pair. **Pay close attention to your assigned return time and make sure you are back in lab on time.** You may travel anywhere within a 5-min walking radius. The total length of time for your observations will be given to you when your project is approved (usually about 25-30 min).

5) When you return from your observations, complete the first part of your lab record, up to the dotted line. Fill in all relevant details of your data collection procedure, as indicated on the lab record worksheet (page 65).

6) For homework, after reading Chapter 3 on how to summarize data, you will summarize your data for an informal report to the rest of the class and complete the rest of your lab record.

"I have this creepy feeling that I'm being observed."

CHART 2C – APPLICATION LEARNING OBJECTIVES

2C Introduction to Self-Report Data Objectives	START HERE BEFORE READING THE NEXT SECTION AND DOING THIS RESEARCH Check how well you feel you can accomplish each objective.					FINISH HERE YOUR LAB PROFESSOR WILL TELL YOU WHEN TO COMPLETE THESE COLUMNS (IN LAB)			
	I don't know how 1	I know a little about this 2	I know enough about this to guess correctly 3	I know how to do this and/or have already done it. 4		I don't know how 1	I know a little about this 2	I know enough about this to guess correctly 3	I know how to do this and/or have already done it. 4
1 Describe what it means for a scientific report to be biased.									
2 Define social desirability bias and explain how it can be minimized.									
3 Explain how survey questions with just two opposing answers can produce biased data.									
4 Explain how leading questions and those that make assumptions about the responder could produce biased data.									
5 Recognize examples of ambiguous and complex questions that would produce useless data.									
6 Gain experience writing good survey questions.									
7 Gain experience summarizing and evaluating self-report data.									

After you complete this half of the chart, read pages 69-72. Then go to lab and wait until the instructor tells you to complete the white half of this chart.

STUDY 2C
INTRODUCTION TO SELF-REPORT DATA

Psychologists often want to know what people are thinking and feeling. These variables are difficult to observe, but not impossible. Cognitive psychologists have used many clever research techniques to observe the unobservable – not only how people think, but even unconscious influences on thinking.[1] However, such techniques are limited and not without some controversy. The most direct way to get information about thoughts and feelings is to ask the person doing the thinking and feeling. Questionnaires produce *self-report data*: i.e., data that come from the point of view of the participants in the study, not from the researcher's point of view.

Although surveys are common in many areas of psychology and economic research, information gathered in this way should be interpreted with caution. Participants might not always tell the truth about their thoughts and feelings, especially when the truth is embarrassing or a lie would make them feel better and seems harmless. In health psychology, for example, participants might under-report problems to avoid having to undergo testing, or over-report problems to get attention. Socially unacceptable attitudes like sexism and racism are difficult to study with surveys because participants usually give socially preferred answers when asked about gender or race, even when their answer is not what they are thinking or feeling. This produces data that reflect a *social desirability bias*. Even honest people sometimes lie on questionnaires, perhaps because they are reporting what they think the researcher wants to hear, or to feel better about themselves, or in the mistaken belief that the answers don't really matter.

AVOIDING BIASED QUESTIONS

Another important consideration with self-report data is the way questions are asked. Have you ever felt the frustration of trying to answer a multiple choice question about yourself where none of the choices were quite right? Ever been tempted to rewrite the choices on a questionnaire? Chances are, those surveys were producing *biased* data. The term *biased* means that the data lean away from the truth about what we are studying, in one way or another. Of course, a question that purposefully misleads the responder to support the researcher's claims is biased, but bias is not always purposeful. Poorly written questions can lead to data that *accidentally* support (or refute) the researcher's claims. The data would still be biased simply because they do not reflect the truth. Several types of biased questions are listed below with examples.

1) FORCED (LIMITED) CHOICES

Which statement describes your attitude toward children?

a. Children are always wonderful, well-behaved, and sweet.
b. Children are always terrible, obnoxious, and mean.

---

[1] Page 498 of your lecture textbook describes ways of measuring unconscious racial prejudice. Results from these types of studies reveal hidden biases that can influence decision-making, even among people who feel very strongly that they have no racial prejudices.

A question with only two choices generally leads to biased data. Assuming adult respondents are about equally drawn to each answer, the data would suggest that 50% of adults think children are always terrible (if so, human population growth would no longer be a problem). The truth about most adults' attitudes probably lies somewhere between one of the two choices. Consider the difference in the final report if we remove the forced choice and ask this question instead:

Which statement describes your attitude toward children?

a. Children are always wonderful, well-behaved, and sweet.
b. Children are always terrible, obnoxious, and mean.
c. Children are sometimes wonderful and sometimes terrible.

Adding the last option would certainly decrease the number of respondents who choose either a or b. Most would probably choose c, and our final report might say that less than 5 or 10% of adults think children are always terrible or always wonderful, rather than 50%. So a question with comprehensive choices, covering all possible responses, leads to better, more accurate data.

2) LEADING QUESTIONS

We all know that questions with wording designed to influence the respondents' thoughts or feelings can produce biased data. But this influence can be subtle or even unintended. Researchers' own attitudes can accidentally sneak into their questions without notice. For example, below is a question that started out biased. It was edited to remove the bias by removing a leading phrase ("exhaust-free"). Answer it yourself, but do it quickly, without too much thought:

I am happy about the increasing number of clean-air electric cars in the city.

1	2	3	4	5
Strongly Disagree	Disagree	Neutral	Agree	Strongly Agree

Unless you feel strongly about this issue, you probably answered at least a 3, even if you have some reservations about electric cars. Usually, the questions you see on surveys have undergone editing to remove bias, but sometimes, a little remains. It took several re-reads before I realized the question should have been written this way:

I am happy about the increasing number of electric cars in the city.

1	2	3	4	5
Strongly Disagree	Disagree	Neutral	Agree	Strongly Agree

The words, "clean-air" have become so closely associated with electric cars that I had to review the question several times before I noticed that they were leading words. When you're asking for the truth, watch out for the adjectives you use in your question! If the noun can be clearly understood without them, take them out. The second question would best reflect true feelings on electric cars.

3) MAKING ASSUMPTIONS ABOUT RESPONDERS

What day of the week do you feel sad? _____

This question is biased because it assumes the responder IS sad at least one day a week, and therefore traps the responder into answering in a way that might not reflect his or her true thoughts or feelings. An unbiased way to ask the same question would be:

What day of the week, if any, do you feel the saddest? _____

4) AMBIGUITY/LACK OF CLARITY

When was your first kiss? _____

The responses might vary from "two minutes after I was born," if the responder is thinking of his/her mother or father, to "age 15," if the responder is thinking of a way of describing when the first romantic kiss happened. Note that even the word, "when" is ambiguous. Some respondents might provide an associated event, such as "when I fell in love," or a period of development, like "while I was in middle school." If the researcher wants to know the age at which most people experience their first romantic kiss, a clearer (less biased) way of asking this question would be:

How old were you when you first kissed someone in a romantic way? _____

5) COMPLEXITY

Sometimes asking too many things in one question leads to biased self-report data because the responder doesn't know which question to answer. Consider the following example:

I plan to take the subway instead of driving and install energy-saving lights at home.

1	2	3	4	5
Strongly Disagree	Disagree	Neutral	Agree	Strongly Agree

If the responder agrees with part of the statement but not with the rest, an honest response becomes impossible. The following two questions should replace the one above:

I plan to take the subway instead of driving.

1	2	3	4	5
Strongly Disagree	Disagree	Neutral	Agree	Strongly Agree

I plan to install energy-saving lights at home.

1	2	3	4	5
Strongly Disagree	Disagree	Neutral	Agree	Strongly Agree

Designing good, unbiased questions is a skill that comes with practice. The purpose of the following research application is to provide an opportunity for you to practice designing questions and gathering and summarizing descriptive survey data, and to see how the wording of questions can influence final reports.

PROCEDURE 2C
(more information will be provided by your lab instructor)

1) The class will discuss and decide on several topics of interest to most students. Examples might be environmentalism, study habits, athleticism, or music-listening preferences.
2) The class will break up into groups. Each group will be assigned a topic and asked to come up with an unbiased question on the topic. The questions may be open-ended (one-or two-word answers only) multiple choice, Likert-type (questions that provide a scale, for example from 1 to 5, where 1 = strongly disagree and 5 = strongly agree), or any other type. When that is done, should be handed in immediately.
3) The group will then be randomly assigned a type of bias from the above list of 5 types, and asked to rewrite their original question in a way that exemplifies that type of bias. It must be a question measuring the SAME conceptual variable as your original, unbiased question. This will work best if it is as similar as possible to the original, except for the bias. When it's complete, hand it in immediately.
4) Your professor will type all the questions into a single questionnaire that will be made available to all students, either on paper or electronically.
5) All students will answer the questions anonymously, and summary statistics will be computed either instantly or for the next week's lab.

"This is interesting... 70% of the respondents to our survey said they don't respond to surveys."

GLOSSARY OF TERMS AND EXAMPLES

Where to find these terms: EP = *Experience Psychology!* (this book),
MD = Myers & DeWall, 2018 (lecture textbook). Figures are in EP.

Analog Observation: Observational research done in a laboratory setting.

> ***Example:*** Gibson's original research using the visual cliff to determine whether crawling infants can perceive depth (MD 234). Note that Myers and DeWall refer to these studies as "experiments," but no manipulation of variables is indicated, just one visual cliff and the observation of how babies reacted to it. As described on page 234 (MD), it is an excellent example of descriptive research with analog observations.
> ***Where to find this term:*** EP 50-51, Fig. 2.3

Biased: Reflecting something other than the best measure or estimate of the truth; leaning or leading away from the truth. A biased question leads or traps the responder into giving an answer that does not reflect his or her true thoughts or feelings, whether intentionally or not.

> ***Examples:*** Biased marketing researchers tend to write biased questions about the products they represent to get higher ratings of those products from consumers. As an exaggerated example, "To what extent do you agree with the statement that this beautiful, wonderful, life-saving product is worth buying for this super-low price?" Another example of bias is the infamous forced-choice question, "Have you stopped beating your children yet, yes or no?"
> ***Where to find this term:*** EP 69-72

Case Study: In-depth research focusing on one entity (e.g., one person, one family, one social organization, one animal, or one business) that usually has some interesting or unusual characteristic.

> ***Example***: H.M. was a patient who underwent brain surgery to remove certain areas of his brain as a treatment for severe epilepsy. The epilepsy was cured, but he displayed fascinating changes in his memory functions, which were studied intensely for many years after the surgery. He died in 2008, at which point his real name was revealed. Read more about him online by typing this article title into your search bar: "H. M., an Unforgettable Amnesiac, Dies at 82"
> ***Where to find this term:*** EP 49, Fig. 2.3, MD 26-27

Conceptual variable (CV): An event, characteristic or behavior of interest, singled out for study. CVs are usually given broad labels that can mean slightly different things to different people.

> ***Examples:*** anger, height, quality of education, happiness, intelligence, friendliness...
> ***Where to find this term:*** EP 51-53, 57-59, 63-64

Data Handling: Describes *how* the data were summarized (not the actual data, but what you did with them in order to summarize them).

> ***Examples:*** Assume you measured anger by counting the number of times people shouted. If you simply counted frequency of shouting, your data handling would say that you "calculated the total number of times the behavior occurred during the observation period," or, "reported the sum of all instances of shouting."

If you wanted to report the prevalence of shouting, your data handling would say that you "calculated the proportion [or percent] of students who shouted out of all those observed." To report proportion, you divide the number of participants who shouted by the total number of participants observed, and to get percent, multiply that by 100.

If you quantified certain aspects of a variable, such as durations, distances or sizes, you will most likely compute an average (or "mean"). For example, "we calculated the mean duration of the shouts."

Where to find this term: EP 66, 67 (Lab Record)

Descriptive Research: A study that measures or identifies one or more conceptual variables with the goal of describing it (them) in some useful way.

Examples: Studies that describe the characteristics of love (see MD, p 515-516)
Where to find this term: EP 47-49,5 59, 63, Fig 2.1, 2.2 MD 25-29

Duration Data: Numbers that describe how long something lasts from beginning to end.

Examples: Studies of drug effects often consider the duration of those effects (see tolerance and addiction, MD 112)
Where to find this term: EP 51

Exploratory Research: A study designed to explore, generally without specific goals or predictions.

Examples: Early studies of the brains of humans and animals, and some current studies of the living brains of humans (MD, 66-68).
Where to find this term: 47, 52, Fig. 2.3

Falsifiability see Chapter 1 Glossary

Frequency Data: Numbers that describe how often something occurs in a given period of time.

Examples: Studies of behavior modification might use frequency data to monitor how often a person engages in an undesired behavior over a given period of time, such as the number of cigarettes smoked per day, to observe the effects of therapy on how many cigarettes the patient smokes per day. Keeping track of these data during smoking cessation therapy can help determine the effectiveness of the therapy.
Where to find this term: EP 51

Naturalistic Observation: Research that observes behaviors or events in their natural settings, without interference or manipulation.

Example: Researchers observed college students as they were leaving a parking lot and recorded whether or not they were using their cell phones as they drove away (Cramer, et al, 2007)
Where to find this term: EP 50, 57, 59, 63-64, Fig. 2.3

Observational Descriptive Study: A type of research designed to describe some conceptual variable in great detail by systematically observing it. The variable can be observed as it exists in nature (*naturalistic observation*) or in a laboratory setting (*analog observation*).

Examples: See *Naturalistic Observation* and *Analog Observation*
Where to find this term: EP 49-50, Fig. 2.3

Operational Definition: A way of defining a conceptual variable so that it can be identified and/or measured. Or, defining a variable in terms of the operations used to identify and/or measure it.

> ***Examples:*** Anger might be operationally defined as…
>
> 1) a furrowed brow combined with tight pressing together of the lips in a straight line or the corners of the mouth angled downward.
>
> 2) any instance of yelling directed at another person or object.
>
> 3) for an operational definition of alien anger, see page 52, right-hand box).
>
> ***Where to find this term:*** EP 52-53, 57-59, 63-64; MD 25

Prevalence Data: Numbers that represent how many times a behavior or event happens out of all the possible times it could happen.

> ***Example:*** Beaver and Barnes (2012) counted drunk driving convictions among people who had twins who had also been convicted of drunk driving, and found that having an identical twin who had already been convicted of drunk driving was associated with a higher prevalence of drunk driving convictions than having a previously convicted fraternal twin (MD 130)
>
> ***Where to find this term:*** EP 51

Reliability: The consistency with which an operational definition can be applied by different observers and/or at different times. Reliable definitions are clear and unambiguous. To improve the reliability of an operational definition, ask yourself, "How can I remove any ambiguity from this definition?"

> ***Examples:*** A reliable operational definition of a smile might be "curving the corners of the mouth upward." By this definition, a smile is easily identified and fairly unambiguous. A less reliable operational definition of happiness might be "the expression of pleasure." There are many different ways to express pleasure, only some of which involve smiling. (e.g., clapping and crying)
>
> ***Where to find this term:*** EP 53, 57; MD 369

Results: The *summarized version* of the data. This does not include raw data unless they are being used to stress a point or as an example. Results are obtained from procedures described in the data handling section, and should be reported in full sentences that summarize what was observed using numbers. See Chapter 3 for more information.

> ***Example (correct):*** "Of the participants observed (N=43), 20% shouted at least once during the 30-minute observation period."
>
> ***NOT an Example (incorrect):*** "Participant 1 shouted once. Participant 2 did not shout. Participant 3 shouted…" (These statements report "raw data," not Results, and should not be included in the Results unless they are used to stress a point or as an example.)
>
> ***Where to find this term:*** Lab Records and Lab Reports (e.g., EP 66)

Self-Report Data: Numbers or information gathered from the point of view of the participant in a study, rather than from the researcher's observations.

> ***Examples:*** The answers to these two questions would produce self-report data:
>
> 1) Please state your age, in years: _____ .
>
> 2) Do you feel that psychology is an interesting subject (circle one):
>
> Yes   No   Not Sure
>
> ***Where to find this term:*** EP 69-71

Social Desirability Bias: The under-reporting of socially unacceptable attitudes and behaviors based on self-report data, due to the tendency of responders to choose socially acceptable or preferred (desirable) answers to questions.

    Example: Voter exit polls can reflect social desirability bias, particularly if opposition to an idea or a candidate has been kept quiet due to threats or fear of retaliation.

    Where to find this term: EP 69

Systematic: Having a clearly defined plan or system for completing a task (see Systematic Observation, Chapter 1 Glossary).

    Examples (systematic): Exploration of solar storms by observing the sun at regular intervals and measuring size and temperature of sunspots; Description of parent–child attachments by observing specifically defined behaviors indicating attachment or lack of attachment; Comparing GPA from college records with number of high school math classes taken, from high school transcripts; Studying the effects of money on ratings of happiness by giving precise amounts of money and surveying mood.

    Examples (NOT systematic): Taking a piece of paper and a pencil out onto the quad, intending to write down random notes about the things you see; Simple people-watching; Trying to recall something you saw a while ago, but really can't remember well.

    Where to find this term: EP 49, 50, 63

Validity: The *accuracy* of an operational definition as a measurement of a conceptual variable. A valid operational definition is one that captures the actual meaning of the conceptual variable. To improve the validity of an operational definition, ask yourself, "What can I do to make a better match between what I am trying to measure and what I am actually measuring?"

    Examples: If the conceptual variable is intelligence, a valid operational definition might be "the average speed with which a person solves 10 puzzles testing logic, spatial, and mathematical reasoning." A less valid operational definition might be "average speed with which a person adds, subtracts, multiplies and divides 10 random pairs of single digits." Note that both definitions are very specific and would probably yield fairly consistent results for any one person at different times, but the first is probably more *valid* because it does a better job of capturing the actual meaning of intelligence, which is more than just speed in arithmetic.

    Where to find this term: EP 52-53, 57, 63; MD 370

Variable: Anything that changes or can be made to change.

    Examples: Color of the sky (during sunset, cloudy, etc.); age; environmentalism (from person to person or over time); the color of carpeting (from room to room or over the years); Presidents; Ice cream flavors; Activity; TV programming; Netflix charges; Exercise; Gym equipment; Clothing; Pixar movies; Toe nail clippers (and clippings); Dinner menus; Airplane ticket prices; Couch softness; Couch attractiveness; Couch locations; Couch colors; Couch styles; Couch occupants; How much you miss home; How boring you find this list of examples; How much you love your pets; How many pets you have... (This list could go on forever.)

    Where to find this term: EP 47-48, 50-53, 57-59, 63-64, 69-72 (& most of the rest of EP)

CHAPTER 3
SUMMARIZING DATA
AND GENERATING HYPOTHESES

CONCEPTS

APPLICATION

GLOSSARY OF TERMS AND EXAMPLES

CHART 3 - CONCEPT LEARNING OBJECTIVES

	Chapter 3 Concepts Objectives	**START HERE** ▼ **BEFORE READING THE NEXT SECTION** Check how well you feel you can accomplish each objective.					**FINISH HERE** ▼ **AFTER YOU HAVE READ UP TO THE NEXT CHART** Check how well you feel you can accomplish each objective, and fix any inaccurate answers on the left.			
		I don't know how **1**	I know a little about this **2**	I know enough about this to guess correctly **3**	I know how to do this and/or have already done it. **4**		I don't know how **1**	I know a little about this **2**	I know enough about this to guess correctly **3**	I know how to do this and/or have already done it. **4**
1	Demonstrate correct use of the terms "raw data," "sample," and "population."									
2	Recognize examples of categorical, ordinal, and interval data.									
3	Explain how best to summarize different types of raw data.									
4	When summarizing interval data, explain when it is best to use a mean and when one should use a median.									
5	Describe two ways of expressing how much the scores vary in an interval data set.									
6	Explain what the standard deviation tells you about how the scores vary in a data set.									

		I don't know how 1	I know a little about this 2	I know enough about this to guess correctly 3	I know how to do this and/or have already done it. 4		I don't know how 1	I know a little about this 2	I know enough about this to guess correctly 3	I know how to do this and/or have already done it. 4
7	Enter data and calculate means and SDs using MS Excel.									
8	Explain the difference between a correlational and a cause-and-effect hypothesis and provide an example of each.									

↓

After you complete this half of the chart, read pages 81-92. Then return to page 79 and complete the white half of this chart.

↓

After you complete this half of the chart, go to page 93 and complete the gray half of Chart 3A. Then read pp. 95 to 96 to prepare for the research you'll do in lab.

FROM RAW DATA TO MEANINGFUL SUMMARIES

Every scientific endeavor is an attempt to better understand the truth about the natural, physical world (or universe). In psychology, the reason we make observations is to determine the truth about some behavior, event, or characteristic of interest. Multiple observations are needed because they will be a better representation of the truth than just one observation. But multiple observations must be summarized into a concise, understandable statement that accurately reflects what we observed.

The data collected in Chapter 2 were an attempt to describe the truth about a conceptual variable (CV). These attempts start with **raw data**, the numbers directly produced by our observations (including survey responses). Data may eventually be used to generate testable ideas (hypotheses) describing or explaining relationships between the things we observed, but before that can happen, the raw data must be summarized in an accurate and meaningful way. This chapter will present an introduction to the process of raw data handling. This will not be an exhaustive list of all the ways that data can be summarized. Instead, we will focus on the basic information and skills needed to meaningfully summarize a small data set. We will then see how a data summary can lead to a hypothesis, and define two types of hypotheses that differ in how they are tested. Although we will use your descriptive data to learn terms and practice skills, it is important to keep in mind that these basic skills are necessary in all other types of research covered in this course. A basic understanding of these terms and procedures is increasingly valuable in our data-driven culture.

When summarizing and reporting data, the goal is to clearly express all the *relevant* details of one's observations with as few words and numbers as possible. Consider this report:

> *Over a 30-min period, we observed 15 people using their cell phones as they walked across campus.*

The first problem is that there is no meaningful context in which to consider the number 15. Is that a lot of people using cell phones for a 30-min period? If 150 people were walking across campus, seeing only 15 with cell phones suggests that they are not commonly in use (only 10% of those observed had cell phones). If just 15 people walked across campus during those 30 minutes, then 100% were using phones. Maybe switching to percentage would improve the report:

> *Over a 30-min period, we observed that 10% of people walking across campus were using their cell phones.*

Better, right? But does it tell you everything you need to know? Consider a different example:

> *Over a 30-min period, 100% of the people observed in a gym were walking with a limp.*

If only two people were observed in the gym, the fact that both of them (100% of the people observed) were both limping is no big deal. But if 50 people were observed, and 100% were limping, that should lead to a meaningful hypothesis! Perhaps the equipment in that gym is dangerous, or maybe the "gym" is actually a physical therapy site focusing on leg injuries. Thus, when summarizing with a percent, the number of observations is critically important information. We will call that number "N." Usually, a capital N refers to all the people observed in a single study, and a lowercase n refers to a subset of people in a single study. For example, a study with four days' worth of observations might have N = 100, with n = 25 on each day. There are exceptions to these rules, but we'll save them for a more advanced class in statistics. Case studies, like the fascinating story of Phineas Gage, the man who had a 3-foot-long iron rod pass through his brain and lived to tell about it, are often called "N of 1" studies because they are based on observations of just one person.

Better evidence for or against ideas can be found in studies with a much higher N. The more observations, the more we can trust those observations to represent the real behaviors of a larger set of people, called the research **population** (the people about whom the researcher wishes to draw conclusions). Returning to the cell phone data summaries in the first two examples on page 81, the population is the set of all college students who walk across campus, day after day. As it would be impossible to study every single student walking across campus, a research **sample** is selected. If the sample consists of everyone who happens to be walking across campus during preset, convenient observation periods, it would be called a **convenience sample**, because the people who are included in the study are only those who are (conveniently) walking across campus while the researcher watches. Convenience samples are chosen at the researcher's discretion, not randomly. A **random sample** is one in which every member of the population has an equal chance of being selected for the study. To get a truly random sample of the population of all students who walk across campus, we would have to select our participants using an arbitrary and random process, unrelated to the time of day or day of week that they would be walking across campus. Convenience samples are obviously much easier to obtain, and are more often used in research than truly random samples.

Coming back to our cell phone example, then, critical readers will want to know the value of N. Thus, the best way report the data would be:

> *Over a 30-min period, we observed that 10% of people walking across campus (N =150) were using their cell phones.*

This way of reporting provides all the relevant information for the critical reader to understand the meaning of the data. Also recall that the goal in reporting data is to summarize observations *meaningfully* and *concisely*. By simply inserting "*(N = 150)*" after the description of the sample that was observed, in this case, "people walking across campus," we add important information in the most concise way. But this is just one example. The best way to summarize raw data depends on the type of data.

THE BEST SUMMARY DEPENDS ON THE TYPE OF DATA

Placing observations in categories, such as people who use cell phones while walking versus those who do not, produces *categorical data* (also called *nominal data*). Another example would be the number of students majoring in Math, Science, English, or History. The best way to summarize categorical data is to report either the frequency (number of observations) in each category or the percentage or proportion within the category out of the total observed. The last italicized report of cell phone use above is a good example of how to report categorical data in percent form.

Ranking things in some meaningful order, such as first, second, third place, and so forth, produces *ordinal data*, meaning that the order of the data matters. The number from each observation does not represent a measureable amount, merely a specific order or placement relative to other observations. In other words, a data set that puts observations in order, like the winners in a race, does not tell us whether first and second place were very close at the finish-line or 50 meters apart. Each observation is simply given a rank relative to other observations. These data can be summarized by reporting the *median* (middle) ranking within any ordinal data set, but it must be remembered that the amount of difference between any two rankings cannot be determined from the data. An example of an ordinal data report would be:

> *When college students (N=15) were each given 10 songs to rank from most-liked to least-liked (with 1 being the top rank), the median rank for Lady Gaga's "Bad Romance" was 6, whereas the median rank of an a cappella version of the same song was 3.*

One can interpret this to mean that students more often gave the acapella version a rank closer to the top, while the Lady Gaga version was more often ranked toward the bottom half of the list of songs. Yet, the 3 and the 6 do not tell us how much more liked the acapella version was, any more than race results tell us how close the race was.

Interval data are measurements that can be compared in meaningful units, allowing quantifiable comparisons between different observations. For example, if you observe school spirit by counting the number of school logos being worn by each person on campus, each student you observe provides a number that reflects that individual's amount of school spirit. You can then argue that the difference in school spirit between a 5 (wearing 5 logos) and a 1 (wearing 1 logo) is bigger than the difference between a 3 and a 1. Unlike ordinal data, the difference between two interval measurements (data points) has a real, quantifiable meaning. The same CV can be measured multiple ways, and interval data are generally preferred whenever possible. This makes sense because interval data can be converted to ordinal by ranking the measurements, but ordinal data cannot be converted to interval because those particular measurements are missing. To measure the popularity of musical artists with interval data instead of ordinal data, we could provide the same songs and count the number of times each participant listened to each song over a one-month period of time (assuming people listen to what they like). Then we cannot only say which songs were listened to the most, in order (ordinal data), but we can also say how many more times the a cappella version was played compared to the original, and compared to other songs.

SUMMARIZING INTERVAL DATA

Interval data are usually summarized with an arithmetic average (add all the scores and divide by the number of scores), or with a median, which is simply the middle score when all scores are listed from lowest to highest. The raw data will determine which summary is more appropriate. The arithmetic average (mean) is used to summarize interval data when the measurements look "normal" (Figure 3.1a). That is, the majority of the scores are close to the average, with about the same number of measurements above the mean as below. Loosely defined, this is a normally distributed data set. A median is more often used when the data are skewed (Figure 3.1b). A *skewed* data set has considerably fewer scores above the average compared to below it, or vice versa.

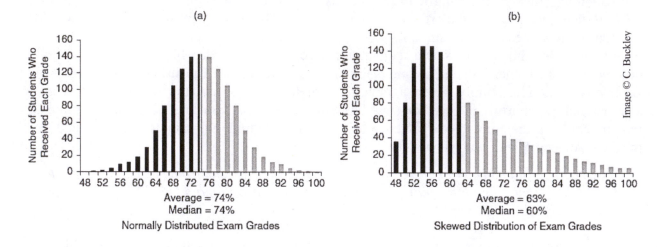

Figure 3.1. A normal distribution of scores is shown on the left (panel a) and a skewed distribution is shown on the right (panel b).

When reporting means, there is another important piece of information (besides N) that the reader will want to know about: **variability**. Even in measuring the length of a piece of rope, perfect precision is nearly impossible. Measuring human behavior is obviously more complicated! There will always be some variability when behaviors are measured. The *amount* of variability is critical information. Imagine a child has a fever and you're using an electronic thermometer to see what her temperature is. To get the true temperature, you take a reading three times and calculate an average. Suppose the three readings are 98, 101, and 104. The average is 101, but the temperatures vary by as much as 3 degrees from the average. Would you trust that the correct temperature was actually 101? For comparison, suppose readings only deviate from the average by 1/10 of one degree, such as 100.9, 101, and 101.1. The average is still 101, but now you instinctively trust that average more. The lower variability is the reason for that trust. Whenever an average is reported, the skeptical reader will always want to know how much the measurements vary around that average.

From now on, we'll call the average a "***mean***," to use the preferred term, and with every mean we report, we will always report an estimate of the variability in the measurements. There are many ways to report variability; the simplest is the ***range***. Range can be expressed by reporting both the lowest and the highest score (e.g., the range of the first set of temperatures in the previous paragraph was 98 to 104; for the second set, the range was 100.9 to 101.1). You can also report the range more concisely with just one number, equal to the difference between the highest and lowest score (e.g., 104 minus 98 equals a range of 6). A range of 6 is greater variability than a range of 0.2 for the second set, meaning you can trust the mean more in the second set. However, range is not commonly used in scientific literature because there are better and more informative ways to express variability, one of which is the standard deviation.

Standard deviation (SD) is a number that reflects exactly what the name implies: a standardized calculation of the deviations from the mean (i.e., differences between each measurement and the mean of all the measurements). The SD is a way of expressing how closely bunched the numbers in a set are around their mean. The *range* can only tell you the how far apart two scores are, the lowest and the highest. The rest of the scores could be anywhere between those two. But the standard deviation allows you to estimate where *most* of the scores are, relative to the mean. You will learn the formula to calculate a standard deviation in more advanced courses. Here, we will focus on how to interpret the SD.

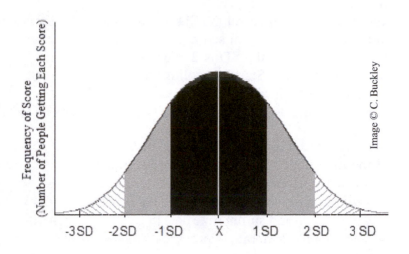

Figure 3.2. The standard deviation (SD) tells how much the scores in a data set differ from the mean of the whole set ($\overline{X}$). In a *normally distributed* data set, 68% of the scores fall within 1 SD of the mean (black area under curve); 95% of scores fall within 2 SD of the mean (black plus gray areas); and 99% of scores fall within 3SD of the mean (black, gray and scored areas). Less than 1% of the scores will fall in the white areas, more than 3 SD from the average of the data set.

In simplest terms, the smaller the SD, the closer the majority of the measurements are to the mean, and the more we can trust the mean as an estimate of the truth. But the SD is much more useful than that. In a normally distributed set of measurements (randomly taken from a large population), we can estimate that most (about 68%) of the measurements will fall within one SD above or below the mean, and almost all (about 95%) of the measurements will fall within two SD of the mean, and all but 1 out of 100 will fall within 3 SD of the mean (Figure 3.2).

For example, suppose creativity was measured in a large group of children with normally distributed creativity scores, and the mean score was 25 with an SD of 4. This means that about 68% of the children scored between 21 (25 minus 4) and 29 (25 plus 4). Doubling the SD to 8, we can also estimate that 95% of the children scored between 17 (25 minus 8) and 33 (25 plus 8). Tripling the SD gives us 12, so we can further estimate that 99% of the scores are between 13 (25 minus 12) and 37 (25 plus 12). This utility makes SD a preferred measure of variability.

Table 3.1. Reporting data summaries

Type Of Data	Report Summary	Also Report
Categorical (nominal)	Frequency, percentage	N (with percent)
Ordinal	Median	N
Interval (normally distributed)	Mean	N, SD
Interval (not normally distributed)	Median	N

Knowing how to interpret the SD is quite practical: Suppose you take a proficiency exam for a job you really want, and you score a 47. You ask the examiner: Is that a good score? Yes, she says; the mean is 40 and the SD is 2. Now you can easily determine how 99% of the people who take this test score on it. Start by tripling the SD (2 x 3 = 6). Subtracting 6 from the mean gives you 34, and adding 6 to the mean gives you 46, so 99% of the people who take this exam probably score between 34 and 46. By this measure, your score is exceptionally high.

In conclusion, summarizing data is a matter of knowing what type of data you have and presenting all the important aspects of the data set in a concise and meaningful way (Table 3.1). Microsoft Excel can be used to calculate all of these data summaries, and many others. Several of them, you probably already know how to calculate by hand. After a brief concept check, we will focus on how to manage and summarize data in Excel. On page 90, we continue with important information on using data to generate hypotheses, and the two basic types of hypotheses you can generate.

CONCEPT CHECK (answers in Appendix B)

1. What would a data set look like if its SD = 0 and its range = 5?

a) All the scores in the data set would be the same.
b) All the scores in the data set would be in the shaded regions of Figure 3.2.
c) It is impossible to have a data set with an SD of 0 and a range of 5.

2. A normally distributed, large sample from the "American Time Use Survey" (2012) found Americans (ages 15 & up) watch an average of 2.8 hr of TV per day. If the standard deviation was 0.4 hr, how many hours of TV would about 68% of Americans probably watch per day?

a) between 0.4 and 0.8 hr
b) between 2.4 and 3.2 hr
c) between 2.0 and 3.6 hr
d) between 3.2 and 3.6 hr

SUMMARIZING DATA WITH MS EXCEL

Microsoft Excel is a data handling (spreadsheet) tool that easily calculates percentages, means, and standard deviations (among many other things), and can be used to create charts and other kinds of data summaries. Students taking this course will probably have varying levels of experience using MS Excel. For this reason, Excel instructions are given here in separate, labeled boxes. If you already know how to sort data in Excel, you can skip Box 3.1. If you already know how to calculate a percentage, a mean, and an SD in Excel, skip Box 3.2. Those who have never used MS Excel should read all the boxed instructions and follow along using MS Excel on any computer. Because new versions of this program are released every few years, please persist through minor differences in appearance that may occur between these instructions and the version you are using. The basic steps will be very similar, whether you are using a PC or a Mac, and regardless of versions.

BOX 3.1 – Entering, Selecting and Sorting Data in MS Excel

When you open MS Excel, it will display a blank "worksheet" (one spreadsheet from a "workbook."). You may have to select "open a workbook," depending on your version of Excel. A worksheet is a grid of rows (identified by numbers going down the left side) and columns (identified by letters going across the top). Each box created by the intersection of a column and row is called a cell, and cells are named using row and column headings. In Figure 3.3a, the number 4.5 is in the cell that would be named B3.

Figure 3.3a shows the number of hours of television watched per day by 10 different people. To recreate the data set on your own computer, click on each cell, typing the data for that cell, and hit <enter>. Excel will automatically move you to the next box down (or over). Each cell is its own small document or writing space. With one notable exception (described in Box 3.2), clicking on a new cell starts a new writing space in that cell. If something is already there, Excel will automatically replace it with whatever you type.

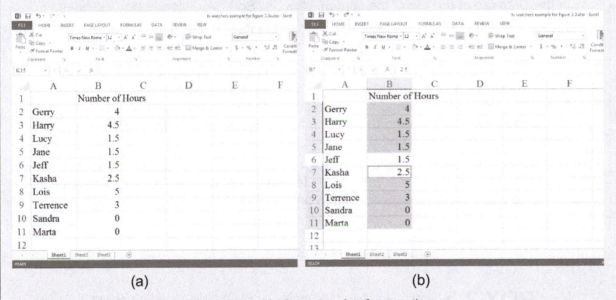

(a)   (b)

Figure 3.3. MS Excel spreadsheets with data samples for practice.

To edit the contents of a cell without completely erasing it, double-click inside the cell. This will produce an insertion cursor, which allows editing just like a normal text document. To erase everything in a cell, click on it once and hit backspace or delete. When strange things happen that you didn't want, click on everyone's best friend: the undo button at the top of the screen. For example, you might type "1.5," hit <enter>, and see "Jan 5." You might have accidentally typed "1/5," which Excel interpreted as a date rather than a number. It will now auto-format every attempt to correct this mistake into as a new date, so typing over the date won't work. (Excel will politely interpret every attempt as another date.) The undo button is the best way to fix these problems. It's at the top left of the worksheet on a PC (near the save icon), or top left-center on a Mac (near the paintbrush icon).

To work with the data, you have to select the cells containing the data you want to use. Left-clicking in any cell selects *only* that cell. Multiple adjacent cells are unfortunately called a "range," not to be confused with the range that expresses the variability in a data set. To select a range of cells, click and drag from the beginning to the end of the selection. Most of the selected cells will turn blue or gray, but one will remain white (any typing you do while multiple cells are selected automatically goes into the white cell). To select cells that are not adjacent to each other, hold down the control key (command key on a Mac) while making separate selections. Try it now. Select cells B2 through B5 and B7 through B11 in one selection. It should end up looking like Figure 3.3b. Cell B6 is white because it has not been selected. Cell B7 is white with a darker border because it is part of the selected set, and anything you type at this point will go into cell B7.

Excel's superpowers include the ability sort, summarize, and make charts from the information in multiple cells (numbers or words) quickly and easily. Sorting data is one of Excel's most useful features (and that is saying something!). To sort the set of data in order from those who watched TV most to least:

Select all the data, including names, by clicking on A1 and dragging to B11. Make sure you include BOTH columns (A and B) in your selection in order to keep names linked to the correct data. Note that your selection includes the "header" or label for the data set, "Number of Hours."

In the Data tab at the top of the screen, click on "Sort." A dialogue box will open.

Check the box for "My data has headers" to tell Excel that the top row is a label, not data. Using the drop-down menu labeled "Sort By," choose "Number of Hours."

Using the drop-down menu labeled "Order," choose "Largest to Smallest," and click "OK." Your data will instantly rearrange from most to least hours spent watching TV. The names should rearrange as well to stay with the correct data points. If they don't, then undo everything and go back to the first step (Select all the data). Make sure you select BOTH columns, A and B.

Try sorting the data alphabetically by name, or from smallest to largest number of hours. When you feel comfortable with the sorting feature, click the "undo" button repeatedly to return the data to their original order before proceeding to Box 3.2.

BOX 3.2 – Summarizing Data: Calculations in MS Excel

Start by creating a data file that looks like the worksheet shown in Figure 3.3a.

Calculations sometimes require typing special characters into a cell. To avoid excessive use of quotation marks, we will use bold font and extra space around anything you should type into a cell, like this: **hello** For the most common calculations, you won't need to type anything because Excel has built-in formulas for a wide variety of data summaries. If your data are set up in one column, a calculation can be performed without even having to select the range of cells containing the data. Simply click on the next cell at the bottom of your column of data cells, choose a formula, hit <enter>, and excel will provide the answer! For example, to calculate the mean number of hours that these people watched TV (based on data shown in Box 3.1, Figure 3.3a), click in cell B12, then go to the top of the screen and click on the "Formulas" tab. Look for the "AutoSum" option to the left. Click on the small triangle below the word "Autosum" to see a list of other automatic formulas. Select "Average" from the list. Then hit <enter>. To borrow an old Southern phrase, Excel gives you the average "faster than green grass through a goose."

Recall that whenever you report a mean, you will always want to report the standard deviation (SD) along with it. Here's how to calculate the SD: Click on the cell where you want the SD to appear and type **= stdev(** Then select the range of cells and hit <enter>. The SD of the cells you selected will appear in the box (again, much faster than that goose can process green grass). Excel has a built-in SD button, as well, but the path to get to that function will depend on the version of Excel, and you can always type **= stdev(** to get the same information.

It is also possible to type a formula of your own to "manually" calculate the sum (or average, or anything else) for any set of cells. Typing **=** in any cell starts a formula, which changes the way Excel responds when you click on the next new cell. Recall from Box 3.1 that clicking on a new cell should start a new writing space. But typing **=** tells Excel that the next cell you click should be entered into the formula. As an example, let's use cell D10 to calculate the sum of cells B3, B5, and B7.

Click on D10 and type **=** . Excel is now ready for you to enter a formula.

Click on cell B3. Notice that Excel enters "B3" after the = sign.

Type **+** and then click cell B5.

Type **+** and then click cell B7.

Hit <enter>, and the sum of cells B3, B5, and B7 will appear in cell D10. (It should be 8.5.)

You can also sum any set of cells by typing **= sum(** and then selecting each cell you want to add, using the control key as described in Box 3.1 to select nonadjacent cells. Try that in cell D11. Hit <enter>, and you should have the same answer in cells D10 and D11. Thus, you can use built-in formulas or you can type out formulas to perform any mathematical calculation you want on the content of any cells.

Let's calculate a percentage using a formula. From our TV-watching data set, we have already calculated the total number of hours watched by three people, Harry (B3), Jane (B5), and Kasha (B7). What percentage of that total time was contributed by Harry, who watched for 4.5 hr?

To get that percentage:

Type **=** in the cell where you want the answer (any blank cell).

Click B3, as this contains the part of the total that we want to translate into percentage.

Type **/** (the symbol for "divided by").

Click on the cell containing the total (either D10 or D11).

Type ***100** to convert the proportion into a percent. (Excel uses * as a multiplication symbol).

Hit <enter>. Excel returns the percentage of time that Harry contributed to the total watched by all three people. (About 53%! Harry should probably watch less TV.)

Play with Excel's features! Next time you have a set of numbers to add for any class or project, type them into Excel instead of a calculator. When working with larger data sets, it's much easier to find and fix mistakes in MS Excel than on a calculator!

GENERATING AND TESTING HYPOTHESES

In trying to understand the natural, physical world, it is not enough to merely describe conceptual variables. Often, the more interesting and important questions lie in the relationships between those variables. Descriptive or exploratory data, once summarized, can inform our guesses about relationships, and those guesses are called hypotheses (singular: hypothesis).

It is important to note that the same data used to *generate* a hypothesis cannot be used as *evidence for* that hypothesis. The data might suggest a pattern, and that pattern might make you think that something is true. But the only way to know whether it has any evidence is to test it, and your descriptive data haven't done that yet. For example, maybe while you were watching students walk across campus, a lot more females were using phones than males (or vice versa). That makes you think: Maybe phone use is related to apparent gender. This would be your hypothesis, but you do not have *evidence* to support it! Not yet!

The human mind is very good at spotting patterns. Often, they are no more than accidental happenings, like finding a potato chip shaped like a dog. One observation does not allow you to generalize to all the chips in the bag. Neither does observing a surprising or unique relationship make it generalizable to a broader population. You can't know whether or not any observed relationship is unique until you test it. Let's say while you're watching students walk across campus, every person you identify as male has his phone out, and every person you identify as female does not. This suggests that a relationship *might* exist between apparent gender and phone use, but no generalizable hypothesis has *evidence* unless some unique event is *predicted* based on that hypothesis, *and* subsequent observations fall in line with the prediction. Why?

When testing hypotheses, a scientific attitude is still necessary, but no longer sufficient. We have to turn to the scientific method, and the steps of the scientific method must be followed *in order*. (see page 24 for a refresher of the steps). This requires that a hypothesis logically leads to a prediction that must be made *before* evidence for or against the hypothesis can be examined. Even if a descriptive study shows 100% of the people using phones were male (or female), that still does *not* count as evidence for the hypothesis that gender is related to phone use. One would have to predict before the observations that there will be more males (or females) using phones, *then* properly collect the data. *To test a hypothesis, predictions must precede observations.* If this seems repetitive, it's because it is a very common mistake in logic to make an observation and call it evidence for a hypothesis without ever having predicted it. The reasons for this will become clearer in Chapters 4 through 8, where each research application will involve testing a research hypothesis.

But before we test any hypotheses, let's clarify our definition of the word and the distinguish the two main types.

MORE THAN JUST AN EDUCATED GUESS: TYPES OF HYPOTHESES

People often use the word "hypothesis" to describe any idea, but a scientific hypothesis is not just any idea. The popular definition of a hypothesis as "an educated guess" is sadly lacking in clarity. A guess about what? If a performer at a fair guesses your age based on your style of dress, that's an educated guess, but is it a hypothesis? If so, it is an extremely limited one, and not very useful. A better, more specific definition would be that a **hypothesis** **is a declaration of a testable relationship between two or more conceptual variables.** A hypothesis may be one of two types, defined with examples below. Notice that the CVs are exactly the same for each example with the same number; only the words describing the type of relationship are changed from a correlational relationship to a causal relationship.

Correlational Hypothesis — Declares that a relationship exists where changes in one conceptual variable are associated with changes in another, so that a score for either variable can be used to predict the score for the other (within a limited range, depending on the strength of the relationship). Some examples:

1. The desire to own a pet rat <u>is related to</u> experience watching *Ratatouille*.

2. Smoking <u>is linked to</u> heart disease.

3. Happiness <u>increases as</u> time spent in nature increases.

4. Purposeless Internet surfing <u>is correlated with</u> depression.

These hypotheses would be tested with **correlational research** (see Ch 1 glossary and Ch 4).

Cause-and-Effect Hypothesis (Causal Hypothesis) — Declares that a relationship exists where changes in one conceptual variable (the cause) directly influence changes in the other (the effect). Some examples:

1. Experience watching *Ratatouille* <u>increases</u> the desire to own a pet rat.

2. Smoking <u>causes</u> heart disease.

3. Happiness <u>is increased by</u> spending time in nature.

4. Purposeless Internet surfing <u>leads to</u> depression.

These hypotheses would be tested with **experimental research** (see Ch 1 and Ch. 5, 6 & 8).

Go back and forth between 1 and 1, 2 and 2, etc., reading just the underlined parts, and focus in the difference in sound between a correlational and a causal hypothesis. This difference is extremely important, as it determines not only the type of research that should be used to test the hypothesis, but also the conclusions that can be drawn from that research.

Note that all cause-and-effect relationships between variables are, by default, also correlational, because changes in the cause will always be correlated to changes in the effect. However, the opposite is not true: *Cause-and-effect relationships cannot be assumed from correlational data.* To test correlational hypothesis #1 above, a researcher only has to ask two questions of each participant: "How many times have you seen *Ratatouille*?" and "On a scale of 1 to 5, where 1 is not at all and 5 is a lot, how much do you want a pet rat?" If the answers to these questions appear to be related in some predicted way, the researcher will have evidence for correlational Hypothesis #1. If so, that does not say anything about cause or effect, only that the two variables are related in a predictable way. Maybe love of pet rats causes one to immediately want to download *Ratatouille* the moment it's released. Or maybe it takes several times seeing the movie to cause one to want a pet rat. Or maybe there is some other explanation for the relationship. This correlational study will tell us nothing about any of those maybe's.

To test one of the "maybe's", such as cause-and-effect hypothesis #1 (that "Experience watching *Ratatouille* increases the desire to own a pet rat,") a researcher would have to randomly place people to different groups, one group (R5) that watches *Ratatouille* five times, one group (R2) that only watches it twice, and another group (R0), that watches it not at all. Everyone would then be asked to rate how much they want a pet rat. If scores on the pet-rat-desirability scale are different among the three groups, with R5 > R3 > R0, then we have evidence for the causal hypothesis that experience watching *Ratatouille* increases the desire to own a pet rat (though there might be some disappointment when the R5 people realize that rats can't cook).

Image © Cartoonresource/Shutterstock

"Let's shrink Big Data into Small Data...
and hope it magically becomes Great Data."

CHART 3A - APPLICATION LEARNING OBJECTIVES

3A Using MS Excel to Summarize Data and Generating Hypotheses Objectives	**START HERE** ▼ BEFORE READING THE NEXT SECTION AND DOING THIS RESEARCH Check how well you feel you can accomplish each objective.					**FINISH HERE** ▼ YOUR LAB PROFESSOR WILL TELL YOU WHEN TO COMPLETE THESE COLUMNS (IN LAB)			
	I don't know how **1**	I know a little about this **2**	I know enough about this to guess correctly **3**	I know how to do this and/or have already done it. **4**		I don't know how **1**	I know a little about this **2**	I know enough about this to guess correctly **3**	I know how to do this and/or have already done it. **4**
1 Sort data using MS Excel.									
2 Calculate means using MS Excel.									
3 Calculate standard deviations using MS Excel.									
4 Calculate percentages using MS Excel.									
5 Distinguish between correlational and cause-and-effect hypotheses.									
6 Generate logical correlational and cause-and-effect hypotheses from descriptive data summaries.									

▼

After you complete this half of the chart, read pages 95-96. Do not complete the white half until asked to do so in lab.

STUDY 3A
SUMMARIZING DATA WITH MS EXCEL & GENERATING HYPOTHESES

© Thomas Reichhart/Shutterstock

The United Nations Development Programme (UNDP) works with governments, financial organizations, and private organizations in many countries around the world to improve the quality of life for all people. As part of their mission, they frequently report descriptive data on many factors related to quality of life all over the world. Their data sets are freely available on the Internet (as of July 2017) at hdr.undp.org/en/data. The data sets provided with this book are subsets of the online data from 2005-2016, to be used for practice in sorting and summarizing data. If the information is of interest to you, please refer to the website, where you can see full data sets from almost 200 countries and for many more variables than the few we provide here. The UNDP provides data on many different variables: education factors like years of schooling; health factors like mortality and fertility rates; economic indicators like cell phone use, carbon emissions, and the labor force; and social factors including trust in the government and in other people, life satisfaction, gender inequality, and homicide and suicide rates.

Your lab instructor will provide the data in an MS Excel file. You will be asked to produce data summaries that will give you practice sorting and summarizing data and generating hypotheses. You might also be asked to produce your own meaningful report on any aspect of the data that interests you, and generate correlational and cause-and-effect hypotheses related to your report. Below is one example of a data set. In addition to the variables of interest on the spreadsheet, which shows the number of phones (both cellular and land lines) on record per 100 people in the country, UNDP also provides a Human Development Index (HDI) ranking for each country. The HDI is calculated based on a number of factors, including life expectancy of people living in the country (calculated from birth); the average number of years of schooling expected and the average number of years of schooling actually attained; and the income index, which reflects the average Gross National Income (GNI) per person living in the country. This and other samples provided with this book were designed to include countries from the full range of HDI rankings.

HDI Rank (lower number = better ranking)	Country	Sum of Telephone Lines and Mobile Subscriptions Per 100 People	
		2005	2010
175	Afghanistan	4.3	38.2
70	Albania	57.6	152.3
2	Australia	139.9	139.7
49	Bahamas	113	162.6
38	Barbados	126.1	177.9
85	Brazil	67.8	125.7
30	Brunei Darussalam	87.2	129.1
138	Cambodia	8.2	60.2
132	Cape Verde	32.4	89.5

(continued from previous page)

HDI Rank (lower number = better ranking)	Country	Sum of Telephone Lines and Mobile Subscriptions Per 100 People	
		2005	2010
184	Chad	2.3	24.3
40	Chile	85.9	136.2
91	Colombia	68.6	111.6
142	Congo	16.2	94.2
59	Cuba	8.8	19.2
112	Egypt	32.5	99
173	Ethiopia	1.4	9.4
96	Fiji	38.6	96.3
161	Haiti	6.9	40.5
120	Honduras	25.8	133.9
136	India	12.3	64.3
131	Iraq	9.6	79.9
16	Israel	154.3	172.5
25	Italy	164.7	185.3
85	Jamaica	86.8	127.5
10	Japan	120.9	126.4
12	Korea (Republic of)	129.3	162.3
54	Kuwait	122.9	181.5
151	Madagascar	3.4	37.9
182	Mali	6.4	49.2
61	Mexico	62.6	98.1
129	Nicaragua	24.7	69.6
153	Nigeria	14.2	55.8
146	Pakistan	11.3	59.1
167	Rwanda	2.7	33.8
57	Saudi Arabia	74.9	203
121	South Aftrica	82	109.2
105	Suriname	62.9	185.7
9	Switzerland	161.1	177.7
78	Ukraine	88.5	145.8
3	United States	128.2	139

GLOSSARY OF TERMS AND EXAMPLES

Where to find these terms: EP = *Experience Psychology!* (this book),
MD = Myers & DeWall, 2018 (lecture textbook). Figures are in EP.

Categorical Data: Data that tell how many observations fit one or more defined categories or groups.
    Examples: The numbers of students in each fraternity and sorority on campus would be categorical data. Counting the number of students who are athletes and non-athletes produces categorical data. A report of the number of cars of different colors passing through an intersection would also be presenting categorical data.
    Where to find this term: EP 82, Table 3.1

Cause-and-Effect Hypothesis: A statement that declares a relationship between two conceptual variables whereby changes in one variable cause (lead to, affect, influence, increase or decrease...) changes in the other variable. Also called a causal hypothesis.
    Examples: Drinking heavily leads to poor judgment. Smoking causes cancer. A positive attitude leads to greater happiness. Study habits affect grades. Friendliness toward others increases friendliness received.
    Where to find this term: EP 91-92, 98, MD 34-38

Convenience Sample: A group of people or events chosen for study based on availability.
    Example: If one wishes to know more about the challenges faced by elderly people in a particular community, the population would consist of all elderly people in that community, and a convenience sample of those people might be chosen by visiting local nursing homes and retirement homes, and asking people who are over age 65 if they would be willing to be participate in the study. This is not a random sample of all elderly people in the community because each elderly person in the community does not have an equal chance of being selected for the study (e.g., those who live independently would not have a chance of being selected).
    Where to find this term: EP 82

Correlational Hypothesis: A statement that declares a predictable relationship between two conceptual variables whereby knowledge of a datum for one variable provides information about the datum for the other variable (datum = 1 data point).
    Examples: Shoe size is related to height (given a person's shoe size, one can predict a range for that same person's height). Precipitation is related to barometric pressure. Total revenue generated by arcades is related to interest in computer science educational programs.
    Where to find this term: EP 91-92, 98, MD 29-32

Hypothesis: A sentence that declares or implies a relationship between two conceptual variables.
    Examples: See Correlational Hypothesis or Cause-and-Effect Hypothesis.
    Where to find this term: EP 81, 90-92, 98, MD 24-25, but note that Myers and DeWall are unclear and sometimes use the words "hypothesis" and "prediction" as synonyms. Technically, they are NOT synonyms, as discussed on page 114 of EP (this book, Chapter 4).

Interval Data: Numbers that represent consistent, measureable amounts, where the difference between any two measurements can be quantified and compared meaningfully to the difference between any other two measurements.

> ***Examples:*** Exam scores are interval data (the difference between a 95 and a 90 is the same as the difference between an 85 and an 80, in terms of the number of points earned). A measurement of the number of calories consumed per meal would also be interval data.
> ***Where to find this term:*** EP 83, Table 3.1

Mean: The arithmetic average of a set of numbers. The mean is often used to represent the value of most of the scores in the data set, or as an estimate of the true score of the population from which the set of numbers came.

> ***Example:*** The mean of 8, 9, 10, 11, and 22 is equal the sum of 8, 9, 10, 11, and 22 divided by 5, which equals 60 divided by 5, which is equal to 12. Note that this is a ***skewed*** data set because the mean is higher than four out of the five numbers in the set. Therefore, the ***median*** would be a better estimate of the true score for this data set.
> ***Where to find this term:*** EP 83-86, 88-89, 97, Fig. 3.1, 3.2, Table 3.1, MD 43-45

Median: The middle score when all scores in a data set are ranked from lowest to highest. The median is sometimes used to representation the value of most of the scores in the data set, or as an estimate of the true score of the population from which the set of numbers came.

> ***Example:*** The median of 8, 9, 10, 11, and 22 is equal to 10, because there are two scores lower than 10 and two scores higher than 10. The sample is not normally distributed, so the median is probably a better estimate of the true score of the population it came from than the ***mean***.
> ***Where to find this term:*** EP 83, Fig. 3.1, Table 3.1, MD 43-45

Nominal Data: See ***Categorical Data***

Ordinal Data: Numbers that represent rankings of observations relative to other observations. These data do not provide information about an individual alone, only relative to others.

> ***Examples:*** Class rankings among graduates are ordinal data. The difference between Valedictorian and Salutatorian cannot be quantitatively compared to the difference between the Salutatorian and the third-ranking graduate. Another example would be a taste-test, where three or more drinks are compared and ranked from best to worst taste as 1, 2, and 3.
> ***Where to find this term:*** EP 83, Table 3.1

Population: The larger group of people or events about which a researcher wishes to draw conclusions. Usually, the population is too large to study every individual within it, so we choose a sample of individuals from the population to study.

> ***Examples:*** When advertising executives study the way children react to a new toy, they use a small group of children, but wish to generalize the results to the way most children will respond to the toy. The population consists of all the children to whom the toy will be marketed.
> ***Where to find this term:*** EP 82, 85, 90

Random Sample: A group of people or events chosen for study based on some arbitrary condition that is unrelated to the variable of interest, whereby every person or event that belongs to the population has an equal chance of being selected for the sample.

Example: If one wishes to know more about the challenges faced by elderly people in a particular community, the population would consist of all elderly people in that community, and a random sample might be chosen by going through an alphabetical listing of all community members over age 65 and selecting every tenth person for the study.
Where to find this term: EP 82

Range: A way of expressing the amount of variability in a set of scores. In any set of scores, the range is the difference between the highest and lowest scores.
Example: The range of the data set 8, 9, 10, 11, and 22 is equal to the difference between 22 and 8. The range of this sample could be expressed as "8 to 22," but we usually represent range with one number that is the difference between the high and low score (in this case, 14).
Where to find this term: EP 84-86, MD 44

Raw Data: The numbers recorded during observation.
Examples: In a study on motivation, people are asked questions about how motivated they feel to go to work. The motivation levels for each individual in the study are raw data. In a study on smoking, people are asked how many cigarettes they smoke per day and at what age they started smoking. The answers for each individual are raw data.
Where to find this term: EP 81, 82, 83

Sample: A subset of a population, assumed to represent the population in terms of the conceptual variable of interest. Ideally, the sample should be large and randomly chosen in order to best represent the population.
Example: If one wishes to know more about the challenges faced by elderly people in a particular community, the population would consist of all elderly people in that community (too many to interview). Those who are included in the study would be a sample.
Where to find this term: EP 82, 86

Skewed: Describes a data set where a great majority of the numbers are either above or below the *mean*. This happens when one or a few numbers in the set are either much higher or much lower than the rest of the numbers in the set.
Example: A single very high number (compared to all the other numbers in the data set) can increase the mean so that it is much higher than most of the numbers in the data set, so the mean does not truly represent most of the numbers. The mean of 2, 3, 4, 6, 12, and 1000 is about 171. Five out of six of the numbers in the sample are way below the mean, and one is way above. These data are skewed. Also see examples for *mean* and *median*.
Where to find this term: EP 82, Fig. 3.1, MD 43, 44, MD Fig. 1.8

Standard Deviation (SD): A way of expressing the variability in a data set. The standard deviation is a standardized measure of the differences (deviations) between each number in the set and the mean of the set. In a large, normally distributed data set (see Fig. 3.1), the standard deviation allows us to estimate where 68%, 95%, and 99% of the scores fall. Sixty-eight percent of scores fall within one SD above or below the mean, 95% fall within two SD, and 99% fall within three SD of the mean.

Examples: "The average child will eat 1,500 peanut butter sandwiches before he/she graduates from high school." (Source: National Peanut Board, nationalpeanutboard.org.) Of course, there is quite a lot of variability around that mean. The National Peanut Board does not offer complete descriptive statistics on their website, but if, for this example, we assume that the SD is 300, then 68% of children would eat between 1,200 and 1,800 peanut butter sandwiches before they graduate from high school, 95% of children would eat between 900 and 2,100, and 99% of children would eat between 600 and 2,400 peanut butter sandwiches. It takes an average of 540 peanuts to make a 12-oz jar of peanut butter. This is much easier to accurately measure than the number of sandwiches eaten per child over several years, so the SD is probably much smaller. A reasonable guess is about 25 peanuts (approximately half an ounce). This would mean that 68% of 12-oz. peanut jars contain between 515 and 565 peanuts. About how many peanuts would you find in 95% of all 12 oz. jars? 99%? The answers are upside down at the bottom of this page.

Where to find this term: EP 85-86, Fig 3.2, Table 3.1, MD 44

Variability: How much the scores in a data set differ from the mean. The greater the variability, the less we can trust the mean as an indication of the most representative score in the sample or as an estimate of the true mean of the population from which the data points came. There are several ways to express variability, but two of them are discussed in this chapter: see ***range*** and ***standard deviation***.

Example: In measuring friendliness of workers at a fast-food chain, the manager records the percentage of time spent smiling per customer being served. She finds employees smile an average of 50% of the time per customer, but there is variability: One employee never stops smiling (he smiles 100% of the time) whereas another smiles just 2% of the time. The range is from 2% to 100%, or 98%. However, those measurements are unusual, and the SD is only 10%, so most of the employees smile between 40% and 60% of the time (assuming the measurements were normally distributed).

Where to find this term: EP 84-85, MD 44

Image © Cartoonresource/Shutterstock

"He thinks all his lost data files are just repressed memories."

95% of 12-oz jars contain between 490 and 590 peanuts, and 99% contain between 465 and 615 peanuts.

CHAPTER 4
CORRELATIONAL RESEARCH: TESTING RELATIONSHIPS

CONCEPTS

APPLICATIONS

GLOSSARY OF TERMS AND EXAMPLES

CHART 4 – CONCEPT LEARNING OBJECTIVES

Chapter 4 Concepts Objectives	START HERE ▾ BEFORE READING THE NEXT SECTION Check how well you feel you can accomplish each objective.					AFTER YOU HAVE READ UP TO THE NEXT CHART Check how well you feel you can accomplish each objective, and fix any inaccurate answers on the left.			
	I don't know how **1**	I know a little about this **2**	I know enough about this to guess correctly **3**	I know how to do this and/or have already done it. **4**		I don't know how **1**	I know a little about this **2**	I know enough about this to guess correctly **3**	I know how to do this and/or have already done it. **4**
1 Define and discuss the goals and value of correlational research.									
2 Provide at least two examples of correlational hypotheses.									
3 Recognize and distinguish between examples of positive and negative correlations.									
4 Estimate the relative strength of correlations from scatterplots and correlation coefficients.									
5 Explain the role of the null hypothesis when testing the significance of a correlation.									
6 Explain the meaning of the term "significant correlation" and the role of probability in making objective decisions about whether or not a correlation is "significant."									

		I don't know how 1	I know a little about this 2	I know enough about this to guess correctly 3	I know how to do this and/or have already done it. 4	I don't know how 1	I know a little about this 2	I know enough about this to guess correctly 3	I know how to do this and/or have already done it. 4
7	Explain one important limitation of correlational research in terms of what one can (and cannot) conclude from a significant correlation.								
8	Explain how the "third variables" and "bidirectionality" play a role in the consideration of new, causal hypotheses from correlational findings.								
9	Distinguish between a hypothesis and a prediction in terms of conceptual variables and operational definitions.								
10	Give at least two good reasons why scientists are careful *not* to use the word "proof" when discussing the evidence from one study for or against a research hypothesis.								

After you complete this half of the chart, read pages 107-116. Then return to page 105 and complete the white half of this chart.

After you complete this half of the chart, go to your assigned application chart(s) and complete the gray half. Then read about that study to prepare for the research you'll do in lab.

CORRELATIONAL RESEARCH

In Chapters 2 and 3, you operationally defined and measured conceptual variables, summarized them quantitatively, and generated hypotheses about relationships between them. We now turn to how these hypotheses can be tested, beginning with correlational research. Recall that a *correlational hypothesis* declares that a predictable relationship exists between two conceptual variables. Recall from Chapter 1 that finding evidence for a hypothesis is not a matter of verifying or confirming it, but of testing it. Correlational hypotheses lead to predictions, which can be tested with observations.

Consider the correlational hypothesis, "*Musical talent is related to artistic talent.*" Assuming we can quantify musical and artistic talent, this relationship can be tested by measuring both variables for each individual in a group of people, and determining the strength of the association between the two variables within the whole group. If the research hypothesis is true, we would predict a relationship between scores, such that people who score high for musical talent would also tend to score high for artistic talent. If our observations are in line with our prediction, we have evidence in favor of the hypothesized relationship. *Correlational research* is similar to descriptive research, but instead of describing conceptual variables in isolation, we describe the pattern of the relationship between pairs of data: As one measurement changes, what happens to the other? Like descriptive studies, correlational studies cannot test or support cause-and-effect hypotheses,(see p. 92) but can be used to generate good ideas for new cause-and-effect hypotheses that can be tested with true experiments. (Chapters 5, 6 & 8)

The data we collect through correlational studies can be visualized and summarized with a *scatterplot*, a graph that shows, for each participant in our study, the value of both variables with one dot. For example, to test the research hypothesis that SAT scores are related to GPA, we would record both scores for each participant in our study (a group of college students). Our scatterplot would show SAT scores on one axis (x-axis or y-axis) and GPA on the other axis, and we would plot a single dot for each student on the graph where his or her SAT score and GPA intersect.

A *positive correlation* (Fig. 4.1) occurs when **low** values in one variable are associated with **low** values in the other variable, and high values in one are associated with high values in the other. Using our example, as shown in the scatterplot to the right, high SAT scores are associated with high GPAs. The scores for each variable are matched for every student (dots show where each student's SAT score and GPA meet). Because low SAT scores tend to be associated with low college GPAs, and high SAT scores with high GPAs, the dots are all included within an oval (shaded area) from the lower left to the upper right of the scatterplot. The predictability of this

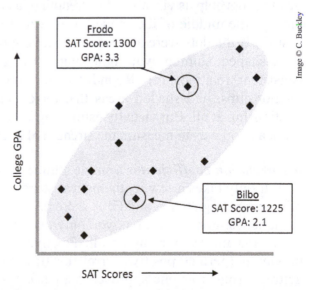

Figure 4.1. A scatterplot of a positive correlation.

relationship means that our correlational hypothesis has resisted falsification. We now can predict, given a student's SAT score, the range for that student's GPA. Our predictions will not always be correct, but the existence of a correlation can greatly improve our accuracy in predicting GPA from SAT scores. However, we cannot conclude that getting a high SAT score causes one to get high grades in college.

A *negative correlation* (Fig. 4.2) occurs when **low** values in one variable are associated with **high** values in another variable. This new sample scatterplot shows imaginary data comparing seat choice to GPA. The pattern suggests that if students are allowed to choose, sitting a great distance from the front of the classroom is associated with having a low GPA, whereas sitting in a lower numbered row (Row 1 or 2) is associated with having a high GPA. Plotting the points for every student where each student's seat choice and GPA meet produces a pattern of dots that are all included within an oval (shaded area) from the upper left to the lower right of the scatterplot. If we had predicted this relationship before seeing these data (and

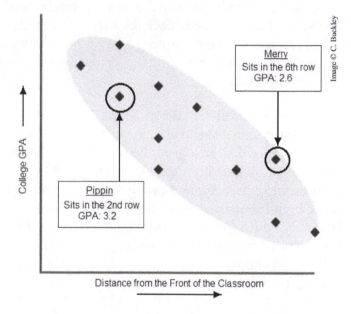

Figure 4.2. A scatterplot of a negative correlation.

if these data were real), we could conclude that as the distance one sits from the front increases, GPA tends to decrease. But remember that correlational studies do not imply cause-and-effect relationships. We could not conclude that professors assign grades based on seating choices! However, if these data were accurate, then it would make sense to test that cause-and-effect hypothesis with a true experiment (not a correlational study).

Scatterplots help us visualize the strength of a correlation. Imagine a straight line drawn lengthwise through the middle of the shaded oval, a *regression line* for the data points, also called a line of best fit. If the dots were all close to a sloping regression line, the shaded area would be a skinny, cigar-shaped, sloping oval, indicating a strong relationship (the dots show little variation from a consistent relationship). Rounder ovals and flat (horizontal) regression lines show weaker relationships, and shaded areas that look more like circles than ovals tell us that there is no relationship at all. But visually estimating how round the oval appears or how much the line slants is not a good way to measure the strength of a relationship. Instead, we use correlation coefficients.

A *correlation coefficient* is a single number that summarizes the strength of a relationship (Figure 4.3). It only takes a few mathematical steps to calculate a correlation coefficient for any two sets of numbers (e.g., SATs and GPA scores). You will learn how to do this if you go on in psychology or statistics. For this course, you only need to know how to interpret a correlation coefficient: 0 represents no relationship at all. Positive coefficients represent positive correlations, up to a maximum (perfect) positive correlation of 1. Negative coefficients represent negative correlations, getting stronger as one approaches a perfect negative correlation of −1. Coefficients above 1 or below −1 are mathematically impossible.

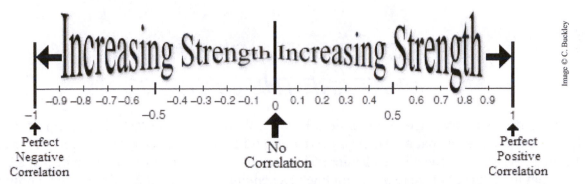

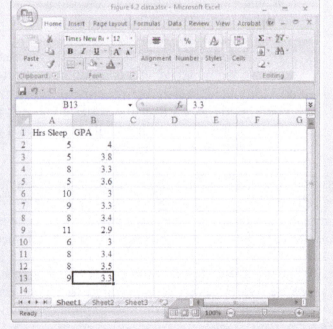

Image © C. Buckley

Figure 4.3. Correlation coefficients can vary from -1 to 1. The closer the coefficient is -1 or 1, the stronger the relationship. Correlation coefficients in the middle of the scale, closer to zero, are weaker relationships. A coefficient of zero means that there is no predictable relationship between the two variables, while coefficients of -1 and 1 indicate equally strong, perfect correlations.

The **strength of a correlation** is shown by the absolute value of the correlation coefficient. The direction of the relationship, positive or negative, does not affect how strong, useful, or important it is. A correlation coefficient of 0.70 is equal in strength to −0.70, and would be equally useful in describing any relationship, given the same number of data points on the scatterplot.

Note that while perfect correlations (−1 and 1) are mathematically possible, they are extremely unlikely in practice. A perfect correlation would mean that knowing the value of one variable would tell us precisely the value of the other. Many factors impact behavior, making this level of association between any two behavioral variables extremely unlikely.

BOX 4.1 -- Creating Scatterplots in MS Excel

Open MS Excel and recreate the spreadsheet shown to the right. To make a scatterplot of the relationship, select all the cells containing labels and data (click and drag from A1 to B13). Click on the insert tab at the top of the screen, then "scatter," and click on the icon in the top left corner (which looks like a scatterplot). You now have a scatterplot. To get a regression line, look for the "Chart Tools" tab at the top of the screen. "Chart Tools" only appears when you select the graph by clicking on it. If you click anywhere outside the scatterplot, the Chart Tools tab will disappear. Under Chart tools, click on the "layout" tab, click on the "trendline" icon, and select "linear trendline" from the options that appear. You can label your x- and y-axis under the layout tab by selecting "Axis Titles," then typing in your labels for the "Primary Horizontal Axis" and the "Primary Vertical Axis." What does your scatterplot suggest about the relationship between the number of hours of sleep and GPA in this imaginary sample?

OBJECTIVE DECISION MAKING:
"WHAT ARE THE ODDS...?"

Now we come to a very important question: How weak does an observed relationship have to be to falsify the hypothesis that a relationship exists? In other words, given a scatterplot, how can we make an objective decision about whether it shows evidence for a real relationship or just a bunch of dots that look sort of close to a sloping line? Depending on the number of dotes (data points), a small amount of scatter from a regression line might represent a real, predictable relationship, or it might represent an accidental sampling of data points that, just by chance, happen to fall in a shape resembling a slanted oval, even though no real relationship exists in the population from which that sample was drawn.

In most cases, evidence for or against a relationship cannot be "eyeballed" from a scatterplot. The human mind is prone "apophenia," a tendency to see patterns where none exist (an example would be seeing the face of Dwayne "The Rock" Johnson in your toast). When we have only a few data points, the chances that they might all fall close to one line are greater than the chances of many data points falling along a line. But the tendency when there are many data points is to imagine lines where none exist. How many data points do we need to test our correlational hypothesis? How close should they be to the regression line? How much should the line slope in order to logically conclude that we have evidence to support a correlational hypothesis? Answering all these questions will essentially boil down to answering just two questions:

1) *"What is the correlation coefficient of our observed measurements?"* The answer to this question, easily calculated mathematically (with a calculator or MS Excel) condenses all our scatterplot data into a single number that represents the strength of the relationship (Fig. 4.3).

2) *"What are the odds?"* That is, what are the chances that in a sample the same size as ours, we would arrive at a correlation coefficient at least as strong as ours, if in fact no relationship exists between these two variables in the population? This can be called "odds-based decision making," and it forms the basis of objective decision making in much (though not all) of science. Let's examine the logic first, then walk through the three-step process.

Assume you have measured two variables that you hypothesize are correlated. The scatterplot hints at a relationship, but maybe your eyes are deceiving you. Is that really a cigar-shape, or is it more roundish than oval-ish? The correlation coefficient is a much more precise indicator, but what absolute value of the correlation coefficient do you need to support the hypothesis?

Here's where scientists get really clever: We know that when there is no predictable relationship between two variables measured within in a *population*[Ch 3], the correlation coefficient for any *random sample*[Ch 3] taken from that population should be zero (see Fig. 4.3). We also know that just by chance, if we repeatedly take random samples from that population, the actual correlation coefficients of those samples will vary – sometimes they will be more than zero and sometimes less – even when there is no predictable relationship in the population. We can this knowledge and probability theory to decide whether we have evidence for our research hypothesis.

MAKING A DECISION BASED ON PROBABILITY: IS YOUR RESEARCH HYPOTHESIS SUPPORTED?

Once we have collected the data and boiled them down to a single number representing the strength of the correlation in our sample, making an objective decision based on probability is a three-step process. Of course, nothing is perfectly objective, but using probability makes our decisions much less subjective. Here we zoom in on the logic behind each step of probabilistic reasoning:

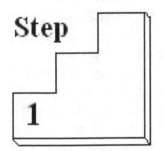

Assume no real relationship exists. That is, assume your research hypothesis is wrong. This may sound a bit pessimistic, but it is an essential first step. To test our research hypothesis, we must first negate it, and assume instead that the ***null hypothesis*** (null = bupkis = nothing = nada = zilch) is true. This is an either-or view of reality. The hypothesized relationship either exists or it does not. If the *null* hypothesis is correct, and we repeat this study many times, the correlation coefficient would vary a bit each time we test another sample from the population, but the mean correlational coefficient for all our attempts would be zero. We need to know that in order to take the next step.

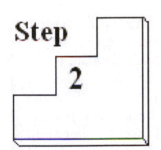

Considering the size of our sample, and the "fact" (assumption) that there is _no_ relationship, determine the probability of producing the observed result. For a correlational study, we must ask ourselves, if there is really is no relationship at all in the population from which we drew our sample, what are the odds that this much data would, just by chance, produce a correlation coefficient like the one we observed? What are the odds that a scatterplot like ours would have happened? Those "odds" are called the ***p-value*** (or "probability value.")

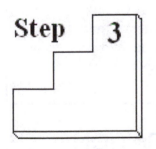

Apply a decision rule. Knowing the *p*-value – the odds that we would see what we saw if the null is true -- we can now make a decision based on one simple rule: If that *p*-value is *less* than 0.05, we have evidence for our *research* hypothesis. Why? Because a *p*-value less than 0.05 means the observed correlation coefficient is quite unlikely. In a world where the null hypothesis is true, our observations would have a less than one in 20 chance of happening. In other words, we observed a much stronger relationship in our sample than we should have if the population's relationship is truly zero. If it's very unlikely to see such a strong correlation coefficient when the null hypothesis is true, then the null is probably NOT true, which means our research hypothesis probably IS true. Stated another way, a sample correlation coefficient that has a less-than-1-in-20 chance of happening (when random samples are repeatedly drawn from a population where no real relationship exists) is evidence that a real relationship probably *does* exist in the population. We will call this sample's observed relationship "statistically ***significant***," meaning that our observations support our *research* hypothesis. Remember that this is an either-or decision about reality: either there is no relationship, or there is one. If our observations are unlikely when there is *no* relationship, we will conclude that there probably *is* a relationship.

These three steps (**the words in bold, underlined type**) form the basis for most (though not all) hypothesis testing in psychology and other natural sciences. We will apply this "probabilistic reasoning" to all our future research projects, whether we are testing correlational or cause-and-effect hypotheses.

BOX 4.2 -- Probabilistic Reasoning

Many students have trouble working with the three-step decision process just described. If it's all perfectly clear for you, ignore this box. If it seems a little foreign or confusing to you, consider this: Everyone (including you) makes probabilistic decisions like this every day. Imagine a decision to buy an expensive item that you really want. You're just not sure whether it will be worth the money. The conversation in your head might go something like this: "I don't think this thing is going to be worth the cost [you're assuming the null hypothesis is true]. Let me ask some friends who've tried it and see what they say [you're comparing data to the null hypothesis]. Hmmm . . . what are the odds that six people would love it if it's really not worth the cost? [you're about to apply a decision rule based on the odds of getting your data when the null hypothesis is true]. The odds of six people loving it if it's worthless are pretty low [that's a very low p-value], so I'm going to reject the idea that it's not worth the cost, and go out and buy it [reject the null hypothesis in favor of the research hypothesis]." Here's another example, this time where you would *not* reject the null hypothesis: "I think this guy likes me, and I'd like to ask him out, but what if he doesn't really like me? Let's assume he does not like me [assuming the null hypothesis is true]. If that's true, what are the odd he would be friendly toward me? [comparing the data to the null]. Everyone says he's a really friendly person all the time, no matter who he's talking to, so the odds are pretty high that he would be friendly toward me, even if he doesn't "like" me [so if the null is true – he does not "like" you – and your observations have a high p-value under that assumption – he's just being friendly – you are ready to apply the decision rule]. So I think I'll wait for more convincing evidence that he likes me [you're not ready to reject the null hypothesis in favor of the research hypothesis]." If you're really thinking like a statistician, you might then say, "If he does something more unlikely under the null, like call my cell number just to talk about nothing important, that would have a much lower p-value, so then I could reject the null and ask him out." But of course, if you ever do ask him out, you won't want to put it in those terms.

CORRELATION DOES NOT IMPLY CAUSATION

Imagine that we have just observed a statistically *significant* relationship (we observed a correlation coefficient in our sample that was less than 5% likely to occur if the population's correlation coefficient is actually zero). How should be interpret that? Of all the mistakes made by the popular media (and even by some scientists!) as they interpret significant correlations, the most common mistake is the use of the word "effect" when describing the relationship. A significant correlation means that two variables were *measured* and found to vary together in a predictable pattern. The factors that may have *caused* the variables to end up as they did were not tested. Nothing was purposefully changed (manipulated) to see how it affected anything else. It is therefore inappropriate to use any word that suggests a cause-and-effect relationship exists when interpreting a correlation. To borrow a phrase from the classic movie *Stripes*, when we see a significant correlation, we should "treat it like a UFO sighting." We saw something, so we're pretty sure it exists, but we don't know where it came from; no reason for its existence can be assumed. This does not devalue correlational findings – they can be very useful! Having evidence for a relationship allows us to make predictions about one variable when we know the value of the other, which can be useful – like predicting sales from website visits or a medical prognosis from a patient's mental health record – or not, like predicting the number of people who will drown from falling out of a fishing boat from the number of marriages in Kentucky.[1]

Beyond its usefulness for making predictions, correlational research is often a starting point from which to generate new hypotheses to explain what we saw. Two variables might be correlated because they are both influenced by some other variable (often called a ***third variable*** explanation). For example, the negative correlation between seat choice and GPA (Fig. 4.2) might be due to a third variable like motivation to do well. Such motivation might affect where students sit (in front, to minimize distractions, or in back, which would make it easier to get away with texting during class). Motivation might also directly increase GPA (by increasing overall effort).

"Bad news. We've discovered a negative correlation between the number of CEO's and company profits. The next step is an experiment..."

Another possible explanation for a correlation is that changes in one variable cause changes in the other. The challenge when formulating this kind of causal hypothesis from a correlation is ***bidirectionality***: If two variables (A and B) are correlated, A might cause B, or B might cause A. The correlation itself does not give us a clue. Based on the data in Figure 4.2, we could hypothesize that having a high GPA causes one to feel like the stereotypical "good student," and therefore to sit in the front. Or we could hypothesize that sitting in the front makes it easier to hear and follow directions, thereby causing increased GPA.

Like exploratory and descriptive studies, correlational data cannot provide evidence for any new cause-and-effect hypotheses that arises from the observed correlation. A true experiment must be done to test causal relationships. To test whether sitting in front causes a higher GPA would require randomly assigning students' seats in class and then comparing grades of those in the front to those in the back. True experiments need purposeful manipulation of the cause and measurement of the effect.(Chapters 5, 6 & 8)

---

[1] Yes, this is a real and documented relationship with a significant correlation coefficient of .95! To see the data for this and more "spurious correlations," See tylervigen.com/spurious-correlations. For more discussion of this fabulous website, see page 128.

While tests of hypotheses generally develop from correlational research to experimental (see cartoon), sometimes correlational research is done after a cause-and-effect relationship has already been tested and supported with laboratory research. This is one way of checking to see that the findings from lab research can be applied outside the lab. If two conceptual variables are shown to be causally related in lab research, the same two variables should also correlate in the real world. If they do not, the generalizability of the lab results is called into question. For example, an experiment showing that inhaling smoke causes cancer in laboratory rats would be less meaningful if smoking and cancer were not significantly correlated in humans.

HYPOTHESIS VERSUS PREDICTION: A CRITICAL DISTINCTION

Hypotheses declare relationships between conceptual variables. To test any hypothesis, we must operationally define the conceptual variables so that we can measure them (and, in the case of an experiment, manipulate them). *We hypothesize a relationship between conceptual variables, but our test of that relationship is based on the operational definitions of those variables*. In order to test a correlational *hypothesis*, we have to make a *prediction* that the scores on the measurements for both variables will vary together. The difference between the hypothesis and the prediction is shown in Figure 4.4.

	IF.. HYPOTHESIS	VS.	THEN... PREDICTION
What is it about?	Conceptual Variables		Operational Defintions
What is it?	A broad statement about a relationship between conceptual variables.		A *test* of the hypothesis. A specific statement about what will happen if the hypothesized relationship is true.
How is it worded?	In the present tense: "A relationship (correlational or cause-and-effect) *exists* between two conceptual variables."		In the future tense: "Something specific *will* happen."
Provide an example?	"Cursing is related to the amount of television watched." (This is a correlational hypothesis)		"The number of F-bombs used in a 5-min monologue on an emotional topic will increase with the number of hours of TV-watching over the previous 7 days (by self-report)."
Explain the example?	Cursing is a conceptual variable that can be defined in many ways: Should the listener matter? The topic? Which words count as curses? TV-watching is a conceptual variable that can be defined different ways. Self-reported hours watching TV will produce different data than asking a roommate or using an automated timer on the TV that counts hours in use.		The above operational definitions of cursing and TV-watching are the ways we have selected to test the hypothesis. If these measurements turn out as predicted, we will have *support* for our hypothesis, *not proof*, partly because we only tested the hypothesis in one, very specific way.

Figure 4.4. Distinguishes between the terms "hypothesis" and "prediction." Note that references to a hypothesis as an "if-then" statement are somewhat misleading. Technically, the hypothesis is the "if" part. What happens in the experiment (the predicted result) is the "then" part. E.g., If traveling increases tolerance (hypothesis), then people who have traveled outside their native country will have higher tolerance scores than people who have not (prediction).

The difference between a hypothesis and a prediction might seem trivial, but it has very important implications for critically evaluating research, which will become clearer in the next section Applications section of this chapter and throughout the rest of this course.

EVIDENCE IS NOT "PROOF"

If you've watched TV in the United States for longer than 10 minutes, you've probably heard a claim that something or other was "clinically proven." The phrase is so overused that it seems to have lost its meaning, if it ever had one. Clinically "proven" generally refers to the results of randomized, controlled trials, where the conclusion is a three-step, probabilistic decision, as explained on page 111 (and again on page 153, as applied to experiments). Always remember: One scientific study does not prove that a hypothesis is correct (or incorrect). If we accept that the word "proven" means "established as truth," then it is possible to establish the truth in mathematics, through logic and deductive reasoning, but not in science, where we use inductive and probabilistic reasoning. In science, we infer from evidence, based on observations. The scientific attitude recognizes that the truth can change with new observations. Scientists must always accept the possibility that they could be wrong about things, which makes them very uncomfortable claiming that they have "established the truth," or "proven" a hypothesis to be "true" or "correct" based on one study (all the words in quotes make scientists uncomfortable).

If a few uncomfortable scientists are not a good enough reason to avoid a word, there are plenty of other very good reasons to avoid speaking of "proof," presented here and throughout this book. We'll begin with two reasons related to what you already know about psychological science.

First, as you saw in Figure 4.4, there is a critical difference between a hypothesis and a prediction. A hypothesis, which claims a relationship between conceptual variables, can only be *indirectly* tested by first operationally defining those variables, then testing the relationship using the measurements dictated by those operational definitions. Remember from Chapter 2 that operational definitions are almost never perfect. They might lack *validity* or *reliability*(Ch. 2 glossary). **The strength of the evidence for any hypothesis depends on the validity and reliability of the operational definitions for the conceptual variables!** It is certainly possible to obtain statistically significant results with operational definitions that are not valid! This is partly why science must be a collective process, and must be communicated clearly: to allow others to critically evaluate the validity and reliability of our operational definitions and to replicate our findings.

Recall, for example, the hypothesis that grades are related to where students sit in their classrooms. If grades are defined by "the average of the first semester's grades," that might lead to a very different result than defining it by "the final grade for one class." There might be a significant correlation between grades and seating arrangements in one class, but not over multiple classes. Therefore, it would be unwise to claim that one study, using specific operational definitions, establishes the truth about a hypothesis.

A second very good reason for not claiming proof of a hypothesis after one study is that scientific decisions are based on probability, specifically, on *the odds of getting the observed results under the assumption that the null hypothesis is true.* If that likelihood is very low (less than 5%), then we decide that the null hypothesis is probably *not* true, and we reject it in favor of our research hypothesis. Hence, there is still a chance (albeit a small one—less than 5%) that the null hypothesis *is* true, and we just happened to get very unusual results. We can never be 100% sure that what we observed wasn't just a lucky accidental sampling of data that happened to fit our prediction. Unlikely things *do* happen, although rarely. So, **based on our odds-based decision-making process, there is always a small chance that our decision to reject the null hypothesis in favor of our research hypothesis was wrong.** Therefore, we cannot call our hypothesis "established truth."

Another good reason that scientists can't claim one study "proves" a hypothesis has to do with the design of our research, and will be discussed in other chapters.

Meanwhile, two more essential points must be made: First, just because we don't claim to have "proof" of our hypotheses, **this does not mean that scientific evidence is any less useful or important, or that it should be dismissed.** Evidence is still evidence; it is much better than guessing. Second, when a general, broad hypothesis explains multiple observations and is repeatedly supported by many different studies, as is the case with evolution, for example, it reaches the status of *theory*. The National Academy of Sciences defines a theory as "a comprehensive explanation of some aspect of nature that is supported by a vast body of evidence."[2] So saying something is "just a theory" is actually saying that it is "just" an idea that explains a lot and has been repeatedly tested and supported by tremendous amounts of research. Often, when people say "just a theory," what follows is not a theory at all. As in: "I have this idea that if you're watching a football game on TV, pointing out how long it's been since the quarterback fumbled causes him to fumble…but it's just a theory." No it's not. At best, it's a hypothesis, and not a very good one, as it is easily falsified. As painful as that experience can be, the fact that it happened once (or more) is not proof of a relationship.

In conclusion, whether you major in psychology, some other science, or a nonscience field, it will be useful to know how objective decisions about scientific evidence are made and how to evaluate the strength of that evidence. This means knowing how to ask the critical questions that will tell you whether to trust a conclusion or not. So far, some questions that should be on your list are:

- ☐ How valid and reliable are the operational definitions used by these researchers?
- ☐ How many observations (participants) were included in the study?
- ☐ How much variability was there in the measurements?
- ☐ How strong was the reported relationship?
- ☐ How likely was this result, assuming the authors of this study were wrong about their research hypothesis?
- ☐ Do other studies support the same hypothesis, with different research designs and different operational definitions?

Asking these questions and others (explored in other chapters) will help you to become a better consumer of scientific information.

---

2 nas.edu/evolution/TheoryOrFact.html

CHART 4A – APPLICATION LEARNING OBJECTIVES

4A Anxiety Sensitivity and Handedness Objectives	**START HERE** ▼ BEFORE READING THE NEXT SECTION AND DOING THIS RESEARCH Check how well you feel you can accomplish each objective.				**FINISH HERE** ▼ YOUR LAB PROFESSOR WILL TELL YOU WHEN TO COMPLETE THESE COLUMNS (IN LAB)			
	I don't know how **1**	I know a little about this **2**	I know enough about this to guess correctly **3**	I know how to do this and/or have already done it. **4**	I don't know how **1**	I know a little about this **2**	I know enough about this to guess correctly **3**	I know how to do this and/or have already done it. **4**
1 Describe one example of how the lateralization of basic brain functions can be studied without brain imaging.								
2 Explain why cause-and-effect observations should not be called "correlations," even though they must be correlated.								
3 Gain practice distinguishing between a hypothesis and a prediction.								
4 Gain practical experience with inventories and computer-based data collection techniques.								
5 Observe the creation of an APA-style scatterplot in MS Excel.								
6 Draw conclusions regarding the strength and direction of the relationship between two variables based on data.								
7 Determine appropriate subsection content for the Method section of a lab report (materials vs procedure).								

▼

After you complete this half of the chart, read pages 119-122. Do not complete the white half until asked to do so in lab.

ANXIETY SENSITIVITY AND HANDEDNESS: IS THERE A RELATIONSHIP?

Image © abandsb/Shutterstock, modified by C Buckley

STUDYING THE BRAIN WITHOUT SEEING IT

One human brain has about a hundred trillion synapses. That's roughly 500 times as many sites for interneuronal communication *in one human head* as the number of stars in our galaxy. As you read this, many synapses in your own head are active right now, allowing you to see these words, comprehend their meaning (hopefully), and begging you to stop reading for a moment to marvel over their very existence. Your brain is the ultimate cooperative system, with different areas at least partially devoted to different tasks, and the whole brain functioning as one unit. In lecture, you learned about the general functions for different areas of the brain, and that complex thoughts and behaviors are not isolated in any one area of the brain. Even a simple task like reading the word "laughter" out loud, or actually laughing out loud, involves multiple areas of the brain.

We have much to learn about this complicated network of specialized areas, overlapping functions and individual differences. In addition to the brain imaging techniques described in your lecture textbook (Myers & DeWall, pp 66-71), psychologists have other, less expensive ways to investigate which areas of the brain are involved in different thoughts and behaviors, and we can use what we know to find out more, as we will in this correlational study.

For example, recall from Myers & DeWall (p 68 & Fig. 2.15) that the right side of your brain controls voluntary movement on the left side of your body, and the left side of your brain controls movement on the right side of your body. We call this ***contralateral motor control***, and it is true for all human brains, due to the organization of the cranial nerves. For about 96% of right-handed people and about 70% of left-handed people, the left side of the brain is also responsible for basic language functions (understanding and producing words). So if you're one of this majority, and we ask you to tap a spacebar with your right hand as fast as you can and try simultaneously speaking, your tapping rate would slow down, but that would not happen if you tapped with your left hand while speaking. This is because speaking and using your right hand would both use the left side of the brain (see Figure 4.5). Asking the left brain to do two things at once (language and tapping) slows down the rate of tapping with the right hand. If your left-handed tapping rate is more affected by speech than your right-handed tapping rate, you might be one of the relatively small number of people for whom language is on the right side of your brain (or on both sides). You can test this out for yourself using this website: clickspeedtest.info/mouse-test, which will measure your mouse-clicking speed. Set the timer to 30 seconds (10 seconds is usually not enough to see an effect). Click as fast as you can with your right hand for the whole 30 sec, and record your number of clicks as "RH, S" (right hand, silent). Then pick up some good reading material (this book will do) and restart the timer, clicking as many times as you can while reading aloud. Record your number of clicks as "RH, L" (right hand, language). Repeat these steps with your left hand (LH, S and LH, L). If the difference in tapping speed is much greater between RH-S and RH-L than it is between LH-S and LH-L, you probably process language on the left side of your brain, like most of us. If you get the opposite pattern, you might be someone who processes language on the right side of your brain. Remember: One round of data collection is not sufficient to "prove" either of those conclusions, but it's fun to see what happens.

Girl at Computer Image © Glovatskiy/Shutterstock; Brain Image © Myper/Shutterstock. Images superimposed and modified by C Buckley.

Figure 4.5. Language and motor control. Contralateral control via the cranial nerves means that for everyone, the right hemisphere of the brain controls the left side of the body (gray circle 1 and gray arrow) and the left hemisphere of the brain controls the right side of the body (black circle 1 and black arrow). For most people (not everyone), basic language functions are controlled by the left cerebral hemisphere (black circle 2). That's why most people who try to tap with their right hand while speaking will slow down their tapping rate: The left side of the brain is doing two tasks at once (black circles 1 & 2). The same people can tap faster with the left hand while speaking because they're using opposite sides of the brain (gray circle 1 and black circle 2), so the tasks are less likely to interfere with each other.

These observations, which have been replicated many times, support the hypothesis that in most people, the left side of the brain influences language production more than the right side of the brain. (Stop here for a moment: Before reading on, check your knowledge. Is this a correlational or cause-and-effect hypothesis?)

If you identified it as a cause-and-effect hypothesis, you are correct. The biggest clue is the use of the verb "influences," which is a synonym for "affects." When we claim that one variable (the left or right side of the brain) influences another (language production), we are stating a cause-and-effect relationship. Technically, this would also cause a correlation between these two variables, but you should *not* present observations that support a cause-and-effect hypothesis by stating that the variables are "correlated." Doing so is like trading a dollar for a quarter. Yes, a quarter is useful, and correlational studies are useful, too, but educated people don't trade dollars for quarters, because dollars are obviously worth more. **If you have experimental evidence for a cause-and-effect relationship, you should never refer to it as a correlation. Please bookmark this page and refer to the underlined sentence when writing your final lab report for this course!**

Correlational studies are still important! Significant correlations allow us to make more accurate predictions and can help us generate new cause-and-effect hypotheses, as discussed previously.
A variety of conceptual variables have been hypothesized to be correlated with handedness. Popular psychology websites often claim that left-handedness is associated with higher intelligence; however, a recent meta-analysis found no reliable evidence for that hypothesis (Papadatou-Pastou & Tomprou, 2015). A study authored by Christopher Ruebeck (Professor of Economics at Lafayette College) and collaborators at Johns Hopkins University (Ruebeck, Harrington & Moffit, 2007) collected data from 5,000 participants and found that among college graduates, left-handed males earned about 15% more, on average, than right-handed males. Females' income was not related to handedness. The reason for that correlation is an open question, but several hypotheses can be offered: Maybe being left-handed forces children to solve problems more often than their right-handed cohorts. Or, maybe left-handedness increases perseverance, a trait that might affect men and women in the job market differently. When all we have are correlational data, multiple explanations could be equally feasible, and would have to be tested.

APPLYING RESEARCH TERMINOLOGY

In this study, we will test the ***correlational hypothesis*** that **handedness (possibly left or right) is related to anxiety sensitivity.** Anxiety sensitivity is the awareness of, and sensitivity to, one's own bodily signals when one is anxious. It is not the same thing as anxiety; rather, it can be briefly defined as "the fear of fear" (Reiss, et al, 1986), because it measures *how we react* when our body sends us signals that are associated with fear or anxiety. Usually, a correlational hypothesis declares a specific direction for the relationship (positive or negative), but you and your classmates are the participants in this study. In general, it is good research technique to keep specific predictions unknown to participants in a study so that behavior is not affected by their expectations or desire to help. In this case, your knowledge of the prediction could influence how you respond to questions about handedness and anxiety sensitivity. We will therefore discuss the direction of the relationship in lab, rather than explain it here.

This is a good place to practice the correct application of the terms ***hypothesis*** and ***prediction***. Our operational definition of handedness will be the average score on a handedness inventory, and our operational definition of anxiety sensitivity will be the average score on the Reiss-Epstein-Gursky

Anxiety Sensitivity Inventory (ASI), a 16-item questionnaire (Reiss, et al, 1986). A brief version of our **hypothesis** is stated in bold in the paragraph above. Our ***prediction*** is that the scores on the handedness inventory will be correlated with the scores on the ASI. This essential difference between a hypothesis (stated in terms of conceptual variables) and a ***prediction*** (stated in terms of the operational definitions) reminds us yet again that our evidence is not absolute "proof" of our hypothesis. If the evidence *could* be said to "prove" anything, it would be limited to proving the predictions, not the hypothesis. In a well-designed study, of course, evidence for the predictions is also strong evidence for the hypothesis, but good critical thinkers are always aware of this subtle difference (see Figure 4.4, page 114).

PROCEDURE 4A
(more information will be provided by your lab instructor)

This will be a correlational study examining the relationship between handedness and anxiety sensitivity. The specific hypothesis (i.e., the direction of the relationship) will be discussed in lab next week, before we examine the data that we collect this week.

1. Complete the Anxiety Sensitivity Inventory. Take your time and answer each question independently and honestly. Cover your answers, as this information may be personal.
2. Obtain a copy of the handedness inventory (provided in lab) and READ all instructions on the inventory. If anything is unclear or you have any questions, ask! Chances are, if you have a question, others want an answer, too!
3. Beginning with your assigned station, proceed around the room, performing each activity at the station *at least twice* with each hand. You will perform each activity with one hand, then switch hands and do the same activity again. You will then switch back and repeat that process at least one more time. Perform each activity as directed on the instructions at each station. Try to make a good decision about which hand is more COMFORTABLE performing the task. Your accuracy performing the task does not matter; comfort should be the main factor. Record your ratings on the inventory.
4. Stay with your group, and move to another station when your whole group has finished with all tasks. You do not have to do the stations in order – look for any available station.
5. Enter the data from your handedness questionnaire and ASI on MS Excel. (A template is provided on Moodle. It will automatically calculate your mean handedness score and your mean ASI score.
6. To assure confidentiality, you will be secretly and randomly assigned an ID number (on the front page of your ASI). DO NOT TELL ANYONE YOUR NUMBER. Type it in the appropriate space on the Excel worksheet, DO NOT type your name.
7. When you are given permission to print out your data sheet, do so and immediately PICK IT UP FROM THE PRINTER and hand it in FACE DOWN at the front of the room. Do not leave your printed data sheet un attended in the printer.
8. Next week, we will discuss the hypothesis in more detail, discuss our specific prediction, and look at the data for all sections of Intro Psych lab to see if they support the hypothesis.

LAB RECORD FOR STUDY 4A
ANXIETY SENSITIVITY AND HANDEDNESS

Name: _Ric Donati_

Part 1: Complete in lab.

Purpose: *To examine a potential relationship between the asymmetry (lateralization) of the brain and anxiety sensitivity.*

Hypothesis: *Anxiety sensitivity and handedness are related, such that sensitivity to anxiety can be predicted by degree and direction of handedness.*

We measured two variables for each participant. The conceptual variables were:

1. _Handedness_

2. _Anxiety Sensitivity_

The operational definition of the first variable was _Score on handedness inventory_

The operational definition of the second variable was _Score on ASI_

Part 2: Homework – Doing this NOW will help you prepare for your lab report writing practicum!

Materials: (describe the Anxiety Sensitivity Inventory and the Handedness Inventory):

The handedness inventory (HI) is a set of 12 everyday tasks that can be completed using one hand, such as throwing paper into a wastebasket or brushing teeth. For each task the participant was asked to evaluate how comfortable the task was on a 7 point scale from -3 to 3. The tasks were set up around a large laboratory room.

The anxiety sensitivity index (ASI) is a set of 16 questions about how the participant responds to anxiety-inducing conditions such as appearing nervous in front of others and stomach growling in public. For each question the participant ranked whether the condition made them uncomfortable on a 5 point scale from 0-Not at all to 4-Very Much.

Write the procedure immediately after collecting data to get the most accurate records!

Procedure: (how were data collected?) Participants first completed a pencil and paper version of the ASI. The process was anonymos and confidential and took participants about 3 minutes to complete. Participants then broke down into small groups and moved around the lab to complete the HI tasks twice with each hand, alternating hands and rating their comfortableness with each task. When making ratings, participants were instructed to ignore the outcomes and to focus on how comfortable they were. Completion took ~30 mins.

_____

_____

_____

_____

_____

_____

_____

_____

_____

_____

_____

_____

_____

_____

- -

Part 3: Back in lab (after data from all labs has been presented).

Participants: n=162   9 ignored due to injury, so 153.   82 female, 71 male

	Total	Left	Right
female	82	6	76
Male	71	7	64

Data handling: Describe how individual Handedness and ASI scores were calculated.

Mean and STD were calculated for each test.

Describe what was compared to what and how (to look for a correlation).

ASI were compared to HI to check for significant correlation.

Results: The correlation between handedness scores and anxiety sensitivity scores was

(positive (negative) flat), and was (significant (not significant)), r(151) =
    (circle one)   (circle one)

0.22 , p [<] 0.05 .
       (fill in < or =)

Conclusion: We predicted a negative correlation between HI and ASI. However, the observed correlation was actually in the opposite direction, therefore we have no evidence to support our hypothsis.

CHART 4B – APPLICATION LEARNING OBJECTIVES

4B Generating and Testing a Correlational Hypothesis Objectives	START HERE ▼ BEFORE READING THE NEXT SECTION AND DOING THIS RESEARCH Check how well you feel you can accomplish each objective.				FINISH HERE ▼ YOUR LAB PROFESSOR WILL TELL YOU WHEN TO COMPLETE THESE COLUMNS (IN LAB)			
	I don't know how **1**	I know a little about this **2**	I know enough about this to guess correctly **3**	I know how to do this and/or have already done it. **4**	I don't know how **1**	I know a little about this **2**	I know enough about this to guess correctly **3**	I know how to do this and/or have already done it. **4**
1 Compose a reasonable correlational hypothesis from a list of conceptual variables.								
2 Estimate the strength and direction of the correlation for your own hypothesis with a scatterplot.								
3 Explain how testing multiple hypotheses or predictions with one data set can impact the strength of odds-based conclusions.								
4 Clearly express the difference between your hypothesis and your prediction, and describe why the difference is important for interpreting evidence.								
5 Draw conclusions regarding the strength and direction of the relationship between two variables based on a data analysis (provided).								

▼

After you complete this half of the chart, read pages 127-129. Do not complete the white half until asked to do so in lab.

STUDY 4B – GENERATING AND TESTING A CORRELATIONAL HYPOTHESIS

For some fascinating spurious correlations, go to

tylervigen.com

Image © Fenton one/Shutterstock

Any two conceptual variables can be declared to be related to one another. One might declare, "Walking speed is related to hair length." This would be a correlational hypothesis, although seemingly illogical. The hypotheses that walking speed is related to leg length, or that gender is related to hair length, seem more likely to find support. However, if one considers the possibility that walking speed could be related to gender (if males have longer legs, or walk faster for other reasons), then a predictable link between walking speed and hair length becomes a more logical hypothesis because males often have shorter hair. The point is that some correlational hypotheses might seem illogical at first, but upon further consideration, could be worth testing. However, we do not simply throw together any two conceptual variables with no reason at all for their proposed relationship. There should be some logic, whether or not it is immediately obvious to others.

For this research, your research team will be given a set of cards with conceptual variables on them. You will discuss possible relationships between these CVs and write a correlational hypothesis for any two of them. You need a *rationale* for your hypothesis. That is, you must be able to logically make the case that the two CVs you choose are correlated. You will then receive operational definitions of those variables and write specific predictions based on your hypothesis. We will collect data from everyone in the lab and enter them into one MS Excel document. Groups will then use that document to produce scatterplots of their data while the professor runs a correlational analysis for each group. Your group will be provided with the results for the test of your hypothesis, and will informally present your study to the rest of the class.

For this research project, several hypotheses will be tested in your lab with one data set. Therefore, before you begin, it is worth reviewing two important concepts about hypothesis testing from this chapter.

First, recall from pages 115 and 116 that every odds-based decision we make has an accepted chance of being wrong. A less-than-5% chance of something happening means it could still happen up to 5% of the time. So if the null hypothesis is true, our results would be highly *unlikely*, but they can still happen. Indeed, up to 5% of the time, they *will* happen. It may help to think of our decision as one roll of a single die with 20 sides. If we only roll it once and predict that it will land on a 13, for example, our guess is probably going to be wrong, but there is still a 5% chance we could have *accidentally* guessed right. The more times we roll the die, the greater our chances of accidentally getting a 13 (more on this in Box 4.3). The main point is that we must never forget the small possibility that significant results might have accidentally turned out the way they did, even with no actual relationship between the variables, and that the more predictions we make, the more likely it is that at least one of them will be significant, just by chance. Keeping this in mind should help us remember that one study cannot "prove" a hypothesis; it can only provide evidence.

There is a highly entertaining website that illustrates this point nicely. Visit tylervigen.com to see what happens when we just compare any and all variables, looking for correlations. It turns out, many unexpected things happen to be spuriously correlated. Over a 5-year period from 2006 to 2010 (inclusive), Pandora's net market losses (in millions of dollars) was significantly correlated with the number of people who drowned by falling in a bathtub (the correlation coefficient was .87!). You can search the website database freely and select from thousands of variables to see what correlates with them. This is fun, but largely meaningless, since no one would predict that per capita cheese consumption is logically related to the number of lawyers in Hawaii ($r = .98$!).

BOX 4.3 - Another Reason We Don't Say "Prove"

In this research, your class will test more than one hypothesis in the same study, with the same data set. Every hypothesis your instructor tests will lead to a specific prediction that will require an odds-based decision about whether or not to reject the null hypothesis, with a 5% chance of being wrong. Consider a 20-sided die. If you roll it 100 times, it's easy to see that the odds of getting at least one 13 in all those tosses are greatly improved, compared to just one toss (although still not certain—only about 99.4%).[3]

If, in this research, your instructor tests six hypotheses, each with a 0.05 chance of being accidentally supported, then you would have about a 26.5% chance[4] of accidentally rejecting the null hypothesis for *at least one* of your class's predictions. We've suddenly gone from a 1 in 20 chance for just one conclusion being wrong (when it is tested alone) to more than a 1 in 4 chance of any one of our conclusions being wrong when we test six predictions in the same study! As you increase the number of predictions in a single study, the odds that you will *accidentally* draw the wrong conclusion on at least one of the predictions can quickly go from very unlikely to very likely, making your evidence for each single prediction quite weak. This is important to realize when interpreting the meaning of your significant relationships, if your class finds any. This does not mean that any significant relationships you find are wrong; only that the chances of them being wrong are greater than they would be if only one prediction had been tested.

There are ways around this problem when we want to make multiple decisions about data in one study. One way around it is to divide your acceptable *p*-value (usually 0.05) by the number of decisions you plan to make. So, if you plan to make five decisions (test five predictions), you would divide 0.05 by 5, which equals 0.01. In that case, you would only reject the null hypothesis for any particular decision if the *p*-value is less than 0.01, rather than 0.05. The total chance of being wrong on any one of the five decisions then still adds

---

[3] There is a formula for determining the precise probability of observing any independent event with a known probability on any known number of attempts to observe it. In other words, the formula can be used to calculate the probability of observing at least one 13 when a single, 20-sided die is tossed 100 times (Appendix A).

[4] Using the same formula described in footnote 4 (Appendix A).

up to no more than an acceptable 0.05. Another way of dealing with this issue will be discussed in Chapter 8, where we will test one hypothesis with more than one prediction.

To review a second reason we don't speak of proof, remember that a ***hypothesis*** declares a relationship between conceptual variables, whereas a ***prediction*** is based on the operational definitions of those variables (Figure 4.4, page 114). Hypotheses are tested somewhat indirectly, through predictions. For example, you might hypothesize that walking speed is related to hair length, but in order to test that hypothesis, you would need operational definitions of walking speed (e.g., distance covered in 10 sec) and hair length (e.g., length in inches of the longest piece of hair).

Your *prediction*, then, is not that walking speed is correlated with hair length, but that *the distance covered in 10 sec will be correlated with the length in inches of the longest piece of hair*. This distinction is an important reminder that the strength of the conclusion for any hypothesis depends on the validity and reliability of the operational definitions used to test it. Consider two different operational definitions of walking speed:

1. Walking speed is the distance covered in a 10-sec period.
2. Walking speed is the number of steps taken in a 10-sec period.

Someone with long legs might score high by the first definition, but low by the second one. The reverse could be true for people with shorter legs, leading to very different results. Furthermore, is walking speed measured on the way to work? To the gym? In the gym? Again, different operational definitions lead to different results. The fact that we are directly testing the prediction (based on operational definitions), and not the hypothesis (based on conceptual variables) is an important reason why one study does not "prove" a hypothesis.

Happens every time someone uses the word
"prove" in a scientific report.

GLOSSARY OF TERMS AND EXAMPLES

Where to find these terms: EP = *Experience Psychology!* (this book),
MD = Myers & DeWall, 2018 (lecture textbook). Figures are in EP.

Bidirectionality: The possibility that an observed correlation between any two variables, A and B, *could* be because changes in A cause changes in B, or because changes in B cause changes in A. If one variable influences the other, we would have no way of knowing which one is the cause and which one is the effect from correlational data.

    Example: If musical performance is positively correlated with math scores, this could be because learning how to play music increases attention to numbers and math (e.g., fractions), OR, it could be because practicing math makes learning music easier. Simply measuring math performance and musical performance would not tell us, either way.

    Where to find this term: EP 113

Cause-and-Effect Hypothesis: A testable declaration that changes in one conceptual variable cause changes in another.

    Examples: Reading cartoons improves mood. Masturbation causes blindness. Walking backwards leads to backward thinking. Petting an animal decreases stress levels. (Note that whether these statements appear true or not, they are all testable ideas about cause-and-effect relationships, so they are all cause-and-effect hypotheses.)

    Where to find this term: EP 108, 120-121

Contralateral Motor Control: "Contra" = opposite, "lateral" = side. This term refers to the way each cerebral hemisphere of the brain (left or right) controls voluntary muscle movement on the opposite side of the body.

    Example: Using Electrical Stimulation of the Brain (ESB) during brain surgery, doctors can stimulate an area of the motor cortex in the right cerebral hemisphere and observe the patient's left arm move.

    Where to find this term: EP 119, Fig. 4.5; MD 68 (not by name).

Correlation Coefficient: A number between -1 and +1 representing the strength of a correlation between two variables, derived from data representing multiple pairs of measurements of those two variables. The absolute value of the coefficient reflects the strength of the relationship, and the sign of the coefficient reflects whether the relationship is direct (positive) or inverse (negative).

    Examples: Ratings of happiness and the number of times people smile might have a correlation coefficient of .85, while ratings of happiness and the number of times people punch someone else in the face might have a correlation coefficient of -.85. Ratings of happiness and the number of times people use the word "the" would probably have a correlation coefficient of 0.00.

    Where to find this term: EP 108-112, 128, Fig. 4.3; MD 29-31

Correlational Hypothesis: A testable statement declaring that two conceptual variables are predictably related to one another, so that the value of one can be used to predict the value of the other (within a range).

    Examples: The number of new pregnancies and the frequency of power outages across different locations are positively correlated.

    Where to find this term: EP 107, 108, 110, 114, 121, 127

Correlational Research/Study: A study designed to measure two conceptual variables in matched pairs, in order to test the hypothesis that they are predictably related to each other.

    Example: Sherman and Flaxman (2001) measured average annual temperatures in different locations around the world and the amount of hot spices used in traditional recipes at those locations (climates and recipes were matched by location) to test the hypothesis that use of hot (bacteria-killing) spices is positively correlated with the intensity of heat experienced in a given climate (MD, p 399).

    Where to find this term: EP 107, 113, 114, MD 29-31

Hypothesis: A sentence that declares or implies a testable relationship between two or more conceptual variables. The relationship can be correlational, cause-and-effect, or null (see *correlational hypothesis* and *cause-and-effect hypothesis, null hypothesis*).

    Examples: See *correlational hypothesis, cause-and-effect hypothesis, null hypothesis*

    Where to find this term: EP 107-108, 110-116, 120-122, 127-129, Fig. 4.4 Box 4.2, Box 4.3; MD 24 (Note that MD's definition of a hypothesis does not distinguish between hypotheses and predictions, but in this lab, you must know the difference – see EP 114-115 and Fig. 4.4).

Negative Correlation: A relationship between two conceptual variables such that as one increases, the other decreases.

    Example: Squirrel population size and chipmunk population size at a single food source are negatively correlated. As squirrels approach the food source, chipmunks run away.

    Where to find this term: EP 108, 113 Fig. 4.2, 4.3

Null Hypothesis: A statement that negates (nullifies) the research hypothesis. It simply says that the research hypothesis is NOT true.

    Examples: A research hypothesis might say that two variables, X and Y are positively correlated. The null hypothesis would be that X and Y are not correlated. If the research hypothesis is that X and Y are negatively correlated, the null hypothesis would *still* be that X and Y are not correlated. If a scientist hypothesizes that there is a cause-and-effect relationship between X and Y, the null hypothesis would be that there is no cause-and-effect relationship.

    Where to find this term: EP 111, 115-116, 127, Box 4.2, Box 4.3

p-value (probability value): The odds of getting whatever result we get (e.g., a particular correlation coefficient), assuming the null hypothesis is true. If the *p*-value is very low, the null hypothesis is probably not true, meaning the alternative (our research hypothesis) is supported. If the *p*-value is high, the odds of getting our results under the null hypothesis are high, so we can't reject the null hypothesis, and we have no support for the alternative (research hypothesis).

    Example: A researcher notices that whenever her college's football team does well, their basketball team also does well. She tests the research hypothesis that the football team's record is positively correlated with the basketball team's record. Going back 20 years, she compares the number of wins for both teams each year. If the **null hypothesis** (that the football team's record is not at all related to the basketball team's record) is true, the correlation coefficient should be zero. But she calculates a correlation coefficient of 0.43, and the ***p*-value** (odds of getting a coefficient that strong by chance when it should be zero) are just 0.02, or 2%. She therefore rejects the null hypothesis, and claims support for her research hypothesis. She can now offer better predictions about the basketball team's success at the end of each football season.

    Where to find this term: EP 111, Box 4.2, Box 4.3

Positive Correlation: A relationship between two conceptual variables such that as one increases, so does the other.

Example: Height and shoe size are positively correlated: Taller people wear larger shoes.
Where to find this term: EP 107-108, Fig. 4.1, 4.3

Prediction: A statement about what will be observed in a study, based on the operational definitions of the variables being studied and assuming the research hypothesis is true.

Example: To test the ***hypothesis*** that intelligence and income are positively correlated, one might operationally define intelligence as "IQ score" and income as "self-reported annual salary." The ***prediction*** would be: "IQ scores will be positively correlated with self-reported annual salary." A similar study was done by Zagorsky (2007) (see MD, page 362).
Where to find this term: EP 107-108, 113-116, 121-122, 127-129, Fig. 4.4, Box 4.3

Regression Line: In correlational research, a straight line through the points on a ***scatterplot*** that is as close as possible to the maximum number of data points. The slope of the line and the average closeness of the data points to the line tell us about the strength and direction of the relationship between the variables, which are represented on the X and Y axes.

Example: (below)
Where to find this term: EP 108, 110, Box 4.1

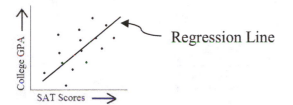

Regression Line

Each point on the scatterplot represents the X-score (SAT) and Y-Score (GPA) for each individual.

Scatterplot: A graph showing the relationship between paired measurements of variables (for example, height and weight), with the value of one variable on the X-axis and the value of the other on the Y-axis. One point is drawn for each pair of measurements at the point on the graph where the X-value and the Y-value intersect.

Examples: The image above shows a scatterplot for GPA and SAT scores. A scatterplot from a study on IQ scores and income (Zagorsky, 2007) is shown on page 389 of Myers & Dewall.
Where to find this term: EP 107-111, 127, Box 4.1

Significant: Refers to a data set that would have had less than a 5% chance of occurring if the null hypothesis were true. Significant ***positive or negative correlations*** allow us to reject the null hypothesis and conclude that we have evidence to support a ***correlational hypothesis***.

Example: As described on pages 374-375 of Myers & DeWall, a study by Deary, Whiteman, Starr, Whalley, and Fox (2004) found a significant positive correlation between IQ at age 11 and IQ at age 80. They had records for over 500 participants whose IQ had been measured at age 11, and again at age 80. The correlation coefficient was + .66. The correlation is ***significant*** because **if** IQ scores at age 11 and age 80 were completely unrelated, the chances of seeing a correlation coefficient of .66 for that many participants would be less than 5%. Therefore, we can reject the null hypothesis, and claim evidence for the hypothesis that IQ in childhood is related to IQ in late adulthood.

Where to find this term: EP 111-115, 121, 128, Box 4.3; MD 45 (Note that the explanation in Myers & DeWall refers to significant *differences*, not significant *correlations*. We will discuss significant differences in the next chapter. They also avoid using the term "null hypothesis," and so are less clear about how significance is actually determined.)

Strength of a Correlation: The predictability of the relationship between two variables, based on measurements of both variables (based on correlational data).
    Example: To test the hypothesis that the number of books read correlates with the size of one's vocabulary, Study A asks people to self-report how many books they read each week and the approximate size of their own vocabulary. Study B actually observes people for several weeks to see how many books they read per week, on average, and then measures vocabulary with an objective test. Researchers in Study A observe a correlation coefficient of .09, while Study B produces a correlation coefficient of .39.   Study B shows a stronger correlation (see below).
    Where to find this term: EP 108-109, Fig 4.3

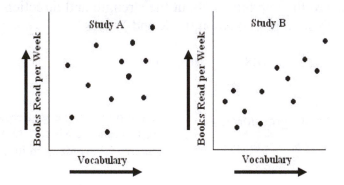

Theory: A unifying idea that explains multiple observations and has evidence to support it from multiple perspectives. Note that Myers & DeWall (p 24) define a theory as a more general hypothesis that organizes evidence into a single explanation and suggests multiple testable predictions. These two definitions are different ways of saying the same thing. Evidence to support an idea from multiple perspectives is what comes from multiple predictions. In order to be called a "theory," an idea must be applied, tested and supported from multiple perspectives, such that there is wide agreement among scientists that it is true or at least plausible.
    Examples: Five theories of emotion are presented in Chapter 12 of your lecture textbook (pages 426-430, especially Table 12.1, p. 230). The evidence for each is presented and discussed.
    Where to find this term: EP 116; MD 24 (but see definition above)

Third Variables: Any variable that *could* influence both conceptual variables in a correlational study, and therefore cause the two variables to correlate. Correlational research does not tell us anything about what these variables are, nor if they exist.
    Examples: A researcher tests the hypothesis that illness and hand washing are negatively correlated by secretly observing hand washing of employees in a company restroom and comparing that to the number of sick days each employee claims at work. She finds a significant negative correlation. This could be explained by general laziness (people who are lazy might be less likely to wash their hands AND more likely to call in sick, even if they are not actually sick). Laziness would be considered a possible ***third variable***.
    Where to find this term: EP 113.

CHAPTER 5
EXPERIMENTAL RESEARCH I:
TESTING CAUSAL RELATIONSHIPS

CONCEPTS

APPLICATIONS

GLOSSARY OF TERMS AND EXAMPLES   177

CHART 5 - CONCEPT LEARNING OBJECTIVES

Chapter 5 Concepts Objectives	**START HERE** ▼ **BEFORE READING THE NEXT SECTION** Check how well you feel you can accomplish each objective.				**FINISH HERE** ▼ **AFTER YOU HAVE READ UP TO THE NEXT CHART** Check how well you feel you can accomplish each objective, and fix any inaccurate answers on the left.			
	I don't know how **1**	I know a little about this **2**	I know enough about this to guess correctly **3**	I know how to do this and/or have already done it. **4**	I don't know how **1**	I know a little about this **2**	I know enough about this to guess correctly **3**	I know how to do this and/or have already done it. **4**
1 Compare the goals and methods of experimental research to correlational research.								
2 Given a simple two-group experiment, identify the independent, dependent, extraneous, and confounding variables.								
3 Identify two levels of the independent variable in a two-group experiment.								
4 Define and contrast the terms representative sample, random selection, and random assignment.								
5 Explain why scientists do not claim that one experiment "proves" a hypothesis.								
6 Explain why variability is so important when comparing two sets of numbers.								

		I don't know how 1	I know a little about this 2	I know enough about this to guess correctly 3	I know how to do this and/or have already done it. 4		I don't know how 1	I know a little about this 2	I know enough about this to guess correctly 3	I know how to do this and/or have already done it. 4
7	Define measurement error and how it relates to variability.									
8	Describe three important factors when assessing the amount of difference between two sets of numbers.									
9	Explain what "significantly different" means on a basic, conceptual level.									
10	Describe what a p-value tells you about the results of an experiment.									
11	Describe how the null hypothesis and probability play a role in testing a cause-and-effect relationship.									

After you complete this half of the chart, read pages 143-155. Then return to page 141 and complete the white half of this chart.

After you complete this half of the chart, go to your assigned application chart(s) and complete the gray half. Then read about that study to prepare for the research you'll do in lab.

THE ANATOMY OF EXPERIMENTATION

In Chapter 4, we tested a correlational hypothesis by collecting data on two variables and summarizing the strength of their relationship as one number (a correlation coefficient). To make an objective decision about whether that number supported our hypothesis, we then applied a three-step, probabilistic decision-making process where we (1) assumed the null hypothesis was true and (2) examined the odds of getting a particular correlation coefficient under that assumption. If those odds were extremely low, then we (3) rejected that null hypothesis in favor of the research hypothesis. Our conclusion from correlational research would be that the two variables are (or are not) related in some predictable way.

The logic behind this decision-making process will be the same for experimental research. We will summarize our experimental raw data with a single number, just as we did with correlational data. The correlation coefficient represented the strength of the association between two sets of numbers. In experimental research, the single number will have a different name[1] and will represent how much two sets of numbers differ from one another (e.g., measurements for Group A versus Group B). Once we have that single number representing our results, the three step process is the same: We will (1) assume the null hypothesis is true, (2) statistically test the odds of getting our observed result under that assumption, and (3) apply the decision rule: If the odds are greatly against getting our result (less than 5% chance), then we will reject that null hypothesis in favor of the research hypothesis. The logic of the statistical decision regarding support for the hypothesis is identical, but the design, goals, and conclusions of experimental research are different from correlational studies.

Experiments are the only type of research that can directly test cause-and-effect relationships. Doing so requires **manipulation** (of the cause), **control** (of other variables), and **measurement** (of the effect). The logic of experimentation is best explained with an analogy: Assume you have been given, absolutely free, a sound system with *amazing* speakers. There's only one catch: It has no labels on the buttons. No problem . . . you can figure out what each button does and label them yourself. Logically, all you have to do is push or turn one button (manipulation), making sure the other buttons stay still (control) and listen for changes in the sound quality (measurement). Repeating this process for each button would eventually tell you what all the buttons do. Pushing more than one button at a time would be useless because you couldn't determine which button was causing any differences you hear in the sound quality.

 "One button at a time" is the way science progresses, particularly with true experiments. Where correlational research often considers multiple variables simultaneously, experiments work best when the cause and effect are isolated for study. We *directly manipulate* only the cause we want to test (the hypothesized cause). We *control* (keep constant) everything else that might also cause any changes, and we *measure* the hypothesized effect.

The terminology associated with experimentation can also be demonstrated using our sound system analogy (Figure 5.1). For each button, we hypothesize a cause-and-effect relationship between moving the button and sound quality, where the button is the cause and the sound quality

---

[1] Actually, this number can have several different names, depending on how the difference is measured, which is why we are not giving it a single name here. Most often, for this class, we will use a "*t*-statistic."

is the effect. Each hypothesis is tested with a separate experiment, and each experiment will have an independent variable, a dependent variable, and extraneous variables. The conceptual ***independent variable*** is the hypothesized cause, which we manipulate (by setting the button to "low" or "high"). The conceptual ***dependent variable*** is the hypothesized effect, which we measure (sound quality). Other factors that could also cause changes in sound quality, which we must control or try to keep constant, are called ***extraneous variables*** (the other buttons, the power source, etc.). If there are any extraneous variables we can't control or that we accidentally don't control, such as interference from nearby electronic equipment, or power surges in the outlet we're using, these would be a special subset of extraneous variables called ***confounding variables*** because they would confound or confuse the results of the experiment.

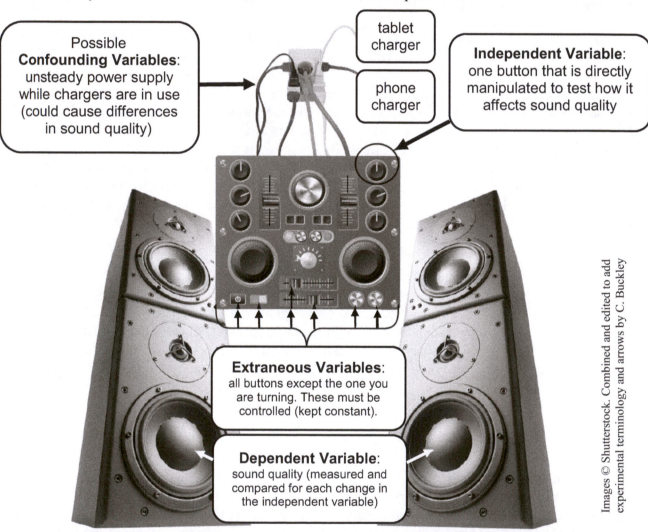

Possible **Confounding Variables**: unsteady power supply while chargers are in use (could cause differences in sound quality)

tablet charger

phone charger

Independent Variable: one button that is directly manipulated to test how it affects sound quality

Extraneous Variables: all buttons except the one you are turning. These must be controlled (kept constant).

Dependent Variable: sound quality (measured and compared for each change in the independent variable)

Images © Shutterstock. Combined and edited to add experimental terminology and arrows by C. Buckley

Figure 5.1 Terminology of Experimentation. We hypothesize that a certain button affects sound quality. That button (the cause) becomes the ***independent variable***, which we will directly manipulate in our experiment by turning it all the way clockwise and all the way counterclockwise for comparison. The sound quality (the effect) is the ***dependent variable***. We measure it to see how turning the button affects it. Anything else that can affect sound quality, for example, the other buttons or the power supply, are ***extraneous variables***. We must control them and keep them still while we see what our single-button manipulation does to the sound quality. Any extraneous variables (things that can vary and affect sound quality) that are NOT controlled (like power drains due to chargers) can become ***confounding variables*** if they happen to change at the same time we turn the knob, because they can also affect sound quality and would confuse the results of our experiment. We do our best to **avoid confounding variables by keeping all extraneous variables constant.**

MANIPULATION AND CONTROL

That heading might sound nasty, but in true experiments, manipulation and control are essential. Measurement is obviously important, too, but that's the relatively easy part. It's all pretty easy when you're dealing with an unlabeled sound system, but when you're trying to unravel the mysteries of thought and behavior, manipulation and control get more complicated. When studying brains and behavior, extraneous variables are everywhere, not just in the power supply or on the face of the stereo; they're much harder to control, and some of them are hidden and might just become confounding variables if you don't spot them and find some way to control them.

Consider this simple hypothesis: *Exposure to classical music improves children's math performance.* Before we go on, note that you can easily determine the conceptual independent and dependent variables for an experiment. Recall the definition of a hypothesis: It is a claim regarding a relationship between two conceptual variables. Therefore, both conceptual variables are stated in the hypothesis. Check your knowledge (answers in Appendix B):

What is the conceptual independent variable? _____

What is the conceptual dependent variable? _____

What might be one extraneous variable? _____

To test this hypothesis, we could expose a group of kids to classical music each day. We could measure the effect on math performance by giving them a math test. But even if they got high scores, that alone would not be enough to support the research hypothesis. We would have to show that they got *higher* math scores than kids who were *not* exposed to classical music. So we would have to directly manipulate exposure to music the same way we would manipulate the stereo button (high and low). Our experiment would have two *levels of the independent variable* (two levels of exposure to classical music): These can be thought of as our operational definition of exposure to classical music: One group listens for three hours per day, and a second group does not. The group that gets classical music is called the *experimental group*, and the group that gets no music (the comparison group) is called the *control group.* Our *dependent (conceptual) variable* would be math performance, and it would be measured (operationally defined) by the score on a simple math test given to all kids in both groups.

Extraneous variables in our experiment would be anything that could affect scores on the math test (other than whether or not the kids listen to classical music). We would try to keep things like age, grade level, and previous experience with the math test the same for both groups. But what about IQ? What about motivation to succeed or enjoyment of math? These extraneous variables have the potential to mess up our results, but would be difficult to control. Therefore, instead of directly controlling them, we will use a process called *random assignment*. Each child would be assigned to either the music or the no music group using some truly random process, such as the flip of a coin. With random assignment, each child in the study has an equal chance of ending up in either group, thereby making it quite likely that things like IQ and enjoyment of math will be distributed about evenly between the two groups. Based on probability theory, the larger the groups, the more effectively random assignment will even out any extraneous variables between the groups. Random assignment is one of the most common techniques used by psychologists to control extraneous variables.

But why use a coin flip? Wouldn't it be easier to just assign the first 20 kids who show up for our music experiment to the classical music group, and the rest to the control group? Although it might seem like people show up "randomly," it's quite likely that the first participants who show up will be the most highly motivated, and might do better on the math test for that reason alone. Motivation to participate would then become a *confounding variable* (something other than the independent variable that could cause a difference between groups when we measure the dependent variable). By not using a truly random process to assign kids to groups, we would be stacking the odds in favor of supporting our research hypothesis, because the most motivated people would have a better chance of getting into the classical music group. Always remember that we are trying to *test* our hypothesis, not *verify* it. Truly random assignment would require that each participant has an equal chance of being placed in one group or another. Therefore, coin flips or some other genuinely random process should be used to assign participants to groups. One might also use an alternating assignment, where the first participant is assigned to Group A and the next to Group B, then A, and so forth. This would not be truly random, but it would create a better match between groups in terms of motivation level (more on this in Chapter 6).

The issues of control and the design of the *control group* are so critical to experimentation that we need to discuss them a bit more. Without the control group, of course, we would have no way of knowing what math performance would have been like without the music. Furthermore, the way the control group is set up directly affects the conclusions we can draw from our results.

Suppose we found that the kids exposed to classical music scored much higher on our math test than the control group. Can we conclude that classical music improved math test scores? Only compared to no music at all. It is also possible that listening to any music might improve math performance, compared to no music. To be able to say that it is the classical nature of the music that makes a difference, we should design our experiment with another comparison group that hears a different type of music, or a variety of other types of music. Or, we could address this question by repeating the whole experiment several times, but with other types of music. But each experiment takes time and money and requires participants who are usually volunteers. We want to get the most information with the fewest experiments, but as more groups are added to a single experiment, results can become more complicated and difficult to interpret. Decisions about how to design experiments depend on a number of factors, including the number of participants available and other practical considerations. We'll learn more about these factors as we design experiments throughout the rest of the semester.

Another control issue is making sure the people in our experiment accurately represent the *population*(Chapter 3) about whom we wish to draw conclusions. A sample of people from a larger group who accurately represent the larger group is called a *representative sample*, and this is what we strive for in all types of research (not just experiments). The easiest way to get a representative sample is by *random selection*. Recall from Chapter 3 that randomly selecting participants produces a *random sample*.(p.82) Mathematically, the larger a random sample is, the better it is as a representative sample. Regardless of the size of our sample, the random selection process assures that no single person from the larger group has a greater chance of being included in the study than anyone else from that group. For example, we could select every person whose social security number ends with zero, or every 50th entry in a phone book. Unfortunately, in practice, random selection is not the norm. Instead, people tend to voluntarily sign up for experiments, so that helpful people generally have a greater chance of being included than others. Although there is some disagreement about this among scientists, in most cases, it doesn't noticeably influence the results, depending on the topic of research. Nevertheless, *researchers and consumers of science should always be aware of how the selection process might impact the behavior of participants*.

Random selection is often confused with ***random assignment***. Random selection is a process by which we *select* participants for our study from a larger population. Random assignment occurs *after* that selection process. Random assignment is the process by which we *assign* those participants to the experimental and control groups, or to different levels of manipulation of the independent variable. Random selection is used for all types of research (descriptive, correlational, and experimental), whereas random assignment only applies to certain types of experimental research. We will clarify which types of experiments use random assignment as we design different experiments this semester.

MAKE YOUR OWN EXPERIMENT (CONCEPT CHECK)

Imagine you want to test this hypothesis: *Offering ice cream at a dining hall increases the dining hall's popularity*. Answer the following (suggested answers in Appendix B):

LEVEL 1 (DIRECT APPLICATION) QUESTIONS:

1. What would be the conceptual independent variable? _____

2. What would be the conceptual dependent variable? _____

3. What might be one extraneous variable? _____

LEVEL 2 (CREATIVE THINKING) QUESTIONS:

4. How many levels of the independent variable would you use? _____

5. Describe your levels of the independent variable. _____

_____

6. How would you measure the dependent variable? _____

_____

LEVEL 3 (ADVANCED APPLICATION) QUESTIONS:

7. What would be the operational definition of your independent variable? _____

_____

8. What would be the operational definition of your dependent variable? _____

_____

Now that we know the terminology and basics of designing a simple experiment, we come back to the question of how to interpret the results.

OBJECTIVE (ODDS-BASED) DECISION MAKING IN EXPERIMENTAL RESEARCH

NOTE: <u>You will not have to do any statistical analyses in this class</u>! You will not be asked to use any mathematical formulas. You only need a basic, theoretical understanding of the roles of probability and variability in making decisions about data. Our goal here is to make sure that all students who complete this course successfully are informed consumers of science.

We'll start with a description of an experiment, then discuss how we apply objective decision making to interpret the results.

Suppose someone in your class claims that drinking a cup of ginseng tea just before studying helps retain information. Some students agree; others don't. Your professor points out that it is an empirical question. In other words, it is a testable hypothesis. She recommends that each student who wants to know whether ginseng improves memory should do an experiment. In reality, no professor can ethically ask students to perform experiments on other students without approval from his or her Institutional Review Board (more on this later), but for the sake of this explanation, we'll pretend the assignment was approved. The experiment is as follows:

> Find 20 friends who are not allergic to ginseng. Use random assignment to split them into two groups: 10 people in one group each receive a 12-ounce cup of tea with ginseng (Group G), while 10 other people each receive a 12-ounce cup of the same brand of tea, but with no ginseng (Group NG). Do not tell participants their group name and do not mention whether or not their tea has ginseng in it. After drinking the tea, ask each participant to memorize a list of 40 words by studying the list for 10 minutes. After studying, each participant should play video games for 3 minutes and then try to recall as many of the words as possible. Record the number of words correctly recalled by each participant and calculate the average (mean) for each group. Your research hypothesis (that ginseng improves memory) leads to the prediction that the group that got ginseng (Group G) will recall more words than the group that got no ginseng (Group NG).

Image © Deamles for sale/Shutterstock

CONCEPT CHECK:
Answers in Appendix B

Before you read on, try labeling the
- ***Conceptual Independent variable,***
- ***Conceptual dependent variable,***
- ***Operational definitions of each,*** and
- A few ***extraneous variables*** in this experiment.

Also state the ***null hypothesis.*** (See Chapter 4 glossary for definition and examples of null hypotheses.)

Since the assignment was optional, and fairly labor-intensive, only the most ambitious and curious students in the class completed it. Below are the *raw data* [Chapter 3] collected by four ambitious students. Their names are Nia, Kiri, Shawn and Antonio. **Each student got a different outcome for the same experiment:**

	Nia's Data		Kiri's Data		Shawn's Data		Antonio's Data	
	G	**NG**	**G**	**NG**	**G**	**NG**	**G**	**NG**
	40	2	19	15	13	10	2	3
	38	1	15	19	19	12	4	6
Number of words correctly recalled by each participant	38	0	19	18	21	13	15	11
	36	3	21	16	23	15	21	15
	39	5	10	12	25	17	23	17
	40	2	21	20	25	18	25	18
	30	4	15	21	25	21	31	20
	35	6	24	20	26	22	35	24
	40	1	15	12	27	24	39	29
	39	2	14	13	30	29	39	38
Averages →	37.5	2.6	17.3	16.6	23.4	18.1	23.4	18.1

If we only look at the means for the number of words recalled in Nia's experiment, it's pretty clear that the ginseng group (G) recalled more words than the no-ginseng group (NG). Nia's experiment would **support** the hypothesis that ginseng improves memory. Note that it would **not "prove"** that hypothesis. Maybe something happened that only affected the people in Group NG. Maybe some major distraction in their testing room interfered with their memory. It is also possible (though unlikely with random assignment), that Nia ended up accidentally putting all the people with the better memory into Group G, and all the memory-challenged folks in Group NG. Although we do our best to assure that the independent variable is the only systematic difference between the groups, other systematic differences (confounding variables) can happen. **The possibility of undetected confounding variables is another good reason why you should think of the results of one study as evidence rather than proof** (see pages 115 & 116 and Box 4.3 for more good reasons).

Now look at Kiri's data. The mean is less than one point higher for Group G than for Group NG. This is not a convincing outcome. Even if she had treated both groups exactly the same (e.g., if everyone in her study had the exact same tea), we would still expect to see some difference in their ability to recall the lists (they are two different groups of people). Is a less-than-one-point difference enough to support our hypothesis? Probably not, but let's reserve judgment for now.

Interestingly, Shawn and Antonio both observed the exact same means for their ginseng groups (23.4 words remembered) and their no-ginseng groups (18.1 words remembered). In both experiments, the mean was more than five points higher for Group G, but there was some overlap; the highest Group NG scores are higher than the lowest Group G scores. A five-point difference in means between groups G and NG seems to suggest an effect of ginseng on Group G's memory, but how do we know when two sets of numbers are different enough to support our hypothesis?

Just as in correlational research, where we had a single number that summarized the strength and direction of the relationship (recall the correlation coefficient from page 109, Fig. 4.3), *We need a single number to summarize the amount of difference* between Group G's scores and Group NG's scores. Unfortunately, we can't just use the difference between the means.

WHY CAN'T WE JUST COMPARE THE AVERAGES?

At first glance, it might seem like subtracting the means of any two sets of data would be a good way to summarize how different they are with just one number (the difference between means). But means can be deceiving! *Variability*[(Chapter 3)] —how much the scores within a group differ from the mean of that group—plays a huge role in how well the mean represents the true value of whatever you are trying to measure. A small town of 100 people can be below the poverty level, with each person making just $15,000/year. If one famous actor making two million dollars a year moves in, the mean income would suddenly be about $35,000/year, even though 99% of the population still makes only $15,000. Imagine another nearby town where everyone actually makes $35,000/year. Before the movie star, the mean incomes in these two towns were very different ($35,000 minus $15,000 equals a difference of $20,000/year). After the actor moves in, if we only compare the mean incomes, we would have to say that one person suddenly erased a $20,000/year difference in incomes between these two towns. Obviously, that would be inaccurate, because with or without Chris Pratt, there is still a $20,000/year difference in the amount of money *most* people make in these two towns.

Therefore, when calculating a single number that represents the actual difference between two groups, we have to consider two main factors: (1) the difference between means and (2) the amount of variability in each data set. You do not need to know how to calculate variability in order to interpret its meaning. But you do have to appreciate the role of variability in determining differences between groups, because it strongly impacts how we design our experiments.

WHERE DOES VARIABILITY COME FROM, AND CAN'T WE GET RID OF IT?

Almost nothing in life can be measured with perfect precision. Chemists and physicists, when they measure the rates of chemical reactions or the magnitude of a force, must accept some degree of **measurement error**, although at the introductory level, they don't often emphasize the uncertainty of these measurements. All psychologists must pay careful attention to measurement error, because measurements of cognition and behavior are, by nature, imprecise. So many factors influence cognition and behavior that it is impossible to hold all of them constant. Even the instruments for measuring our variables can vary a lot. Therefore, psychologists, like all scientists, accept measurement error as a natural part of science. We can't get rid of it, but we can minimize it.

One very important way to minimize error is to take multiple measurements and calculate an average. This is why, in the ginseng experiment, the professor recommended 10 participants (i.e., 10 measurements) in each condition (with ginseng and without). Experiments in psychology measure the same thing repeatedly under each condition in order to get the best estimate of its true value under each condition. The more measurements we can get, the more we can trust the mean as an estimate of the true score. Ideally, that ginseng experiment should have had at least 20 or 30 participants in each group (100 would be great!) but practical considerations often keep us from getting as many participants as we would like. Regardless of the number of participants, there will always be some with higher or lower scores on our measurement than the actual (true) value (whatever that may be), so we must understand how variability impacts our objective decisions.

HOW DOES VARIABILITY AFFECT OBJECTIVE DECISION MAKING?

Back to the ginseng experiment. Note that Shawn and Antonio got the exact same means, but they differed in the amount of variability in their scores. Spoiler alert: One of these two outcomes supports the research hypothesis (that is, it shows a **significant difference** between Group G and Group NG), and the other does not. We're not saying which one yet. . .

	Shawn's Data		Antonio's Data	
	G	**NG**	**G**	**NG**
	13	10	2	3
Number	19	12	4	6
of words	21	13	15	11
correctly	23	15	21	15
recalled	25	17	23	17
by each	25	18	25	18
participant	25	21	31	20
	26	22	35	24
	27	24	39	29
	30	29	39	38
Averages →	**23.4**	**18.1**	**23.4**	**18.1**

In the table to the left, the scores from Shawn's and Antonio's experiments have been rearranged from lowest to highest in each column. For Shawn's study, we can now easily see that Group G's scores ranged from 13 to 30 (a difference, or range, of 17 points), and Group NG's scores ranged from 10 to 29 points (a 19-point range). If you calculate the ranges for Antonio's experiment, you should get 37 for Group G and 35 for Group NG. The greater range (variability) in each of the two sets of scores for Antonio's experiment makes those means less meaningful (less trustworthy) than the means for Shawn's.

Range is just one simple way of determining variability in a set of scores. A better, more sophisticated way is to calculate the **standard deviation**.[Ch 3] This course does not require that you calculate a standard deviation by hand. If you need it, Box 3.2 shows you how to get MS Excel to calculate a standard deviation for you. When comparing two sets of scores on the same scale, the higher the standard deviation, the greater the variability, and the less you can trust the mean as an estimate of the real or true value of whatever you measured.

To test their hypotheses, scientists use means and SDs (among other things, including the number of observations) to perform a **statistical analysis** of the data (see Box 5.1). Applying mathematical formulas and tools designed to summarize the results, we can statistically determine the likelihood of getting those results if our research hypothesis is wrong (i.e., if the null hypothesis is true). Without this, we are too easily fooled into seeing what we want to see. The correct statistical analysis depends on the type of research we do and the type of data we collect.

For correlational research, our analysis produced a correlation coefficient: one number that represented the strength of the relationship between two variables. For our ginseng tea experiment, the statistical analysis will also produce a single number, but it will represent the amount of difference between Group G and Group NG. Box 5.1 provides more information on the factors that contribute to that number. Once we know the amount of difference between the groups, we can determine the p-value, or the probability of getting that result if the null hypothesis is true.

BOX 5.1- What Makes Two Sets of Numbers Different?

For our experiment on ginseng tea, we want to compare the scores in Group G to those in Group NG in order to arrive at a single number that represents the amount of difference between two sets of scores. We'll call this number "t." [2] **Three factors affect the value of t: (1) the number of scores in each set, (2) the difference between the two means, and (3) the variability in each set of scores.** The impact of the first factor, the number of scores, can be most easily understood with a simple rule from Chapter 3: The more scores there are in a sample, the more you can trust the sample to tell the truth about the whole population. The other two factors can best be understood as a "signal-to-noise ratio," where the difference between the means is the signal, and the variability is the noise. As shown below, the value of t will increase as the difference between the means of the two groups increases, but a lot of variability in the scores will decrease t:

t can be thought of as a signal-to-noise ratio

$$\frac{\text{The difference between the averages of the two groups} \leftarrow \text{SIGNAL}}{\text{The variability among the scores in each set} \qquad \leftarrow \text{NOISE}}$$

The bigger the difference between means, the louder the signal, and the easier it is to detect the difference (just as ¾ is larger than ¼, a bigger numerator leads to a higher value of t). The greater the variability in the scores, the louder the noise, and the harder it is to detect the signal (just as ¼ is less than ½, a bigger denominator leads to a smaller value of t). Don't forget that the number of scores in each set plays a role as well, but in our four attempts at the ginseng experiment, we have the same number of scores in every set, so we can more easily focus on the signal-to-noise ratio and how that affects our calculation of the actual difference between groups (the value of t). Here are the actual values of t for the four imaginary outcomes of our ginseng experiment:

> For Nia's Experiment, $t = 30.11$
> For Kiri's Experiment, $t = 0.41$
> For Shawn's Experiment, $t = 2.20$
> For Antonio's Experiment, $t = 0.99$

Compare these numbers to the pairs of averages you see for each student's experiment on page 149. Nia's data produced a very high value of t, and Kiri's data produced a very low value, as we would expect, because t represents the amount of difference between Group G scores and Group NG scores. Note that even though Shawn and Antonio collected data with the exact same averages for G versus NG participants, the value of t (the estimated difference between the sets of scores in Group G and Group NG) is larger for Shawn's data, just as we would expect, because there was less variability in the scores for Shawn's participants than there was for Antonio's participants. Less variability equals less noise, so the same signal (the exact same difference between means) counts for more in Shawn's experiment, leading to a higher value of t than Antonio obtained. It's the same idea we introduced in Chapter 3: More variability = less trust in the means (if we can't trust the means, we can't trust the difference between them!).

---

[2] For this experiment, t is a two-sample, independent t-test, which you will learn how to do if you take a statistics course.

DO WE HAVE A SIGNIFICANT DIFFERENCE?

The graphics below should look familiar.[(p 111)] Just as with correlational research, the main goal of the statistical analysis is to decide whether or not we have support for our research hypothesis. Going back to our experimental research hypothesizing that ginseng improves memory, we must decide whether *significantly* more words were recalled by people in the ginseng group than the control group. **Note that a significant difference does NOT mean an important difference.** It is merely a statistical term that reflects unlikely odds of getting the results we got if the null hypothesis is true. To make our decision, we'll use the same three-step decision-making process we used in our correlational research:

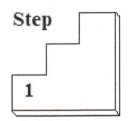

Assume there is no causal relationship. Your experimental research hypothesis states that there is a cause-and-effect relationship between two variables. Just as in correlational research, we must begin the decision-making process by negating the research hypothesis. For the hypothesis is that ginseng improves memory, the null hypothesis declares that ginseng does NOT improve memory. Under the null hypothesis, we predict no difference in the number of words recalled between the ginseng group and the no-ginseng group (i.e., we predict a difference of zero).

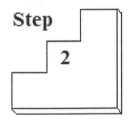

Considering the size of our sample, and the "fact" (assumption) that there is no causal relationship, determine the probability of producing the observed result. We can ask ourselves, if there really is no difference in memory between a group given ginseng and a group given no ginseng, what are the odds that two groups with this many people would, just by chance, score as differently as they did on our memory test? (From Box 5.1, what are the odds of observing our value of *t* when comparing two random sets of people who should not differ?) Those odds are call the *p*-value.

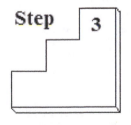

Apply a decision rule. Knowing the p-value, we can make a decision based on one simple rule: A difference that is so unlikely that it has a *p*-value less than .05 (a less-than-5% chance of happening when the null hypothesis is true) suggests that the null hypothesis is NOT true. In other words, a difference between our groups that is so large that it would have occurred by chance less than 1 time out of 20 repetitions of this experiment *when, in reality, no difference exists,* counts as evidence that a real difference probably *does* exist. We will call this probable difference a "***significant difference***," meaning that our data can be used as evidence to support our research hypothesis.

DEFINING AND INTERPRETING THE *p*-VALUE

Whether we are looking at results from a correlational study or an experiment, we always start by assuming the null hypothesis is true, then determining the ***p-value***, which is the probability of getting the observed results under the null hypothesis. You might be wondering why we have to assume the *null* hypothesis is true. Wouldn't it make more sense to assume the *research* hypothesis is true, and then calculate the probability of getting the observed results? That way, results that are unlikely would falsify the research hypothesis. But there is a really good reason we can't do that: If we assume a correlational research hypothesis is true, what should the correlation coefficient be? Would it be 0.98? 0.65? 0.33? There is no way of knowing. Similarly, if we assume there is a real difference between conditions in an experiment, what should that difference be? It could be huge, or it could be moderate. If we don't know the actual strength of the correlation, or what the actual difference between groups in an experiment *should* be, we can't figure out probability of getting the difference we observed between groups.

Let's instead assume the null hypothesis is true. What would be the correlation coefficient? Zero. (See Figure 4.3, if you're not sure why.) In an experiment, what would be the actual difference if there should be no difference between groups? Zero. By assuming the null hypothesis is true, we know exactly what the correlation coefficient or the difference between groups should be: zero. That information is absolutely required in order to figure out the probability of getting our observed results (the p-value).

It may help to think of this as a bet. In order to make a wise bet on whether or not it will rain, you have to know something about the conditions outdoors. Similarly, in order to determine the probability of obtaining a certain result, we have to know about the conditions under which we observed it. If conditions are such that the *research* hypothesis is true, we won't know enough about those conditions to work out the probability of getting our results. If, for example, ginseng does improve memory, we would have to know *exactly how much memory should improve* in order to calculate the probability of getting the differences in memory we observed. But our research hypothesis only says ginseng improves memory, not *how much* it improves memory. The only condition where we know for sure what the difference between our samples *should* be is when the null hypothesis is true, and the difference should be zero.[3]

Although in theory, the null hypothesis states that the difference between groups *should* be zero, in reality, the difference will *not* always be exactly zero. Remember that any two groups in an experiment are two randomly chosen samples from the same population. They are still different people, and will probably be at least a little bit different. But if they're large samples of people, they usually won't be *very* different. To test the null hypothesis statistically, we'll assume a difference of zero. We are using exactly the same logic when testing for a significant difference as we used to test for a significant correlation: Our decision is still based on the ***p-value***, the probability of getting our observed results when the difference should be zero (under the null).

Let's apply objective decision-making to our ginseng experiment. Table 5.1 shows the from each ambitious student's research. In each case, statistical formulas have been applied to arrive at t-statistics and p-values for each student's experimental results.[4] Nia observed a huge difference in word recall between her two groups, represented by the t-statistic of 30.11. If there really is no effect of ginseng on memory, the odds of observing a t-statistic as large as Nia observed are crazy small… this would happen only eight times in one quadrillion replications of this experiment!

---

[3] In truth, we can statistically determine the p-value for any *known* difference between means. Occasionally, researchers do statistically test the probability of *known* differences other than zero. But this is rare; most of the time, the condition under which we know the difference between means is when the null hypothesis is true, and the difference is zero.

[4] These probabilities also depend on the number of participants in each group (in this case, there were 10). They were calculated using the "Data Analysis" feature on MS Excel.

Table 5.1 Results from four attempts at the same experiment (raw data on page 149).

	Value of t	p-value
Nia's data	30.11	0.00000000000000787
Kiri's data	0.41	0.689
Shawn's data	2.20	0.041
Antonio's data	0.99	0.335

Based on Nia's data, we would conclude that the null hypothesis is probably wrong; ginseng probably improved memory. Of course, eight times out of a quadrillion, we would be wrong to draw this conclusion, because a difference at least this large is likely to occur by chance that often. Still, if we trust Nia's data, it might be a good idea to buy stock in ginseng tea.

The other students had more realistic data. With no effect of ginseng on memory, the chances of getting a difference as large as Kiri observed are actually pretty good—about 69%. So there is no reason to reject the null hypothesis. A difference as large as Shawn's is quite unlikely—chances are only about 4 out of 100. So if the null hypothesis were true (that is, if ginseng does not improve memory), Shawn's data probably would not have happened. Shawn would reject the null hypothesis in favor of the research hypothesis that ginseng does improve memory. A difference like the one observed by Antonio is likely to be at least that large (given that ginseng does not affect memory) about 34 times out of 100: likely enough that we could not reject the null hypothesis based on Antonio's data. His study would lead to the conclusion that ginseng did not improve memory performance.

In summary, by general consensus among scientists,[5] **"significance" means that if the null hypothesis is true, your observations would have occurred by chance less than 5 times out of 100.** This also means that when p is greater than 0.05, we have no basis for rejecting the null hypothesis; the differences we observed were "too likely" under the null hypothesis (even if $p = 0.06$!). Therefore, Nia and Shawn found support the research hypothesis, whereas Kiri and Antonio did not.

It is now worth revisiting one of the reasons that significant correlations or differences should be taken as **evidence** for the research hypothesis, **not proof.** Rejecting the null hypothesis means that there is still a chance (albeit a small one) that the results we observed *did* happen by chance, even though the null hypothesis was actually true. For every "successful" experiment, scientists know that there is a chance we could be wrong when we reject the null hypothesis in favor of our research hypothesis.[6] We accept this because we know that it is a small chance—less than 5%. **Our statistical evidence does not prove that a real difference exists; it only shows that the lack of a real difference is very unlikely.**

---

[5] This "consensus" may differ depending on other factors you will learn about in a statistics course. In the meantime, it is sufficient to accept 5% as the standard maximum p-value to reject the null hypothesis.

[6] Scientists are so aware of this chance of being wrong, they even have a name for it: Type I Error.

CHART 5A - APPLICATION LEARNING OBJECTIVES

5A Perceptual Aftereffects Objectives	**START HERE** ↓ **BEFORE READING THE NEXT SECTION AND DOING THIS RESEARCH** Check how well you feel you can accomplish each objective.				**FINISH HERE** ↓ **YOUR LAB PROFESSOR WILL TELL YOU WHEN TO COMPLETE THESE COLUMNS (IN LAB)**			
	I don't know how **1**	I know a little about this **2**	I know enough about this to guess correctly **3**	I know how to do this and/or have already done it. **4**	I don't know how **1**	I know a little about this **2**	I know enough about this to guess correctly **3**	I know how to do this and/or have already done it. **4**
1 Give examples of perceptual adaptation and perception-action coupling.								
2 Describe two examples of perceptual aftereffects.								
3 Explain how perceptual adaptation can combine with perception-action coupling to produce an aftereffect.								
4 Experimentally test a hypothesis regarding the physical location of an aftereffect.								
5 Collect data and interpret an analysis (provided) to draw conclusions about whether or not the hypothesis is supported.								

↓

After you complete this half of the chart, read pages 159-164. Do not complete the white half until asked to do so in lab.

STUDY 5A – LOCATION OF PERCEPTUAL MOTOR AFTEREFFECTS

Image © bikeriderlondon/Shutterstock

To experience a visual aftereffect: Cut out the shape below on the dotted line and glue or tape it to a piece of paperboard or cardstock. Push a pin or thumbtack through the center from behind. Spin the image smoothly and continuously while staring at the center (without looking away from the center at all!). Do this for about 45 sec. Then look *immediately* at the man on the boat and see what happens.

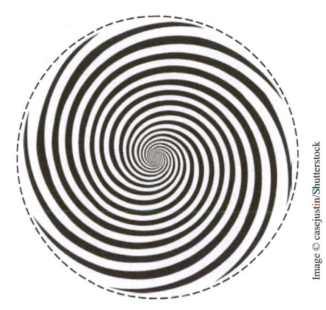

Image © casejustin/Shutterstock

PERCEPTUAL ADAPTATION AND AFTEREFFECTS

Have you ever been on a boat or cruise ship for an extended period? How did you feel when you first got off the boat? You might have still felt the gentle rocking of the waves, as though your brain didn't get the memo that you were back on land. This strange feeling is called a ***perceptual motor aftereffect,*** and it is due to the interplay of two different processes, perception-action coupling and perceptual adaptation. ***Perception-action coupling*** is a concise way of saying that we move our bodies in ways that accommodate what we sense in our environment. This coordination of muscle movements with perceptual information is demonstrated in the picture above by the man's ability to stay on the boat. As his brain perceives the tilt and sway of the boat, it sends signals to the muscles of his body to coordinate their activity to lean back when the boat tips forward, and vice versa (lucky for him!). Perception-action coupling is probably the most underappreciated way that your brain takes care of your body. It is happening all the time, all day, every day, and we completely ignore how amazing it is. Each time you reach for a pencil to jot down a note, perception-action coupling is guiding your movements.

The space to the left is blank so that you can cut out the image on page 159 without cutting any text. Don't cut off the boxes above! But do cut out the spiral and try the visual after effect! (which wears off in a few seconds).

How do we perceive reality? We like to assume that the way we do this is unchanging; but is that a correct assumption? The answer is no. An accurate perception of reality starts with **sensation**, which is the process by which sensory organs transduce energy from our environment into electrochemical signals that the brain can understand. **Perception** is the interpretation of those signals, i.e., the interpretation of sensory information. During **perceptual adaptation**, the way we interpret that information *changes*. As sensory input repeats itself, we begin to interpret it differently – to perceive it differently. We adapt to it. This can throw off the accuracy of our perceptions of reality. A perceptual ***aftereffect*** occurs if our adaptation is no longer correct when the old information *stops* repeating. Something about the sensation/perception process changes during repetition, causing us to misinterpret reality when the repetition stops. Why does this happen?

In order to interpret what one is seeing (or hearing, or touching), the brain must extract information from the stimulation it receives. Information comes in the form of differences, not sameness. For example, compare the two boxes at the top of this page. The left box contains more information, because there are more differences in color, pattern, and shapes. Sameness is not only boring; it lacks information.

To get the most information out of our environment, our brains are specialized to detect differences, and not waste time on sameness. If a stimulus remains the same, like the background noise at a party, we adapt to it by raising our voices to be heard. We don't keep asking ourselves, "Is there a lot of noise?" so we can adjust our own volume each time we speak. We simply get used to speaking louder. It is not until a difference happens—the room suddenly goes quiet (usually just as we are saying something peculiar or embarrassing)—that we perceive the new sensory information about the lack of background noise, usually too late to save our dignity. But most of the time, perceptual adaptation is great; it helps us focus on important information by allowing us to put "sameness" on autopilot.

Dark adaptation is what happens as your eyes adjust to dim light. Your perception of the amount of light changes as you spend more time in a dim room, even though the actual amount of light in the room (i.e., the light energy being transduced by your eyes into electrochemical signals) does not change. Where is dark adaptation happening? Where is the mechanism that allows you to see more clearly? Are your *eyes* transducing light energy more effectively, sending more information to the brain? Or is your *brain* becoming more sensitive to very low levels of incoming sensory information, perhaps getting better at interpreting it? Let's use the logic of scientific reasoning to figure this out:

Next time you wake up in the middle of the night, look around in the dark. If you've been asleep for a while, you will be maximally dark-adapted, so you should see well enough to identify some items in the room. Close or completely cover one eye (but do not put pressure on it). Turn the light on to expose the other eye to a bright room for a few seconds; then turn it off. Using just the eye that was exposed to the light, the room will be very dark. But if you close that eye and open the other, the room will immediately brighten without turning on any lights!

Practically speaking, this means that if you just use one eye and keep the other one closed or covered, you can turn on the bathroom light at night (useful for improved aim or to make sure the seat is down). You can then turn off the light and use the eye that was closed (which is still dark-adapted) to see very well on your way back to the bed, so you won't trip on a cat toy or stub your toe.

Scientifically speaking, this observation supports the hypothesis that dark adaptation happens in the *eye* rather than in the *brain* (the causal hypothesis that a change in the eye causes the adaptation). If dark adaptation meant your *brain* was changing, getting more sensitive to signals from the eyes, then briefly exposing one eye to light wouldn't make a difference—your *brain* would be dark-adapted, so when the lights go out, you would detect the same amount of light, no matter which eye you use. Since this does not happen, and only the eye that was *not* exposed to light remains dark-adapted, we can conclude that dark adaptation is happening in the eye itself.

THE EXPERIMENTAL DESIGN: OUR HYPOTHESIS, CONCEPTUAL VARIABLES, OPERATIONAL DEFINITIONS, AND PREDICTION

If you haven't read the paragraph above, you should do that now and make sure you understand how the evidence supports the hypothesis that *dark adaptation happens in the eye rather than in the brain.* In this research, we are going to use the same logic to address the question of whether perceptual-motor aftereffects happen in the muscles that are used during adaptation, or whether the brain is incorrectly providing information about the environment. We will test the research hypothesis that *perceptual-motor aftereffects are located in the muscles rather than in the brain.*

It may be difficult to spot the conceptual variables in this hypothesis unless we reword it as a direct statement about cause and effect: *A change in the muscles that are used during adaptation causes a perceptual-motor aftereffect.* We have not changed the meaning of the research hypothesis, only the order of the words so that the cause and effect are clearer. Read both italicized hypotheses again out loud if you need convincing that their underlying meaning is the same. With the cause-and- effect statement, we can now more easily identify the conceptual independent and dependent variables. Our conceptual independent variable is the cause: "the muscles that are used during adaptation," and the conceptual dependent variable is the effect: "the perceptual-motor aftereffect." If we thought these effects were located in the brain, we would hypothesize that a change in the brain causes perceptual-motor aftereffects.

To test our research hypothesis (italicized above), we will randomly split the class into two groups, A and B. Every participant will measure his or her baseline accuracy throwing a bean bag at a target. Everyone will then go through an adaptation phase, tossing the bean bag while wearing "prism glasses" that shift the tosser's visual field to the left. When you first put on the glasses, your throws will be off-target, but using perception-action coupling, your throws will generally get more accurate. Eventually, you'll be able to hit the center line four times in a row while wearing glasses that are giving you misinformation about where that line is! This is perceptual adaptation at its best: Repeated sensory input tells you that everything in your environment is actually further to the right than it is, and your perception adjusts to this repeating stimulus and modifies your behavior accordingly. You will then take the glasses off and measure any perceptual aftereffect by re-testing your accuracy without the glasses. Both baseline and re-testing will be done with the same arm, and without the glasses. The goal is to see how your accuracy changed due to adaptation that occurs between baseline and retesting.

During this adaptation period, we will manipulate the independent variable (*the change in muscles that are used during adaptation*) by manipulating which arm is used for adaptation. Group A will adapt with the same arm they use during the baseline testing and retesting, so that any changes during adaptation involve the same muscles that were used for baseline and re-testing. Group B will switch arms during adaptation only (Figure 5.2), so the muscles of the arm they use for baseline and testing will not be used during adaptation. The test of perceptual aftereffects is whether there is any change in tossing accuracy from the baseline measurements to retesting, and the test of the hypothesis is whether that change in tossing accuracy differs for people who use the same muscles during baseline, adaptation, and retesting (Group A) versus those who use different muscles during adaptation from those used during baseline and retesting (Group B) (Figure 5.2).

The operational definition of the independent variable has two levels: (1) Group A, using the same arm muscles for the test of aftereffects that were used during adaptation and (2) Group B, using different arm muscles for the test of aftereffects than those used during adaptation. The dependent variable is the perceptual motor aftereffect, and it is operationally defined by the change in tossing accuracy from baseline to retesting.

Go back and re-read the research hypothesis, stated in italics in the second paragraph of this section. If it is true, we predict that there will be a bigger change in tossing accuracy for Group A (the group that tests the same arm used during adaptation) than for Group B (the group that tests the arm that was *not* used during adaptation). Why? Explain this to yourself (or better yet, to someone else until they say they understand it!). If you can't explain why, go back and re-read from the beginning of this research application (page 159). If you still can't explain it, please ask questions in lab, or go to your PLA's or professor's office hours to get a better understanding.

For this experiment, as for all experiments, we will have to control *extraneous variables*, such as the level of adaptation attained while wearing the glasses and which arm was used to adapt to the glasses (dominant or nondominant). We'll do our best to avoid *confounding variables*, although you might notice one or two, if you think about it afterward. If these terms are not clear, review the information on experimental research on page 143-147, and/or ask your instructor for help.

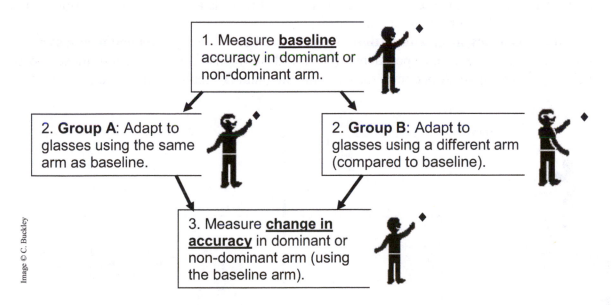

Figure 5.2 Experimental design for the perceptual adaptation study. 1. Both groups start by measuring their tossing accuracy. 2. Then both groups put on glasses and toss until adaptation occurs. Group A always uses the same arm for all three phases; Group B switches arms during adaptation, then goes back to the baseline arm for testing. 3. Both groups test the change in accuracy for the same arm they used during baseline.

PROCEDURE 5A

1. Watch the instructor demonstrate proper data collection technique.
2. Work in pairs. Decide who will be Participant A and who will be Participant B. While A tosses, B is the Experimenter, and while B tosses, A is the Experimenter. Each pair takes one clipboard, one pair of prism glasses, one beanbag, a pen or pencil, and a data sheet, and finds an available target station.
3. General rules for tossing and measuring: Tosser stands with toes on the launch mark (Figure 5.3A). Starting with the appropriate throwing arm (Steps 4 & 6 below), he/she tosses the bag, aiming for the red X on the target. The Experimenter records where the bean bag lands when necessary (Figure 5.3B). IMPORTANT: Tosser must STAY at the launch mark for ALL tosses, NOT pick up his/her own bean bag. After each toss, the Experimenter must WALK the bag back to the Tosser and PLACE IT IN THE SAME HAND FROM WHICH IT WAS THROWN. Do not throw the bag back, not even gently. If the Tosser has to use the other hand to catch the bag, he/she might adapt using those muscles.
4. Participant A Tossers will ALWAYS use the same arm, for all three phases. To control for the extraneous variable of hand dominance, half of Participant A Tossers will use their dominant arm, and half will use their nondominant arm for all tosses.
   a. **Measure baseline accuracy:** The Experimenter (B) measures the horizontal displacement (horizontal distance between the target and the landing place) for each of 10 tosses.
   b. **Adapt to left-shifted visual field:** Tosser (A) puts prism glasses on. Using the SAME arm, he/she completes 25 tosses with no measurements, then keeps tossing until at least four in a row land touching the vertical line (up to a maximum of 20 additional tosses, 45 total). After 25 tosses, the Experimenter (B) starts counting and records the number of additional tosses required to get 4 in a row, up to 20.
   c. **Measure accuracy after adaptation:** Tosser (A) takes off the glasses and then tosses three times with the same arm. Experimenter (B) records horizontal displacement of those 3 tosses.
5. Switch roles. Participant A becomes the experimenter, and B becomes the Tosser.

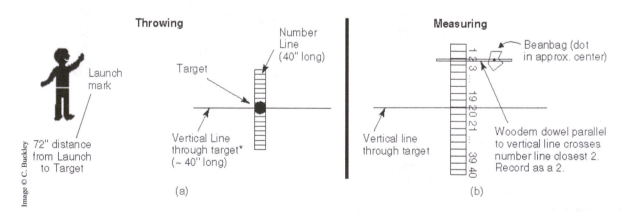

Figure 5.3 (a) Target station, showing where the Tosser should stand and the target station distances. **(b)** To record tossing accuracy, use a straightedge (wooden dowel or imaginary line) going through the approximate center of the beanbag, parallel to the vertical line (vertical from the perspective of the person throwing the beanbag). Record the whole number closest to the point where the parallel line crosses the number line. We are only interested in horizontal tossing accuracy.

6. Tosser (B) will use the dominant OR nondominant arm for baseline tossing as instructed on the data sheet, then use the OTHER arm for adaptation, then go back to the baseline arm for testing. To control for the extraneous variable of hand dominance, half of the Participant B Tossers will start with their dominant arm, and half will start with their nondominant arm. All B Tossers will switch to the other arm for adaptation, then switch back after adaptation.

   a. **Measure baseline accuracy:** The Experimenter (A) measures the horizontal displacement (horizontal distance between the target and the landing place) of each of 10 tosses.

   b. **Adapt to left-shifted visual field:** Tosser (B) puts prism glasses on (adaptation phase). Using the OTHER arm, Tosser (B) completes 25 tosses with no measurements, then keeps tossing until at least four in a row land touching the vertical line (up to a maximum of 20 additional tosses, 45 total). **After** 25 tosses, the Experimenter (A) starts counting and records the number of additional tosses required to get 4 in a row, up to 20.

   c. **Measure accuracy after adaptation:** Tosser (B) takes off the glasses and switches arms, back to the arm used during baseline, then tosses three times. Experimenter (A) records the horizontal displacement of those 3 tosses.

7. Return to the lab and calculate your mean accuracy before and after adaptation as demonstrated by your instructor. Then calculate your change in accuracy by subtracting your baseline mean (mean of first 10 tosses) from your postadaptation mean (mean of last three tosses).

BONUS INFO:
AMAZING ANIMAL SENSORY SYSTEMS YOU WISH YOU HAD

© worldclassphoto /Shutterstock.com

A Sensory and Perceptual Marvel: The Mantis Shrimp. The animal pictured above is spectacular in full color, and can see better than any human can. It has the ability to detect 12 different wavelengths of color (we can only detect three: red, green, and blue). It can also see in stereo with just one eye (we need two). To see this beauty, even with your own (limited) visual system is still quite impressive. For full color video and more fascinating facts about them, see Ze Frank's *True Facts about the Mantis Shrimp* at youtube .com/watch?v=F5FEj9U-CJM Warning: NSFW. There is some mild "adult language" in this video.

MORE AMAZING ANIMAL SENSORY SYSTEMS YOU WISH YOU HAD

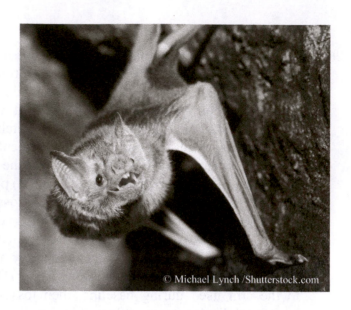

The Vampire Bat. Vampire bats have a type of protein in their noses that allows them to sense temperature gradients with enough precision that they can feel where their victims' veins are located under the skin. This would be a welcome skill for any phlebotomist, who would have a much easier time drawing blood for lab tests.

© Fer Gregory /Shutterstock.com

The Shark. Humans have five senses, and you can probably name them. (In case you forgot, they are taste, smell, hearing, sight, and touch, though). Some would add "proprioception" and many more sensory abilities – up to 20 – but all of these are essentially multiple uses of other sensory systems. Sharks have the same five basic sensory systems, plus two: They can detect motion at a distance using a "lateral line" system, and they have a distributed sensory organ called the "Ampullae of Lorenzini" that can detect tiny variations in electrical fields caused by muscle movements of nearby animals. No kidding. You can do your best to stay perfectly still, but quite literally, if you move a muscle, a nearby shark can sense it.

The Elephant. You might think you have sensitive feet, but not compared to an elephant. They have seismic sensory systems in their feet. Pacinian corpuscles are pressure- and vibration-sensitive cells that are common in mammalian skin (including our own), but elephants have taken them "one step further" (pardon the pun). They have particularly high concentrations of these cells in their trunks, and more buried in the fronts and backs of each foot. They can detect the location and direction of low-frequency seismic vibrations (for example, the rumbles and steps of other elephants) from as far as 6 miles away. Imagine how nice it would be if your feet could tell you when the train you want to catch is miles away and coming toward you.

© Susan Schmitz /Shutterstock.com

LAB RECORD FOR STUDY 5A – PERCEPTUAL AFTEREFFECTS

Name: _____ Date: _____

Research Partner's Name: _____

Purpose: *To investigate the location of perceptual aftereffects associated with perception-action coupling.*

Hypotheses: *A change in the motor neuron pathways (brain-to-muscle communication) during adaptation causes perceptual motor aftereffects. If the hypothesis is true, only muscles that were involved in the adaptation process would show evidence of the aftereffect. Arm muscles NOT involved in adaptation should behave as they did before adaptation.*

Conceptual independent variable (what did we manipulate because we hypothesized it to be the location of the aftereffects?): _____
_____

Conceptual dependent variable (what did we expect our manipulations to affect?):
_____

Operational definition of IV (how, specifically, did we define the IV? What were the two levels of our IV?): _____
_____

Operational definition of DV (what, specifically, did we measure to look for an effect?):
_____

Prediction (if the research hypothesis we are testing is true, what, specifically, would we expect to happen with the measurements in our experiment?): _____
_____

Participants: _____ *college students enrolled in introductory psychology lab participated as part of the course. Gender, age and handedness were not recorded, but gender was mixed and most participants were between 18 and 22 years old and right-handed.*

Materials (list all relevant materials with brief descriptions): _____
_____
_____
_____
_____
_____
_____
_____

Procedure: *Students worked in pairs and took turns as Participant (Tosser) and Experimenter (Measurer). Participants were instructed to stay at the launch line throughout their tossing trials and Experimenters were asked to retrieve and hand the bag back to the Participant and to take measurements of accuracy (horizontal displacement from a vertical line through the center of the target). To measure horizontal displacement, a straight stick was laid across the midpoint of the bean bag at its landing point, parallel to the vertical line drawn through the 20-inch mark center of target). The number closest to where the stick crossed the horizontal number line was recorded. Data collection was a three-step process. During the first step (Baseline), tossing accuracy was measured for 10 consecutive tosses with one arm. For the second step (Adaptation), the Participant wore prism glasses while tossing the bag repeatedly with either the same arm (Group A) or the other arm (Group B) until it landed touching the vertical line a minimum of four times in a row, with no fewer than 29 tosses in all and no more than 45 tosses, regardless of whether or not this criterion was achieved. No measurements of displacement were recorded during Adaptation. For the third step (Testing), participants completed three measured tosses with the same arm they had used during Baseline. All three steps comprised one round of data collection. After the first round was completed, Participant and Experimenter switched roles. Each student completed one round of data collection as the Participant and one round as the Experimenter. Within each group (A and B), half of the participants used their dominant arm during Adaptation and the other half used their nondominant arm during adaptation.*

Data Handling: For each participant (and each arm), how did we calculate the change in accuracy?_____
_____
_____

We used a t-test to compare _____.

Results (see Prediction section for guidance on this) _____
_____
_____
_____
_____

Conclusion

What would we expect to observe if the *null* hypothesis were true? _____
_____

Can we reject the null hypothesis in favor of our research hypothesis?   Yes   No   Not Sure

What can we conclude about the location of perceptual aftereffects associated with perception-action coupling?_____
_____
_____

CHART 5B – APPLICATION LEARNING OBJECTIVES

5B Language and Thought Objectives	START HERE ▼ BEFORE READING THE NEXT SECTION AND DOING THIS RESEARCH Check how well you feel you can accomplish each objective.					FINISH HERE ▼ YOUR LAB PROFESSOR WILL TELL YOU WHEN TO COMPLETE THESE COLUMNS (IN LAB)			
	I don't know how 1	I know a little about this 2	I know enough about this to guess correctly 3	I know how to do this and/or have already done it. 4		I don't know how 1	I know a little about this 2	I know enough about this to guess correctly 3	I know how to do this and/or have already done it. 4
1 Explain the meaning of the term "linguistic determinism."									
2 Describe the linguistic relativity hypothesis in general terms.									
3 Explain how the Stroop Effect can be used to test the effects of language on thinking.									
4 Apply the terminology of experimental research to a study on the effects of language on thinking.									
5 Consider other hypotheses and predictions that can be tested with Stroop-like tests.									

▼

After you complete this half of the chart, read pages 171-173. Do not complete the white half until asked to do so in lab.

STUDY 5B – LANGUAGE AND THOUGHT

LINGUISTIC DETERMINISM AND THE STROOP EFFECT

In 1935, J. Ridley Stroop published an article based on his PhD dissertation entitled, "Studies of interference in serial verbal reactions." He went on to teach Bible studies at a small Christian college in Tennessee, leaving behind a literary battlefield strewn with published reports arguing over the best explanation for the phenomenon he had described. Nearly 90 years later, the Stroop effect remains a popular topic for research in psychology.

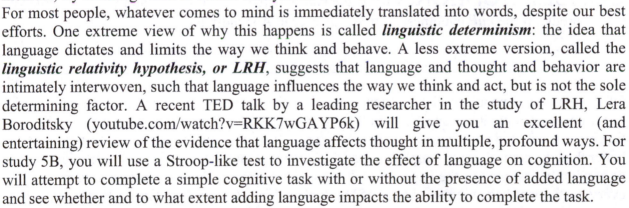

Image © iQoncept/Shutterstock

At least in part, the reason for the popularity of research on the Stroop effect is that it can be used as a way of measuring the impact of language on thought, and vice versa. Try this: For just a moment, try thinking without words. Can you do it?

For most people, whatever comes to mind is immediately translated into words, despite our best efforts. One extreme view of why this happens is called *linguistic determinism*: the idea that language dictates and limits the way we think and behave. A less extreme version, called the *linguistic relativity hypothesis, or LRH*, suggests that language and thought and behavior are intimately interwoven, such that language influences the way we think and act, but is not the sole determining factor. A recent TED talk by a leading researcher in the study of LRH, Lera Boroditsky (youtube.com/watch?v=RKK7wGAYP6k) will give you an excellent (and entertaining) review of the evidence that language affects thought in multiple, profound ways. For study 5B, you will use a Stroop-like test to investigate the effect of language on cognition. You will attempt to complete a simple cognitive task with or without the presence of added language and see whether and to what extent adding language impacts the ability to complete the task.

Typically, the Stroop effect is measured using a color-naming task, where different colors of ink are printed in rows and columns. The cognitive task is to simply name the color of the ink. Due to the complexity and individuality of color perception, the need for excellent lighting, clear color print-outs, contrasting paper colors, and so forth, we will instead use a size-naming task that should work at least as well, with fewer complications.

THE EXPERIMENTAL DESIGN: OUR HYPOTHESIS, DEFINITIONS, AND PREDICTION

Based on the linguistic relativity hypothesis, we can restate our research hypothesis in very general terms as "*language affects thinking.*" This is a cause-and-effect hypothesis, and testing it will require the manipulation of language (the conceptual *independent variable*, or IV) and the measurement of its effect on thinking (the conceptual *dependent variable*, or DV).

We will ask participants to perform a simple cognitive task: naming the sizes of dots inside boxes. There will be five sizes, relative to the size of the box, and participants will practice using the names a few times to make sure they can correctly identify the different sizes:

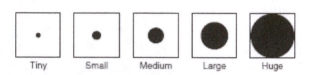

Tiny   Small   Medium   Large   Huge

Image © C. Buckley

We will operationally define our conceptual IV (language) with two levels: People at one level of the IV will see words that might interfere with the task (the *experimental group*, A), and those at the other level of the IV will not see any words with the task (the *control group*, B). The operational definition of our DV (thinking) will be the time it takes to complete the task, which we can measure by observing each other in pairs and using cell phone stopwatches or a publicly available stopwatch at online-stopwatch.com. If language affects thinking, then we *predict* that people who see words should take longer to complete the simple cognitive task than people who do the same task without seeing any words.

CONCEPT CHECK: What is the *null* hypothesis in this case, and what outcome you would predict if the *null* hypothesis is true? (answer in Appendix B)

_____

_____

Of course, some people will be better at naming sizes than others, perhaps because of prior experiences or motivation levels. If we allow people to choose their group assignments, it is likely that more motivated people would want to sign up for the experimental group, and might perform better than the control group simply because they are more motivated. Therefore, participants must be randomly assigned to the experimental and control groups. *Random assignment* means that every participant has an equal chance of being placed into Group A or Group B. We must base group assignments on some random process, such as a coin flip.

We will also have to control *extraneous variables*, such as the way in which the cognitive task is presented and timed and the amount of practice everyone gets with naming the sizes. We'll also do our best to avoid *confounding variables*, although you might notice one or two, if you think about it afterward. If these terms are not clear, review the information on experimental research on pages 143-147, and/or ask your instructor for help.

PROCEDURE 5B

1. You will work in pairs, facing each other, at opposite sides of a desk. Flip a coin to determine which person in each pair will be in Group A and which person will be in Group B. The winner of the coin toss will be in Group A.

2. Your instructor will provide a practice sheet of dots (stimuli) for each pair of students. Keep the sheet facing down until you are asked to flip it over. The arrow should be pointing to the Group A person (the first participant).

3. When both people in the pair are ready, one person (the **participant**) will flip over the practice sheet *horizontally* (keeping the arrow pointing toward him or herself) and immediately begin reading off the sizes of the dots out loud, from left to right, one row at a time. The first row of dots will have the corresponding words that describe them, making the task very easy, and the remaining rows will present the sizes without their descriptions, so that you can practice naming them without their labels. If you make a mistake, you must stop and say the correct size before going on to the next dot. The other person in each pair (the **experimenter**) will be looking at a list of correct answers, making sure that the correct sizes are named. If a mistake is made, the **experimenter** should immediately say "no," and the participant must try again to say the correct size. The participant may not continue until the correct size is named. Neither person should ever be pointing at the dots. It may help the participant to sit on his or her own hands while naming sizes, to avoid the temptation to point at them.

4. The participant should go through the whole sheet, correctly naming the size of every dot for practice. Once all the dot sizes have been correctly named, the experimenter should immediately flip the card over so the dots can no longer be seen.

5. Your instructor will then provide a page of stimuli, face-down so that you can't see the dots. Do not flip it over until the experimenter is ready to begin a stopwatch. (If you're using your phone's stopwatch app, ignore or turn off notifications ringers, lights, or other incoming message signals.)

6. When the experimenter is ready, he/she will start the stopwatch and say "go." The participant should immediately flip the card over and begin naming the sizes of the dots **as quickly as possible.** Ignore any words that are included in the squares with the dots. Just name size of each dot, as you did during practice. The experimenter should watch the answer key carefully, just as you did during practice, and say "no" if a size is incorrectly named. Immediately stop the stopwatch when the size of the *last* dot is named. **Record the number of seconds required to complete the task**.

7. Now go back to the practice sheet and set it face down between the two of you. This time the arrow points to the Group B person, who will become the new participant. The Group A person becomes the new experimenter. Repeat from Step 3. Make sure you wait for your instructor to provide the NEW stimuli labeled "Group B" in Step 5.

8. All scores will be recorded on one Excel spreadsheet. The instructor will compare the mean time to complete the task for Group A versus Group B participants using a statistical analysis, and the *p*-value will be provided for the entire class.

GLOSSARY OF TERMS AND EXAMPLES

Where to find these terms: EP = *Experience Psychology!* (this book),
MD = Myers & DeWall, 2018 (lecture textbook). Figures are in EP.

Aftereffect: After perceptual adaptation, a sudden change in sensory information causes a temporary misperception.

    Examples: For an example of a visual aftereffect, cut out the spiral and follow the directions on page 159.

    Where to find this term: EP 159-160, 162-163

Confounding Variable: A factor other than the independent variable that could *systematically* affect the outcome of an experiment, meaning it is different for different ***levels of the IV***. This makes it difficult or impossible to separate the effects of the IV from any effects of the confounding variable. We do our best to eliminate confounding variables in the design of an experiment.

    Examples: A researcher studies the effect of mild electrical shock on self-reported happiness by asking volunteers to sign up for an electric shock study where only half of the participants will actually get a shock. To encourage those who will have to endure the shock to participate, he offers them cash, but he doesn't have enough cash to offer it to those in the no-shock group. The cash offered will be a confounding variable because it is (1) not the independent variable (shock is the independent variable), (2) it is systematically different between the experimental and control groups, and (3) it is likely to affect the scores on the dependent variable (happiness scores).

    Where to find this term: EP 144-146, 149, 163, 172, Fig. 5.1

Control Group: The comparison group in an experiment. This group gets treated the same way as the ***experimental group*** in every way possible except for differences in the level of the independent variable, so that if we observe any differences between groups when we measure the ***dependent variable***, we can conclude that those differences are due to the ***independent variable***. Usually, the control group is the one where the independent variable is kept at its natural level, not purposefully increased or decreased.

    Example: In an experiment where a new creativity training method is hypothesized to increase problem solving ability, the control group would be a group that does not get any training, or a group that gets a more traditional training method.

    Where to find this term: EP 145-147, 153, 172

Dark Adaptation: When exposed to the dark for an extended period of time, the eyes become better and better at detecting small amounts of light, and the ability to perceive surroundings improves. Brief exposure to light eliminates dark adaptation.

    Example: Being indoors, in a windowless room with no lights, you will slowly be able to detect more and more items in the room. If you turn on a light, then turn it back off, it will be very dark again, until dark adaptation reoccurs.

    Where to find this term: EP 161-162

Dependent Variable: The "effect" in a cause-and-effect relationship. We measure this in an experiment in order to determine whether our manipulations of the *independent variable* made a difference.

    Example: For the hypothesis that caffeine increases irritability, irritability would be the dependent variable.

    Where to find this term: EP 144-149, 162-163, 172, Fig. 5.1

Experiment: The only type of research that can directly test a cause-and-effect hypothesis. Researchers tinker with the cause and measure the effect, while controlling (keeping constant) other factors that might also influence the effect.

    Example: To test the hypothesis that caffeine increases irritability, an experiment could be done where participants are randomly split into two groups; one is given caffeinated coffee while the other is given decaffeinated coffee. The irritability of all participants is then measured. Other factors that could affect irritability, such as time of day, friendliness toward participants, and the belief that the coffee is caffeinated, must be the same for all participants.

    Where to find this term: EP 143-155, 162-165, 172-173, Fig. 5.1

Experimental Group: The group that directly experiences the manipulation of the independent variable in an experiment. This group gets treated the same way as the *control group* in every way possible except for differences in the level of the *independent variable*, so that when we compare the measurements of the *dependent variable* between groups, we can see whether or not the experimental treatment had an effect.

    Example: In an experiment where a new creativity training method is hypothesized to increase problem solving ability, the experimental group would be the group that gets the new training, whereas the other group (the control group) gets a more traditional training method (or no training at all).

    Where to find this term: EP 145, 172

Extraneous Variable: Any factor (variable) other than the *independent variable* that can potentially affect the *dependent variable* in an *experiment*. These must be controlled (kept constant) across different levels of the independent variable. (*Random assignment* is the way that we attempt to even out most extraneous variables between groups.)

    Example: A researcher hypothesizes that watching someone perform a heroic act increases courage. Two groups of participants watch the same video, but with two different endings. In one, a man reaches out to pull a small child from an oncoming train, but in the other, the man must stand on the tracks to get the child's shoelace untangled from the tracks. To measure courage, participants are then asked to climb a ladder as high as they can until they feel too scared to go any higher. Extraneous variables would be things like the gender of the participants, the things that happen in the video leading up to the train, and participants' knowledge of the purpose of the experiment, which should all be kept the same in both groups. Experience with ladders would be another extraneous variable that would probably be evened out between groups using *random assignment*.

    Where to find this term: EP 144-145, 163-165, 172, Fig. 5.1

Independent Variable: The "cause" in a cause-and-effect relationship. We manipulate this in an experiment in order to determine whether those manipulations make a difference in the *dependent variable* (effect).

Example: For the hypothesis that caffeine increases irritability, caffeine would be the independent variable.

Where to find this term: EP 144-149, 162-163, 172, Fig. 5.1

Levels of the Independent Variable: In an experiment, the different ways in which the "cause" from the cause-and-effect hypothesis is manipulated. Levels of the IV can also be thought of as the "operational definitions[Ch 2] of the independent variable."

Example: For the hypothesis that caffeine increases irritability, caffeine would be the independent variable, and different levels of independent variable would be caffeinated coffee and decaffeinated coffee (or caffeine versus no caffeine).

Where to find this term: EP 145

Linguistic Determinism: The idea that language determines how we think and behave; hence, the words and structure of the language we use limits and dictates our capacity for reason and action.

Example: Although it has little empirical evidence to support it, the classic example of linguistic determinism is in the claim that cultures with people who have more words for snow can reason and act in more varied ways with respect to snow than those who only have one word for snow.

Where to find this term: EP 171

Linguistic Relativity: The idea that language influences how we think and behave; hence, the words and structure of the language we use are connected to our capacity for reason and action, but are not the sole determinants.

Example: Both English and Mandarin speakers refer to time along a forward/backward axis (both refer to time as something that is "ahead" or "behind.") However, the Mandarin language also has many more phrases that refer to past events as "up" and future events as "down." Boroditsky (2001) compared how quickly native English and Mandarin speakers answer questions about time, after they were primed to think along a forward/backward (horizontal) axis, or along an up/down (vertical) axis. English speakers did better when primed to think horizontally, whereas Mandarin speakers did better when primed to think vertically, supporting the idea that one's native language has at least some influence on his or her way of reasoning.

Where to find this term: EP 171, 172

Measurement Error: Any source of variability in a set of measurements, such as imprecision or other unknown factors that may affect measurement variability. "Error" is a bit misleading, because anything that keeps us from getting the true or precise value of a measurement is considered measurement error, including unexplained individual differences, which are obviously not "errors."

Examples: If two people use the same operational definition in different ways and get different measurements for the exact same observation, that is one type of measurement error. If they use the same operational definition in exactly the same way, but the observation itself, for some unknown reason, varies from one measurement to the next, that is also measurement error.

Where to find this term: EP 150

p-Value: Assuming the null hypothesis is true, *p* is the probability of getting whatever result we got (e.g., a particular correlation coefficient or value of *t*). If the *p*-value is very low, that suggests the null hypothesis is probably not true, meaning the alternative (our research hypothesis) is supported. If the *p*-value is high, that means the odds of getting our results under the null hypothesis are high, so we can't reject the null hypothesis, and we have no support for the alternative (or research hypothesis).

 Example: In a study on driving while distracted by cell phone conversations, Strayer and Johnston (2001) asked participants to "drive" a computerized simulator where they had to react to signals on the computer screen while driving. The percentage of signals that participants missed more than doubled when they used a cell phone while driving, compared to driving with no distractions. The statistical value calculated to represent the difference in missed signals with and without the cell phone was 8.8. The ***p-value*** for that statistic, given the number of participants observed, was less than 0.01, meaning that if the null hypothesis is true (i.e., cell phones do not affect driving performance), then a statistical difference of 8.8 would have had a less-than-1% chance of occurring by chance, given the number of participants observed. Since 1% is less than 5%, we can conclude that talking on the cell phone significantly affected driving performance.

 Where to find this term: EP 152-155, 173, Table 5.1, see also Chapter 4 Glossary

Perception: The interpretation of sensory information.

 Example: Whenever we look at anything, electrochemical signals passed on by ganglion cells in the retina follow the optic nerve and are integrated with other neuronal information in the brain to help us identify what we see.

 Where to find this term: EP 159-162, 171

Perception-Action Coupling: The coordination of muscle activity with ***perception.***

 Example: When walking a trail with sticks and rocks, you watch where you step, and your feet seem to easily "choose" the best places to land based on your perception of the terrain.

 Where to find this term: EP 159, 162

Perceptual Adaptation: Perception of information from the environment changes due to extended repetition of the information, thereby improving sensitivity to differences when they arise.

 Example: Dark adaptation, smell adaptation, pressure adaptation

 Where to find this term: EP 159, 162

Perceptual Motor Aftereffect: When perceptual adaptation is linked to perception-action coupling, a sudden change in sensory information causes a temporary misperception, often associated with incorrect motor coordination.

 Examples: As you walk on a treadmill for a while, ***perceptual adaptation*** occurs along with ***perception-action coupling.*** You become accustomed to the ***perception*** that the floor is moving backward, and you adjust your center of gravity and your steps to keep your balance. Otherwise, you would fall off the treadmill. Instead, you quickly adapt to the moving floor. But if you stay on for a long time, and that perceptual adaptation is strong enough, when you step off and the sensory information suddenly changes (solid floor beneath you), you will experience a perceptual motor aftereffect. It will feel like the floor is moving forward under your feet, and you may even lean slightly to try to accommodate that feeling.

 Where to find this term: EP 159, 163

Random Assignment: The use of a random process for putting participants into different groups so that they will experience different ***levels of the independent variable*** in an ***experiment***. A random process means that no one in the study has a better chance of ending up in any particular group than anyone else.

    Example: People may be assigned to groups by flipping a coin, rolling a die, pulling numbers from a hat, or any other random process.

    Where to find this term: EP 145-149, 172

Random Selection: The use of a random process for choosing people (or other animals) to participate in a study. A random process means that no one from the larger group (about whom we wish to draw conclusions) has a better chance of being included in the study than anyone else from that same ***population***^(Ch 3).

    Examples: Choosing people who have a "2" in their social security number, or choosing every 10th name in the phone book.

    Where to find this term: EP 146-147

Representative Sample: A subset of people or other animals that accurately represent the larger group about whom the researcher wants to draw conclusions. This is best achieved by using ***random selection.*** When random selection is used, a ***random sample*** ^(Ch 3) is created, which is theoretically representative of the ***population***^(Ch 3).

    Example: A representative sample of all college students in the United States would include students from all kinds of colleges and universities, including 2-year, 4-year, and post-graduate universities.

    Where to find this term: EP 146

Sensation: The transduction of various forms of energy into electrochemical signals by sensory organs.

    Example: Photoreceptors (rods and cones) in the retina respond to light by releasing neurotransmitter.

    Where to find this term: EP 160

Significant Difference: A difference between sets of numbers that would be very unlikely if the null hypothesis is true (by general consensus, it would have a less than 5% chance of occurring).

    Example: On page 255 of MD, an experiment by Ijzerman and Semin (2009) is briefly described. In more detail, the authors found that people who were randomly assigned to hold a warm drink, when compared to those who held a cold drink, were more aware of social closeness to others. In the study, two groups of people, holding either warm or cold drinks in their hands without knowing why, were asked to describe someone and to rate their closeness to that person. Those holding warm drinks rated themselves significantly closer to the person they thought of than those holding a cold drink. Without their knowledge, the temperature of their drinks affected their thoughts of friends. These findings were replicated in 2014 by Schilder, Ijzerman, and Denissen. Isn't psychology fascinating?

    Where to find this term: EP 151-155

Standard Deviation: A way of representing the amount of ***variability***[(Ch 3)] in a set of numbers, or how much most of the numbers differ from the mean. When you arrange a set of numbers from lowest to highest and subtract the lowest score from the highest score, you are calculating the ***range***,[(Ch 3)] which is one way of expressing how much the numbers differ from the mean of the set. But the range only tells you how far two numbers (the maximum and the minimum) are from the mean. The standard deviation is a better representation of variability in a set of numbers because it tells you where *most* of the numbers in the set are, relative to the mean.

    Example: In a ***normally distributed*** data set, [(Chapter 3, Fig. 3.1a)] a standard deviation equal to five points estimates that most of the numbers (about 68%) are within five points (plus or minus) of the mean.

    Where to find this term: EP 151, See also Chapter 3 Glossary

Statistical Analysis: The application of mathematical formulas and probability theory to a data set in order to summarize and draw conclusions from the data.

    Examples: Testing a correlational hypothesis by calculating a correlation coefficient and determining its ***p-value*** is a statistical analysis. Testing a cause-and-effect hypothesis by calculating a number representing the difference between two sets of data from two different groups, then determining the *p*-value for getting that result is a statistical analysis. These are just two of many types of statistical analyses.

    Where to find this term: EP 151-153, 173, Box 5.1

Image © Cartoonresource/Shutterstock

"Guess where I get my best ideas." *

* Alternate caption: *"... and according to my statistical analysis, everything came out okay."*

CHAPTER 6
EXPERIMENTAL RESEARCH II:
MATCHED SAMPLES AND
WITHIN-PARTICIPANTS RESEARCH

CONCEPTS

APPLICATIONS

GLOSSARY OF TERMS AND EXAMPLES

CHART 6 - CONCEPT LEARNING OBJECTIVES

Chapter 6 Concepts Objectives	**START HERE** ▼ **BEFORE READING THE NEXT SECTION** Check how well you feel you can accomplish each objective.				**FINISH HERE** ▼ **AFTER YOU HAVE READ UP TO THE NEXT CHART** Check how well you feel you can accomplish each objective, and fix any inaccurate answers on the left.			
	I don't know how **1**	I know a little about this **2**	I know enough about this to guess correctly **3**	I know how to do this and/or have already done it. **4**	I don't know how **1**	I know a little about this **2**	I know enough about this to guess correctly **3**	I know how to do this and/or have already done it. **4**
1 "Pass" a "test" on experimental terminology and the logic of hypothesis testing.								
2 Explain the goals of experimentation with respect to proof, verification, falsification, and evidence.								
3 Using a signal-to-noise analogy, describe two ways to improve the power of an experiment to statistically detect differences between levels of the IV.								
4 Describe the purpose of matching samples in an experiment and how you would do this with random assignment.								
5 Compare a "between participants" experiment to a "within-participants" experiment, in terms of how data would be collected and what would be compared.								

		I don't know how 1	I know a little about this 2	I know enough about this to guess correctly 3	I know how to do this and/or have already done it. 4		I don't know how 1	I know a little about this 2	I know enough about this to guess correctly 3	I know how to do this and/or have already done it. 4
6	Describe two advantages of a within-participants experiment compared to a between-participants experiment.									
7	Explain what "order effects" are, when (and why) they are a problem, and how they can be avoided.									

After you complete this half of the chart, read pages 187-194. Then return to page 185 and complete the white half of this chart.

After you complete this half of the chart, go to your assigned application chart(s) and complete the gray half. Then read about that study to prepare for the research you'll do in lab.

A REVIEW OF EXPERIMENTAL TERMS AND LOGIC

The remaining chapters will use experimental terminology a lot. Take this quiz to make sure you can correctly apply the terms and understand the logic of hypothesis testing. The answer key is in Appendix B. If you get 100%, great! You're ready to read on. If not, refer to the page numbers after each question to review the necessary information before proceeding.

Professor Stewart tested the hypothesis that relaxing for 15 min immediately before exams leads to better exam performance. Forty students who volunteered to participate were randomly assigned to two groups when they arrived for their 3-hr exam period. Twenty students in Group R were told to study silently for the first hour, then relax for 15 min without studying (they were asked to avoid thinking about course content and instead listen to their favorite music or play simple games on their mobile devices). Then they took the exam. Twenty different students (Group NR) were instructed to relax in the same way without studying for the first 15 min, then study for one hour, then immediately take the exam, without any relaxation between studying and taking the exam. Exam scores were compared between Groups R and NR:

Group R ⟶	Study for 1 hour	Rest for 15 min	Take Exam
Group NR ⟶	Rest for 15 min	Study for 1 hour	Take Exam

What is the null hypothesis? _____ p. 136

What is the conceptual independent variable (IV)? _____ p. 144, 179

What is the conceptual dependent variable (DV)? _____ p. 144, 178

How is the IV operationally defined (what are the levels of the IV?) _____ p. 145, 179

How is the DV operationally defined? _____ p. 145

State the prediction in terms of operational definitions. _____

_____ p. 114

The results are as follows: Group R mean exam score = 86%
                                Group NR mean exam score = 79%

Standard deviations for both groups are about 11 points, and the statistical analysis shows that with 20 participants in each group, the p-value is 0.049. What can Prof. Stewart conclude? p. 148-155, 180

_____

_____

Name an extraneous variable that is effectively controlled and explain how it is controlled. p. 144-147

_____

_____

Name a confounding variable and explain why it is confounding. p. 144-147

_____

_____

DESIGNING EXPERIMENTS TO <u>TEST</u> HYPOTHESES

Testing a cause-and-effect hypothesis with a true experiment takes time, energy, funds, and participants, some of which can be hard to find. For these reasons and for ethical reasons, we don't take experimentation with human participants lightly. Experiments must be designed carefully to have every chance of finding evidence for our hypothesis *if it is true*.

However, it is very important to remember, as discussed in Chapter 1, that our goal in the design of an experiment is to *test* our hypothesis, *not to verify it*. Researchers do *not* set out to "prove" a hypothesis, or to "demonstrate that it is true," or to "illustrate that it is correct," or to do anything of the sort. Instead, we strive to put the hypothesis to the test; *we try to falsify it*. If the hypothesis stands up to this test, then we can say we have evidence to support it. It is the *evidence* we seek, *not* proof, and *not* verification. Even if evidence is found, our (single) study will not allow us to claim we have "proof" for our hypothesis, or even that it is "correct." ^{Chapters 4 and 5} To a scientist, "proof" has a different meaning than "evidence." Proof is usually thought of as established truth, whereas evidence is understood to be dynamic and open to further study.

Attempting to falsify our hypothesis does not mean we believe it to be false, or that we don't want to find support for it. Certainly, if our research hypothesis is true, we want to be able to reject the null hypothesis. We must therefore design experiments that maximize our chances of finding evidence, if it can be found. At the same time, we must avoid stacking the cards in favor of *accidentally* rejecting the null hypothesis and supporting our research hypothesis with an experiment that does not rigorously test it.

For example, consider the experiment described in the quiz on the previous page. It was designed to compare two groups of students: those who relaxed for 15 min just before an exam and those who did not. If there had been no difference in their scores, this would have falsified Professor Stewart's research hypothesis that relaxing before a test improves performance. He could have designed the experiment differently, and assigned his best students to the relaxation group, making it more likely that he would have support for his research hypothesis, because they would probably score higher than the non-relaxation group. Obviously, that would not be a real test of his hypothesis. Using random assignment helped assure that the students in each group came into the exam with about the same chances of success.

Look at the results for Professor Stewart's study on page 187. In order to test his hypothesis, he must ask, with two *randomly assigned* groups of 20 students from the same class, what are the odds that their exam scores would differ as much as these two groups did ("Relaxation" versus "No Relaxation")? Imagine that the groups had not been treated differently. If everyone just came in and took the exam without any differences in relaxation, the null hypothesis would be true, and the odds of observing the difference Professor Stewart reported (between any two random groups) would be 0.049 (that's exactly what we mean by a "p-value."). Since a less-than-5% chance is pretty unlikely, the professor was justified in rejecting the null hypothesis in favor of the decision that there was a real difference in the way these two groups performed. That difference, he can conclude, was probably due to his manipulation of the relaxation time just before the exam.

You might be bothered by the notion that true experiments, though they claim to have the best control over extraneous variables, frequently rely on random assignment to obtain that control. Can random assignment be trusted to perfectly distribute the students into groups with equal chances of success on the exam? Recall from Chapter 3 that the larger the number of observations we make, and the smaller the variability in those observations, the more we can trust random assignment to do its job. If Professor Stewart had been able to test 100 students in each group, with about the same variability in their scores, that would have made his 7-point difference in means much (much!) less likely under the null hypothesis. In other words, there would be a much smaller p-value (somewhere around 0.000004). Two groups of 20 people can differ by 7 points relatively easily, just by chance. But if 200 people are randomly assigned to groups with 100 people in each group, their means are quite unlikely to differ that much, just by chance.

With only 20 participants in each group and so much variability in scores (SD of 11), should Professor Stewart really place that much trust in random assignment? What if, just by chance, even without the relaxation period, these two groups had differed on their exam scores? The p-value tells us that the probability of that happening is less than 5%, but only barely. A few students scoring a little higher or lower could have wiped out his chances of detecting any effect of relaxation. Thankfully, there are ways to improve control over extraneous variables and maximize our chances of detecting differences, if those differences truly exist.

STRENGTHEN THE SIGNAL, MINIMIZE THE NOISE

The decision regarding evidence for Professor Stewart's hypothesis was based on the statistical calculation of the amount of difference between the two sets of exam scores observed for the R and NR groups. The bigger that difference, the lower the p-value, and the better his chances of supporting his research hypothesis. Remember, though, that the actual difference is not just a matter of the difference between the means of the exam scores for each group, but is also affected by the amount of variability around those means.[Chapter 5] The more variability there is, the less you can trust any mean to tell you the truth about the group it is representing. In other words, variability *within* two sets of scores makes it harder to tell whether or not there is a real difference *between* the sets, even when the means appear to differ a lot. It may help to think of the actual difference between groups as a "signal-to-noise" ratio, where the difference between means is the signal, and variability within the groups is the noise.[1]

The **estimated difference** between groups can be thought of as a signal-to-noise ratio $=$ $$\frac{\text{The } \textbf{difference between the means} \text{ of the two groups}}{\text{The } \textbf{variability} \text{ among the scores in each set}} \quad \begin{matrix} \leftarrow \text{SIGNAL} \\ \leftarrow \text{NOISE} \end{matrix}$$

---

[1] The information presented here about the "signal-to-noise ratio" is describing the same concept as "t" in Box 5.1. "t" is the result of a simple t-test, which is a statistical estimate of the actual difference between two sets of numbers, based on the difference between means, the variability, and the number of observations. For more information on the factors that affect t, see Box 5.1.

Imagine being at a party where the music is a bit loud, but you thought you heard your name mentioned in a conversation about 5 ft away. You desperately want to hear the conversation (the signal), but the music (noise) is too loud. What would you do? Either get closer to the conversation (strengthen the signal), or turn down the music (minimize the noise). By analogy, to maximize the chances of detecting a difference between two groups in an experiment, we must design effective manipulations that strengthen the signal by creating real differences between different levels of the IV, or minimize the noise by decreasing the variability in our measurements. Ideally, we should do both.

For example, if Professor Stewart had chosen a 5-min relaxation period instead of 15, he could presumably have expected less of a difference in students' scores (a weaker signal). To strengthen the signal, he could have increased the relaxation time to 30 min, creating a 30-minute difference between experimental and control groups, rather than just a 15-minute difference. But he'd have to be careful! Too much relaxation before the exam could lead to more forgetting. Strengthening the signal (maximizing the difference between different levels of the IV) is made easier by knowing as much as possible about the conditions under which your hypothesis should hold true. The best strategy will depend a lot on the hypothesis. This information often comes from reading published research articles on related topics, including descriptive and correlational research, as well as experiments. Researchers use a combination of published reports, logic, and careful observations to make these design decisions.

In contrast, minimizing the noise (i.e., minimizing variability) can be achieved through various general strategies that are often easier to use. Two of the most useful strategies will be introduced below: **matched samples** and the **within-participants** design. But first, let's take a closer look at where the noise is coming from.

Much of the variability that makes it difficult to detect a difference between means comes from individual differences between participants, whether or not they are in the same group. In the true experiments we've discussed or completed so far, the comparisons have been made between participants in different groups. We call these studies *between-participants* experiments (also called **between-subjects** or **between-groups** experiments). This is a useful form of experimentation, quite capable of detecting differences due to our manipulations. But let's face it; different people differ in a lot of ways, and sometimes two randomly assigned groups of people will differ for reasons other than the manipulation of our IV, especially if those groups are small. So what can we do to minimize the impact of individual differences on our comparisons between small groups of people?

MATCHING SAMPLES REDUCES NOISE

When a between-groups (i.e., between-participants) experiment is the best option (for reasons that will be discussed below), and the researcher wants better control over extraneous variables than random assignment can achieve, using **matched samples** can be a useful strategy. In the simplest form of this between-groups research design, participants are matched as closely as possible in pairs on some important trait; then each pair is split up, with one participant randomly assigned (perhaps by a coin flip) to each of the two different groups.

For example, if Professor Stewart had wanted more control over the differences between his two groups of students in test-taking ability, he could have matched his samples (groups of students) based on their grades on the previous exam. To do so, he would first list all the students in order, from highest to lowest scores on the previous exam. Then he would use some random process, such as the flip of a coin, to place the top student in one of the groups. The next student would be placed in the other group. Another coin toss would determine the placement of the next two students on the list, and so on. Using this modified system of random assignment, each participant would still have an equal chance of being assigned to either group, but both groups should end up about the same in terms of variables related to their scores on the previous exam. In other words, they would be "matched samples."

One caveat when matching samples: It works best when there is good *validity* [Chapter 2] to the measure used for matching. In the example above, the measure used for matching is performance on the previous exam. Is that a **valid** measure of test-taking ability and related extraneous variables that can affect students' scores on the experimental test? It would be unwise to match samples based on an essay exam if the exam that will be used in the experiment is multiple-choice. Many things can affect how students perform on one exam, including the type of content, the style of questions, and individual differences in stress the students are experiencing at the time. It might be better, if the information is available, to match the groups based on their current overall grade in the course. Whatever measure is used, one should never assume it is a perfectly valid measure (these rarely exist in nature). Although matching samples can be a useful technique for decreasing the variability between groups, careful consideration must be given to the measurement used to match the samples, in both the design of the study and the interpretation of the results.

WITHIN-PARTICIPANTS DESIGNS: LESS NOISE, MORE DATA!

Let's return again to Professor Stewart's study. It is clear that even if he matches his samples based on the previous exam grade, there are bound to be some between-group differences in test-taking and study habits. The only way to get rid of all individual differences between groups would be to have the same students in both groups! That sounds impossible, but it's not. We can expose all participants to both levels of the IV, one level at a time. Rather than having an R group and an NR group, we would have an R condition and an NR condition. We'd ask all participants to try both conditions, and compare each participant's score in the R condition to his or her own score in the NR condition. This gives us much better control over extraneous variables associated with individual differences because the individuals are the same at both levels of the IV. There will be less noise (less variability). By decreasing variability, this research design gives us more power to detect differences that are due to the different levels of the IV.

Studies designed in this way are called *within-participants* experiments because the final comparisons are made, literally, within the same participants. They are also called *repeated measures* experiments, because measurements of the DV are repeated for the same participants under different conditions.

In a within-participants experiment, Professor Stewart would test all of his participants twice, perhaps during the midterms and the finals. For the midterm exam, all of the students would be instructed just as they were for Group R: Study 1 hr, relax 15 min, then take the exam. For the final exam, they would all be instructed as they were for Group NR: Relax 15 min, study for 1 hr, then immediately take the exam. Exam scores would then be compared *within* each participant for Conditions R versus Condition NR. Note that we would no longer call them "Group R, Group NR." That would imply that they are different groups of people, which they are not.

Because each student's score on the midterm is compared to his or her own score on the final, individual differences in test-taking ability and study habits should be greatly reduced. There will still be some within-participant variability that cannot be controlled. For example, each individual can still differ in how much stress they are handling during each exam period, and how much time they had available to study for each exam. We cannot completely eliminate all variability between different conditions, even when we use the same participants. As outlined in Chapter 5, variability happens, and the best we can do is to try to minimize its impact.

More importantly, there is a major *confounding variable* Chapter 5 in Professor Stewart's within-participants experiment, as we described it above. Do you see it? Every student is doing the R condition for the midterm exam and the NR condition for the final exam. This means the exam itself might be a confounding variable. Recall that confounding variables are systematic differences between groups other than the IV. Maybe the midterm is easier than the final. This difference can affect the DV (the exam score), and add to the purposeful systematic difference created by the levels IV (relaxation vs no relaxation just before the exams). If students do perform better in the relaxation condition (midterm), we won't know whether it's because of the relaxation, or because the midterm exam was easier than the final. Are students more stressed during finals than midterms? If so, stress levels could be another confounding variable.

The problem gets bigger: Between taking the midterm and taking the final, students can get better at taking exams (*practice effect*) or worse at taking exams (*fatigue effect*). Thus, even if the exams and the levels of stress were the same, a significant difference in exam performance still could not be exclusively attributed to the relaxation, because it could also be due to the effects of practice or fatigue when taking the second exam. In every within-participants experiment, variables related to the order in which the levels of the IV are presented can cause *order effects* (practice or fatigue), making it impossible to determine what, exactly, caused any differences between different levels of the IV. Order effects are also called *carryover effects* because they imply that experience with one level of the IV can be *carried over* to another level, and can affect the way the participant behaves. By either name, that is bad, because it is a systematic difference between levels of the IV other than the IV itself. In other words, order effects are another confounding variable.

Thankfully, these problems can easily be avoided using a technique called *counterbalancing*, in which we vary the order of conditions for different participants. In a two-condition experiment, half of the participants would complete Condition R first, then NR, and the other half would complete Condition NR first, then R. This balances out any differences between conditions that could be caused by the order in which they are presented in addition to fixing the problem of one exam being easier than the other. It counters these effects by presenting all possible orders within each condition, across all participants.

Table 6.1. Summary of the Types of **True Experimental Research Designs** Discussed in This Chapter, Their Advantages, Disadvantages, and Caveats.

Research Design	Is Random Assignment Needed?	Advantages	Disadvantages	Caveats
Between Participants	Yes, random assignment is required.	No order effects; less chance of participants figuring out the hypothesis	Relatively fewer observations per level of IV (given the same number of participants)	Between-group variability
Between-Participants with Matched Samples	Random assignment should be used whenever possible (based on pairing technique in order to match samples)	Same as above, but also has better control over one (or a few) related extraneous variables (decreased between-group variability)	Relatively fewer observations per level of IV (given the same number of participants)	Measure used for matching must have good validity
Within-Participants (Repeated Measures)	Random assignment is not critical, but should be applied to the order of conditions when counterbalancing (see text).	A lot more data from the same number of participants; eliminates between-group variability, which minimizes noise	Not always practical, especially when knowledge of one level of the IV could affect performance or responses at other level(s).	Counterbalancing is needed to avoid order effects (see text)

When Professor Stewart does a properly counterbalanced, within-participants experiment, he will do the same thing he did for the between-participants experiment (page 187), but now he will do it twice, once for the midterm and again for the final exam; and he will switch conditions for his participants from one exam to the next. That is, participants who relaxed before the midterm exam will *not* relax before the final exam, and those who did *not* relax before the midterm *will* relax before the final. In this way, all participants will be exposed to both levels of relaxation (Conditions R and NR), but the order of exposure to R and NR will be balanced across the two types of exams.

Since the mean for Condition R is composed of both midterm and final exam scores, and so is the mean for condition NR, Professor Stewart can now compare means between conditions and ignore the type of exam. There is nothing systematically different about Conditions R and NR, other than the independent variable of relaxation vs. no relaxation just before the exam. With proper counterbalancing, a within-participants design is a very powerful way to decrease noise in order to detect signals. In other words, it is a powerful way to test a hypothesis.

There is another huge benefit to the within-participants research design. By exposing every participant to two levels of the IV rather than just one, we obtain twice as much data with the same number of participants! Recall from Chapter 3 that having more data means we can place more trust in the means, which makes it easier to find evidence for our hypothesis, if it is true. When Professor Stewart designed his study as a between-participants experiment, he was able to compare 20 scores from Group R to 20 scores from Group NR. Each of his 40 students only contributed to one level of the IV. In a within-participants experiment, however, he is able to compare 40 scores in Condition R (20 midterms and 20 final exams) to 40 scores in Condition NR. This, too, makes the within-participants design a much more powerful technique for testing hypotheses.

So why would we ever want to use a between-participants experiment? Sometimes, a within-participants experiment is not practical. For example, Professor Stewart might only have one 3-hr exam period available for his experiment. Another problem is that sometimes, the researcher does not want the participants to have *any* awareness of the other levels of the IV, because this could affect the way participants respond to other levels of the IV. Changing the order for different levels of the IV is not always enough to keep knowledge of one level from affecting another. For example, in an experiment to test the hypothesis that knowing about the benefits of exercise increases workout intensity, one cannot expose participants to information on the benefits of exercise before their first workout, and then expect them to forget those benefits before their second workout. In any study where knowledge or experience with one level of the IV could affect the way participants respond to the other level of the IV, it is best to use a between-participants research design, rather than within participants.

Each research design discussed in this chapter has several advantages and disadvantages, which you will learn about if you take more advanced courses in psychology. In the meantime, a brief summary of some important considerations is presented in Table 6.1.

CHART 6A – APPLICATION LEARNING OBJECTIVES

6A Effect of Encouragement on Grip Strength Objectives	START HERE ↓ BEFORE READING THE NEXT SECTION AND DOING THIS RESEARCH Check how well you feel you can accomplish each objective.				FINISH HERE ↓ YOUR LAB PROFESSOR WILL TELL YOU WHEN TO COMPLETE THESE COLUMNS (IN LAB)			
	I don't know how **1**	I know a little about this **2**	I know enough about this to guess correctly **3**	I know how to do this and/or have already done it. **4**	I don't know how **1**	I know a little about this **2**	I know enough about this to guess correctly **3**	I know how to do this and/or have already done it. **4**
1 Define "hysterical strength" and explain why there has been no experimental research on what causes it.								
2 Describe in general what social psychologists study.								
3 Describe the conditions under which a between-participants experiment should be done with matched-samples, and how that differs from normal random assignment.								
4 Gain experience with the use of an Informed Consent Form for experimentation with human participants.								
5 Gain experience using one type of matched-samples technique.								

↓
After you complete this half of the chart, read pages 197-199. Do not complete the white half until asked to do so in lab.

STUDY 6A – EFFECT OF ENCOURAGEMENT ON GRIP STRENGTH

ARE WE STRONGER THAN WE REALIZE?

Image © Greg Epperson/Shutterstock

It's quite likely you've heard stories of "superhuman strength" displayed by people in high-pressure situations. In July of 2006, Ken Boyle lifted a car off a cyclist who had been hit, dragged, and pinned under the car. Granted, Ken Boyle was a 300-pound power weightlifter, but his maximum dead-lift prior to that experience had been 700 pounds. The car weighed 3000 lbs.

Even if we concede that only one side of the car was lifted, and we're not sure how that weight was distributed, it is quite likely that this was a new record for Ken. The technical term for his experience is "hysterical strength." It is commonly explained as an adrenaline rush—an autonomic nervous system (neuroendocrine) response to an extreme situation, based on what Walter Cannon called the "fight or flight" response (Myers and DeWall, 2018, page 454).

Unfortunately, there is no scientific research that can directly test or fully explain anecdotes like this. A surge of adrenaline can temporarily increase muscle strength, but to what extent this happens in hysterical strength situations remains a mystery. To study these events, we would have to reproduce them, and we can't go around pinning cyclists under cars in front of weightlifters. Biomechanical researchers have examined the physical limits of muscular and skeletal forces, and determined that indeed, our bodies are theoretically capable of strength beyond that which we would each consider our own maximum, though not to the extent reported in Ken's story. Nevertheless, on a much smaller scale, it is possible that we can be stronger than we believe ourselves to be. This research application asks: Can encouragement from others make us stronger?

We ask this question because it is clear that we are social creatures, capable of both nurturing one another and of manipulating others to our own advantage. The flip side of that coin is that in general, we can easily be influenced by others. Social psychologists study how the behavior of individuals is shaped by social situations. Use the index of your lecture textbook to find more information about the seminal studies of Solomon Asch and Philip Zimbardo, and Barbara Fredrickson's work on positive psychology and where happiness comes from. Fredrickson, a prolific researcher in social psychology, specifically positive psychology, has recently turned her attention to the neuroscience of happiness. She was also an influential writer on Objectification Theory (see her 1997 review, listed in the References section of this book) and the subtle influences of cultural gender norms on the mental health of females. Social psychologists have contributed much to our understanding of human behavior. In this study, you will examine whether social influence can affect physical strength.

Yours will not be the first study to ask this question. Jung and Hallbeck (2004) used a small sample of 21 male students and found that encouragement significantly increased peak grip strength measurements. However, 21 participants, as you know, is not a large sample, and no information is available on whether females would respond in the same way. You will use a dynamometer to measure your own peak grip strength, both alone and with encouragement. Grip dynamometers are commonly used by many athletes and their trainers, from gymnasts to weightlifters, and scores vary considerably. Some research suggests that norms can even differ between very large samples of people in different countries (Massy-Westropp, et al., 2011), so we can expect considerable variation in our small classroom groups of participants.

Recall from the Content section of this chapter that in cases where we have a relatively low number of participants ("low N"), and a lot of variability in the dependent measure (in this case, grip strength), it makes sense to use a matching samples technique to reduce the between-groups variability. To minimize the impact of your own expectations on the results, you will see that the procedures outlined below are brief. You will receive more detailed instructions in lab.

In the meantime, note that although published norms exist for different age groups and genders, they are based on professional therapeutic and training techniques and equipment, and will not be comparable to the measurements we take. Furthermore, no one should be embarrassed by his or her grip strength, as it is primarily a measure of forearm strength, not overall strength. It's not even what we usually think of as arm strength, which is in the upper arm. Those who have worked hard to develop forearm strength will generally have higher scores, just as those who work hard at any skill will generally perform better on that skill than the norm. Nevertheless, your scores will remain confidential (no one other than your partner will know them), so you will not have to publicly share your own grip strength. Also know that you do have the option of not participating, without negative consequences.

This brings up an important point with respect to the ethics of research with human participants: Because you are a student in this lab class, you have been asked to participate in multiple studies as part of the course curriculum. Each time, you have been informed of the goals of the study, aware of the risks and benefits of participation, and given the option to decline participation. As students in the class, you may have felt some pressure to participate, or worried that declining participation would affect your grade in lab. These studies are meant to be informative, educational, and fun, and we hope you will want to participate, but you should also be aware that you have every right to decide not to participate, without fear of negative consequences. Your instructor agrees with and follows these guiding principles. However, that does not mean that you can skip lab. If you do not participate, you will still be expected to pay attention to what others are doing in lab and complete lab records.

IMPORTANT NOTES ON PROCEDURE 6A

Rather than a complete procedure section (which you will get in lab), there are three very notes that you should read before participating in this study:

1. If you have either high blood pressure or any reason at all for concern regarding past or future injury to your wrists, arms, or fingers, that has been or could be caused by squeezing a dynamometer as hard as you can, DO NOT PARTICIPATE. Everyone who does participate will be asked to sign an informed consent form, confirming that you have no such concerns, and agreeing to stop squeezing if you feel any pain or discomfort.

2. Research on grip strength is typically performed with very expensive ($500–$1000 ea.), carefully calibrated dynamometers that are recalibrated between each use or every time they are bumped. The dynamometers we will use are very inexpensive, by comparison, not carefully calibrated, and therefore, will undoubtedly be less accurate. While we are hopeful that they will at least be consistent, you should NOT use your readings for diagnostic or competition-related information. As in all psychological research, with the notable exception of research on gambling, no wagering is allowed.

3. Body position affects grip strength readings, so it is important that you follow the directions you are given precisely. Do not change your body or arm position to try to get more comfortable before your measurement.

"Come on, Tabby!"
"You know, you're right! With enough encouragement, Tabby has great grip strength!"

Lab Record for Study 6A – Grip Strength

Name: _____ Date: _____

Group Member Names: _____

Purpose: *To examine the influence of positive social interaction (encouragement) on physical strength.*

Hypothesis: _____

_____

Conceptual independent variable: _____

Conceptual dependent variable: _____

Operational definition of IV:

1. _____
2. _____

Operational definition of DV: _____

Prediction _____

_____

_____

_____

Participants: ____ *male, _____ female, and _____ non-binary college students enrolled in introductory psychology lab participated as part of the course. Age was not recorded, but most participants were between 18 and 22 years old.*

Materials _____

_____

_____

_____

_____

_____

_____

_____

_____

_____

_____

_____

_____

Procedure: _____

_____

_____

_____

_____

_____

_____

Data Handling: _____

_____

_____

We used a t-test to compare _____ .

Results: _____

_____

_____

_____

_____

_____

Conclusion What would we expect if the *null* hypothesis were true? _____

_____

_____

Can we reject the null hypothesis in favor of our research hypothesis?   Yes   No   Not Sure

What can we conclude about the effect of encouragement on strength? _____

_____

_____

_____

We kept grip strength approximately constant across groups in this study using a matched samples technique. Describe another way to control the same extraneous variable using a within-participants experiment. Make sure you include a way to control for order effects, if needed.

_____

_____

_____

_____

_____

CHART 6B – APPLICATION LEARNING OBJECTIVES

6B Effects of Conversation on Reaction Time Objectives	START HERE BEFORE READING THE NEXT SECTION AND DOING THIS RESEARCH Check how well you feel you can accomplish each objective.					FINISH HERE YOUR LAB PROFESSOR WILL TELL YOU WHEN TO COMPLETE THESE COLUMNS (IN LAB)			
	I don't know how **1**	I know a little about this **2**	I know enough about this to guess correctly **3**	I know how to do this and/or have already done it. **4**		I don't know how **1**	I know a little about this **2**	I know enough about this to guess correctly **3**	I know how to do this and/or have already done it. **4**
1 Discuss correlational evidence that phone conversations while driving are related to accident rates.									
2 Correctly use the terms bidirectionality and third variable as you generate at least three hypotheses to explain the correlational evidence that phone conversations while driving are related to accident rates.									
3 Discuss experimental evidence that phone conversations impair driving performance.									
4 Gain experience using a within-participants experiment to test a hypothesis.									

After you complete this half of the chart, read pages 205-207 and your assigned procedure (1 or 2). Do not complete the white half until asked to do so in lab.

STUDY 6B – EFFECTS OF CONVERSATION ON REACTION TIME

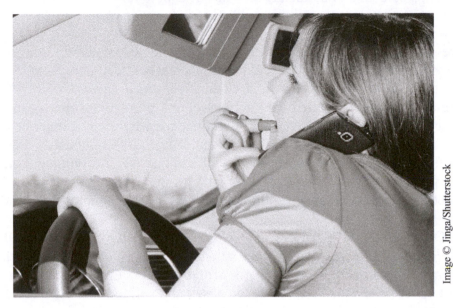

Image © Jinga/Shutterstock

RESEARCH ON PHONE USE WHILE DRIVING

We have all heard the horror stories and been warned a thousand times not to text while driving. As new laws are passed and new distractions for drivers are invented, less and less attention has been paid to the question of whether phone conversations while driving are dangerous. Compared to the outrage over people who text while driving, there is relatively little discussion about placing a call while driving, and most people seem to feel that as long as a hands-free device is used, phone conversations do not impact driving safety.

Empirically speaking, however, that conclusion is not well-founded. First, there is no shortage of correlational research showing a relationship between cell phone conversations while driving and accident rates. In a study of nearly 700 people who had been in car accidents, Redelmeir and Tibishirani (1997) examined phone records and found that nearly a quarter of the drivers had been conversing (not texting) on their phones within a 10-min period approximating the time of their accidents. Comparing this to normative data on accident rates, they concluded that there was a four-fold increase in accident rates among people who converse on phones while driving. Furthermore, they found no difference in this relationship for hands-free (compared to handheld) phones. In other words, they suggested that the increased accident risk was associated with conversation itself, not dialing or holding a phone.

Cramer, Mayer, and Ryan (2007) reported descriptive data indicating that college students are a particularly high-risk group for cell phone use while driving. This correlates strongly with a very high accident rate among young adults. However, critical thinking requires that we consider all possible explanations for these observed correlations, and not come to any cause-and-effect conclusions without experimentation. Other possible explanations for the correlations are not hard to find. Maybe college students talk on the phone while driving because they represent the greatest proportion of cell phone users, in general, and this is no different whether they are driving or not. Maybe cell phone records indicate more phone use within a few minutes of accidents because people are calling someone immediately after an accident to report that they need help or that they will be late for appointments (recall the problem of **bidirectionality.** [Chapter 4])

Furthermore, a relationship between talking on the phone and accident rates might be explained by heavier-than-normal traffic, which could cause increases in cell phone use *and* higher accident rates, rather than phone use causing the accidents (see **third variables** [Chapter 4]). Another third-variable explanation can be called the "self-selection" problem, which is that those who are categorized as cell-phone-using drivers carry with them a whole set of other behaviors that could put them at risk for more accidents. Beck, Yan, and Wang (2007) published a correlational study that documents an association between the use of a phone while driving and other risky driving behaviors (e.g., speeding, ignoring traffic signals). It might be the tendency to engage in those behaviors, and not the phone conversations, per se, that increases the risk of accidents.

Now, IF YOU THINK IT'S OKAY TO USE YOUR PHONE WHILE DRIVING, KEEP READING. *Potential* explanations for correlations, no matter how reasonable they are, do NOT mean that our cause-and-effect hypothesis is wrong. It is a common lapse in critical thinking to assume that any reasonable explanation for an observation eliminates other explanations.

The explanations above have not been tested with experiments, so there is no evidence to support them. However, the hypothesis that talking on the phone causes an increase in accident rates has been experimentally tested several times. Strayer and Drews (2004) found that talking on a hands-free phone in a driving simulator increased reaction time and doubled the number of rear-end collisions compared to driving the simulator without distractions. Alm and Nilsson (1995) and Strayer, Drews, and Johnston (2003) reported similar findings. Strayer, Drews, and Crouch (2003) compared cell phone conversations during simulated driving to driving at the legal blood-alcohol limit of 0.08%, and found more accidents and slower braking time in the cell phone conversation condition, compared to the drunk driving condition. The fact that these studies have been completed with simulators, rather than actual cars, should not detract too much from their importance. In combination with all the naturalistic and correlational research on this topic, the evidence strongly suggests a very real, cause-and-effect relationship between drivers' cell phone conversations and car accidents.

This research project will address the question of how conversation might increase accident rates by slowing reaction time. In fact, since it is quite clear from previous research, including MRI studies, that talking at all (just producing speech) slows reaction time, we are going to compare the effects of normal conversation to a control condition of simply repeating words. In this way, our comparison will more effectively test the effects of real conversation on reaction time and eliminate the possibility that the effects are simply due to the motor control task of producing words.

Because reaction times differ greatly from one person to the next, and in order to get more data from the limited number of participants in our study, we will use a within-participants design for this experiment.

PROCEDURE 6B-1
(for most reaction-time websites and apps)

For example, Humanbenchmark.com/tests/reactiontime/

1. Using a counterbalancing strategy, your instructor will assign half the class to do the word repetition trial first, then the conversation trial. The other half will do the conversation trial first, then the word repetition trial. This will be based on some random characteristic such as the first letter of your last name.

2. In groups of three people, go to the reaction-time website or download the reaction-time mobile app recommended by your instructor.

3. Assign one person in your group as the experimenter (E), one person as the recorder, (R), and one as the participant (P). When all data have been collected for the first P (participant), you will rotate these roles until everyone has completed each role.

4. Each new P should attempt one set of five measurements of reaction time without recording scores, just to get used to how reaction time is measured.

5. When five measurements have been completed, reload the page before starting the first experimental trial. This will reset the trial number on the screen, making recording of data much easier for R.

6. When P is ready, R starts a timer for a 2-min trial. As soon as the timer begins, P begins a set of five reaction-time measurements. At the same time, E begins either asking questions from the script that P must immediately answer (conversation condition), or reading words from the word list that P must immediately repeat (word repetition condition). The condition that is completed first is based on P's assignment from Step 1 above. As each reaction-time score is displayed, R will immediately record it on the data sheet. As each set of five is completed, P will immediately begin another set of five reactions while E continues to ask questions or say words. This continues until timer indicates the 2 min are up. Note to R: if you miss a reaction time, DON'T GUESS. Simply skip it and record the next one.

7. The same participant will repeat Step 6 for the other condition (word repetition or conversation). R takes data for another 2-min interval.

8. Switch roles and repeat Steps 6 and 7. Then switch roles again and repeat Steps 6 and 7 again.

9. Enter all data into excel for each participant and calculate average reaction times for each condition. If you skipped any data boxes, don't forget to subtract the number of missing data points from the total number of scores before calculating the average.

10. Send the data file to your lab instructor and begin work on your lab record.

6B Data Sheet for Use With Procedure 1

Important: In the gray box at the top of each column, indicate the condition for that column (circle "WR" for Word Repetition, or circle "C" for Conversation). You will not need all Trial boxes.

1st Participant			2nd Participant			3rd Participant		
Trial Number	WR or C	WR or C	Trial Number	WR or C	WR or C	Trial Number	WR or C	WR or C
1			1			1		
2			2			2		
3			3			3		
4			4			4		
5			5			5		
6			6			6		
7			7			7		
8			8			8		
9			9			9		
10			10			10		
11			11			11		
12			12			12		
13			13			13		
14			14			14		
15			15			15		
16			16			16		
17			17			17		
18			18			18		
19			19			19		
20			20			20		
21			21			21		
22			22			22		
23			23			23		
24			24			24		
25			25			25		
26			26			26		
27			27			27		
28			28			28		
29			29			29		
30			30			30		

PROCEDURE 6B-2

For use with railroadersleep.org/Explore/Your-Sleep-Toolkit/Test-Your-Reaction-Time

1. Work in pairs. Flip a coin to see who will be Participant 1 and Participant 2. Call heads or tails first.
   WINNER: Participant 1
   OTHER: Participant 2
2. To counterbalance the order of the two conditions, one person in your pair will do the Conversation task first, then the Word Repetition task, and the other person will do the Word Repetition task first, then Conversation. This will be assigned based on where you are sitting in the class, with half the pairs assigned to each order.
3. Fill in the boxes on the data sheet on page 210 (at the top of each column) indicating the order of the conditions BEFORE YOU BEGIN ANY DATA COLLECTION.
4. With your partner, go to the reaction-time website. Click "Ramp up" and "You're all set to go." Do not enter sleep information. Read the rest of these instructions BEFORE you press the spacebar to start.
5. In the following steps, P stands for the participant and E for the experimenter. After all data have been collected for the first P (Participant 1), you will switch roles. E always sits to the right of P, like a passenger in a car (in the US). This is so that E can reach the "bail out" button when the trial ends.
6. When P is ready (read all steps below first!), he/she will hit the spacebar to begin a 1-min trial. At the same time, E begins a 1-min timer and follows the correct instructions from Step 7. While E presents the words or questions, P's goal is to perform the task while reacting as quickly as possible to each picture that pops up in the road by hitting the spacebar to switch lanes. P must wait for each picture before hitting the spacebar. If you hit the spacebar before a picture, you will get a "False Start" penalty added to your score at the end. There will also be a "crash" penalty, so be sure to react quickly to avoid crashes.
7. Directions for Experimenter (E): If P's first condition is WR (word repetition), then as soon as you start the timer, begin reading only the words in red from Word List A. While "driving," P must immediately repeat each word. If condition C is first, then read the entire questions that include the red words from the Word List A. P must immediately answer each question. Correct answers are provided after each question in parentheses. If answer is wrong, E should say, "try again" until a correct answer is given, up to three times. If the third answer is still wrong, proceed to the next question. **When the timer rings at 1 min**, E should immediately click on "bail out." Then click "See results." Record the number of false starts and crashes, and use the data charts to calculate your score.
8. Repeat Step 7 with the same Participant, but use Word List B and switch conditions. (If P just repeated words, he or she must now answer the question for each of the words on List B while doing the driving task. If s/he answered questions on with List A, then s/he will now repeat only the words in red on List B while doing the driving task.)
9. Switch roles and repeat Steps 7 and 8, but use Word Lists C and D. The Experimenter becomes Participant 2. Make sure Participant 2 gets words from Word Lists C & D and does the conditions in the OPPOSITE order compared to Participant 1. If Participant 1 started with Word Repetition, Participant 2 must start with the Conversation condition.
10. Report all four scores to your lab instructor and begin work on your lab record.

6B Data Sheet for Use with Procedure 2

For use with
railroadersleep.org/Explore/Your-Sleep-Toolkit/Test-Your-Reaction-Time

Important: Do TWO coin tosses:

1st COIN TOSS – WINNER is PARTICIPANT 1.

For HALF OF THE PAIRS, PARTICIPANT 1 WILL DO CONVERSATION (C) FIRST, THEN WORD REPETITION (R). ALL OTHER PAIRS WILL DO WR FIRST, THEN C.

For Participant 1, in the box labeled "First Condition" and "Second Condition" write in "WR" and "C" or "C" and "WR" <u>based on the order you were assigned</u>.

Reverse that order for Participant 2.

Participant 1: Is English your first language?		**Yes**		**No**
Word List A: First Condition →		**Word List B**: Second Condition →		
Average Reaction Time →		Average Reaction Time →		
Number of False Starts	×.02 =	Number of False Starts	×.02 =	
Number of Accidents	×.05 =	Number of Accidents	×.05 =	
SCORE (total) →		SCORE (total) →		

Participant 2: Is English your first language?		**Yes**		**No**
Word List C: First Condition →		**Word List D**:: Second Condition →		
Average Reaction Time →		Average Reaction Time →		
Number of False Starts	×.02 =	Number of False Starts	×.02 =	
Number of Accidents	×.05 =	Number of Accidents	×.05 =	
SCORE (total) →		SCORE (total) →		

$$Score = Average + (Fasle\ Starts \times 0.02) + (Accidents \times 0.05)$$

Each false start adds 2% of a second to your average reaction time.
Each accident adds 5% of a second to your average reaction time.

GLOSSARY OF TERMS AND EXAMPLES

Where to find these terms: EP = *Experience Psychology!* (this book), MD = Myers & DeWall, 2018 (lecture textbook). Figures are in EP.

Between-Groups: See ***between-participants.***

Between-Participants: Describes an experiment that uses different participants at each *level of the independent variable.*[Chapter 5] Also called "*between-groups*" or "*between-subjects.*"

 Example: Research by Albert Bandura exposed some children to an adult model who was beating up on an inflatable clown-doll. A different group of children played in the same room at another time, and did not witness this adult's violent behavior. Both groups of children were later observed in a room with a variety of toys, including the inflatable clown. Those who witnessed the adult beating up on the doll displayed significantly more aggressive behavior. Because the children in the two levels of the independent variable (exposure to violent behavior) were different children, randomly assigned to one group or the other, this is a between-participants, true experiment. The aggressive behavior the children displayed (DV) was compared *between participants* or *between groups* of participants.

 Where to find this term: EP 190, 194, Table 6.1

Between-Subjects: See ***between-participants***.

Carryover Effects: See ***order effects***.

Counterbalancing: In an experiment where participants experience more than one level of the independent variable (i.e., a ***within-participants*** experiment), the order in which the levels are presented must be different for different participants. For proper counterbalancing, whenever conditions of the experiment permit, all possible orders should be systematically represented at each level of the IV, and these orders should be randomly assigned to the participants.

 Example: Imagine a within-participants experiment to test the hypothesis that room temperature affects reaction time, with three levels of room temperature, 50 °F, 70 °F, and 90 °F. All participants would take the same reaction time test three times, once at 50 °F, once at 70 °F, and once at 90 °F. Since they could get better at the test each time they take it (***practice effect***) or they could get more bored/tired each time they take the test (***fatigue effect***), the order in which they are exposed to the three temperatures must be counterbalanced. There are six possible orders for three different temperatures, so one sixth of the participants should be randomly assigned to each of those six orders (50-70-90, 50-90-70, 70-50-90, 70-90-50, 90-50-70, and 90-70-50)

 Where to find this term: EP 192, 194, 207, Table 6.1

Fatigue Effect: In ***within-participants*** designs, because participants are exposed to the measurement of the DV more than once, they can get tired and get worse at it each time. If a worse score is observed the second time the DV is measured, that could be due to the fatigue, rather than the manipulation of the IV.

 Example: See example given for ***order effects***.

 Where to find this term: EP 192

Matching Groups: See ***matched samples***.

Matched Samples: A technique used in a ***between-participants*** experiment that is designed to minimize variability related to some extraneous variable by purposefully setting up the groups so that they are matched using some measure of that variable. Participants are first measured for the extraneous variable, then ranked according to their score. Starting with the top ranking, pairs of participants are split and randomly assigned to the different groups to test two different levels of the IV. Also called "***matched groups.***"

    Example: To test the hypothesis that fear of flying can be decreased with her therapy technique, a researcher recruits 50 volunteers. Because they vary a lot in terms of how afraid they are of flying before the experiment, she gives them all a survey to measure their fear of flying. To match her samples (groups), she lists participants in order from the highest to the lowest fear score, and breaks this list up from top to bottom in pairs. She randomly assigns one person from each pair to be in the therapy group and the other in a no-therapy group. In this way, the groups will be closely matched in terms of their baseline fear of flying, but still randomly assigned to different groups.

    Where to find this term: EP 190-191, Table 6.1

Order Effects: In ***within-participants*** designs, the order of exposure to different levels of the independent variable can become a ***confounding variable***.[Chapter 5] Order effects can improve performance each time the participant is exposed to a new level of the independent variable (***practice effect***), or they can impair performance each time (***fatigue effect***). Also called ***carryover effects.***

    Example: In an experiment designed to test the hypothesis that the presence of a female observer affects men's high-jump performance, male participants are first trained on how to jump as high as possible. After a 10-min rest, a female experimenter arrives to measure the maximum height the participant can jump. That experimenter then leaves and a male experimenter arrives to measure the participant's jump height again. Researchers predict males will jump higher for the female experimenter than for the male. Because every participant jumped for a female experimenter first, and then a male, the researchers should be concerned about order effects: If the participants jump significantly lower for the male experimenter, that could be because they were tired out by the time the male experimenter arrived (***fatigue effect***). Similarly, if they jump higher for the male experimenter, that could be because they have gotten better at high-jumping (***practice effect***). To avoid this confounding variable, one half of the participants should see the female experimenter first, and one half should see the male experimenter first (see ***counterbalancing***).

    Where to find this term: EP 192, Table 6.1

Practice Effect: In ***within-participants*** designs, because participants are exposed to the measurement of the DV more than once, they can get better at it. Thus, if a better score is observed the second time the DV is measured, the effect of the purposeful manipulation of the conditions is confounded with the effect of practice.

    Example: See example given for ***order effects***.
    Where to find this term: EP 192

Repeated Measures: See ***within-participants***.

Within-Participants: Describes an experiment that uses the same participants at each level of the independent variable. Also called "***repeated measures.***"

Example: A recent experiment by Vliek and Rotteveel (2012) tested the hypothesis that "when time flies, people are more likely to assess the experience positively than when time drags." All participants were asked to assess the emotion expressed on individually presented faces, and were told that the faces would be presented on a computer screen for 8 sec each. In truth, sometimes the faces were shown for only 6 sec (the "time flies" condition), and sometimes they were shown for 10 sec (the "time drags" condition). People rated the same faces more positively when they were only viewed for 6 sec, compared to when they were viewed for 10 sec. Because each participant experienced both the "time flies" and the "time drags" conditions, this was a within-participants experiment. Ratings of faces were compared for each time condition *within* participants. In other words, there were *repeated measures* of face ratings.

Where to find this term: EP 190-194, 206, Table 6.1

Frankenphobia: the inability to focus on today's experiment because last week's is sneaking up on you.

CHAPTER 7
QUASI-EXPERIMENTAL RESEARCH

CONCEPTS

APPLICATIONS

GLOSSARY OF TERMS AND EXAMPLES

CHART 7 - CONCEPT LEARNING OBJECTIVES

Chapter 7 Concepts Objectives	START HERE ▼ BEFORE READING THE NEXT SECTION Check how well you feel you can accomplish each objective.					FINISH HERE ▼ AFTER YOU HAVE READ UP TO THE NEXT CHART Check how well you feel you can accomplish each objective, and fix any inaccurate answers on the left.			
	I don't know how **1**	I know a little about this **2**	I know enough about this to guess correctly **3**	I know how to do this and/or have already done it. **4**		I don't know how **1**	I know a little about this **2**	I know enough about this to guess correctly **3**	I know how to do this and/or have already done it. **4**
1 Explain the difference between a quasi-experiment and a true experiment.									
2 Discuss the similarities between correlational and quasi-experimental research.									
3 Explain why an experiment comparing two or more groups without random assignment might be called quasi-experimental.									
4 Explain the main benefit of doing true experiments rather than quasi-experiments.									
5 Explain two factors that often cause researchers to choose a quasi-experiment over a true experiment.									

		I don't know how 1	I know a little about this 2	I know enough about this to guess correctly 3	I know how to do this and/or have already done it. 4	I don't know how 1	I know a little about this 2	I know enough about this to guess correctly 3	I know how to do this and/or have already done it. 4
6	Provide an example of a study with non-equivalent groups and discuss at least one confounding variable.								

After you complete this half of the chart, read pages 221-228. Then return to page 219 and complete the white half of this chart.

After you complete this half of the chart, go to your assigned application chart(s) and complete the gray half. Then read about that study to prepare for the research you'll do in lab.

QUASI-EXPERIMENTS VS TRUE EXPERIMENTS

In 2011, Daniel Shechtman won the Nobel Prize in Chemistry for his discovery of "quasicrystals." While true crystals are defined by their three-dimensional, repeating patterns that fit neatly together with no gaps between the patterns, quasicrystals have no obvious repeating pattern in their structure, but still manage to fit neatly together to form a crystal-like substance with no gaps. Shechtman had discovered crystals that other chemists said were "not really crystals." His discovery was so radical when he first reported it in 1982 that he was dismissed from his laboratory and accused of being an embarrassment to other chemists! They were wrong. Since then, due to their hard, yet slippery qualities, quasicrystals have found applications in nonstick frying pans and surgical tools, among other things, and nearly 30 years after the publication of this work, Dr. Shechtman was recognized as having radically changed our understanding of crystalline structures.

There are at least three morals to this story. First, doing real science takes courage. You have to be willing to share your evidence, even (perhaps especially) when it disagrees with common knowledge. Second, it takes clear records, clear communication, and the work of many for science to progress. Shechtman's paper was reviewed, published, scrutinized, replicated, and expanded to arrive at our current understanding of quasicrystals and their applications. Third, the fact that a word starts with the prefix "quasi" does not make it any less meaningful or useful!

The prefix "quasi" means "resembling, but not equivalent to." A quasicrystal has some of the same properties as other crystals, but is different enough that it cannot be called a true crystal. Similarly, a *quasi-experiment* has some of the characteristics of a true experiment, but lacks one very important, defining characteristic: **control over variables that can affect the outcome**.

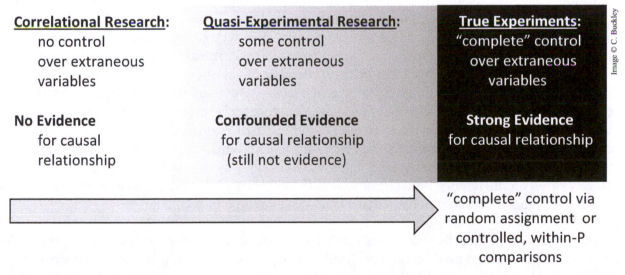

Figure 7.1 A continuum of control, showing types of hypothesis-testing research, from correlational studies, which have no control over any variables, to experimental studies that control extraneous variables using random assignment or within-participant designs. Quasi-experiments are in a gray area indicating no clear evidence for causal relationships. This is because there are different types of quasi-experiments with varying amounts of control over extraneous variables. Some quasi-experiments have no more control than a correlational study, and even those that do have more control still have confounding variables, which means they cannot offer evidence for a causal relationship. Only true experiments, in the black and white area, offer clear evidence (*not proof!*) for causal relationships.

221 ———————————————————— Chapter 7

In previous chapters, we have stated the defining characteristics of correlational and experimental research: Correlational studies measure existing variables. There is no control over those variables or anything that might affect them; True experiments attempt to isolate and directly manipulate one variable (the IV) while keeping complete control over all other relevant, extraneous variables. Those variables that cannot be directly controlled are assumed to be indirectly controlled by random assignment or by making comparisons within the same individuals (within-participants design). If an extraneous variable is not controlled, it becomes a confounding variable, often leading to a dismissal of the results. If we think of "control" on a continuum from none at all to the maximum amount, correlational research and experimental research are at opposite extremes. Quasi-experimental types of research can be placed along the continuum, usually closer to the correlational end, and never sharing the space with real evidence for a cause-and-effect relationship (Figure 7.1).

Quasi-experiments include a wide variety of techniques for testing hypotheses. While they often claim to be testing cause-and-effect hypotheses, and will sometimes (boldly) conclude that a cause-and-effect relationship exists, it is important to note that any one such study cannot provide evidence for a causal relationship. The only type of study that can provide evidence for a cause-and-effect-relationship is a true experiment.

HOW DOES A LACK OF CONTROL MAKE QUASI-EXPERIMENTS DIFFERENT?

Let's first consider what control does for us. True experiments are designed to control everything that can affect the dependent variable. That requires a **control group** (or at least one group or condition for comparison to the experimental group or condition).[Chapter 5] For example, to test whether a new medicine reduces headache pain, we might randomly assign people with headaches to take either the new medicine or simple aspirin. We would then compare the number of headaches that go away in both groups. Due to **random assignment** [Chapter 5] of participants to the different groups, variables that cannot be controlled but might affect the dependent variable, such as caffeine addiction or the intensity of the headache before the medicine, are assumed to be represented equally in the two different groups. Random assignment does not *guarantee* that all other relevant, extraneous variables are equally represented in different groups, but it does make differences between groups unlikely, especially for large groups.[1] Ideally, the consequence of this amount of control (keeping two groups the same in every way except for the levels of the IV) is that any observed difference between groups in the dependent variable (headache relief) can *only* be caused by the differences in the independent variable (type of medicine).[2]

To varying degrees, quasi-experiments don't have control over those extraneous variables. For example, a quasi-experiment on our new headache medicine might simply ask volunteers to try it and report how well it works. (This would be a single-group, posttest quasi-experiment, as

---

[1] This is yet another opportunity to remind ourselves that evidence from one study is not equivalent to proof, and that studies with many participants can produce stronger evidence than those with few participants.

[2] Of course, a big difference can also occur randomly between any two groups, even if everything about those two groups is equal (variability happens!). Our p-values tells us how unlikely that is! If it's very unlikely ($p < .05$), then we can conclude that the difference we observed was due to the different levels of the IV.

described in Box 7.1). With no comparison group, there is no control at all over extraneous variables. We have no way of knowing whether the medicine was more effective than any other, or indeed, if it was effective at all. With rare exceptions, every headache eventually goes away. Did these headaches go away faster than normal? With no "normal" comparison group, we have no way of knowing. We could get some control over some extraneous variables by asking people who decide not to take the medicine to serve as a comparison group. We could make sure both groups are the same age and that they have similar medical histories. But if the participants themselves decide which group they'll be in (take the medicine or don't), then there is no random assignment; therefore no control over other important extraneous variables, such as... Can you name a few?

How about the motivation to get relief, which might be linked to how intense the headaches are to begin with? For some people, headaches tend to go away quickly without medication, so they rarely take anything. These people would probably choose to be in our comparison group. Those who have stubborn or intense headaches that take a long time to go away would probably choose to be in the experimental group. If so, we might find that our medicine appears to extend headache pain, compared to taking nothing at all! Obviously, the lack of control over extraneous variables would cost us the ability to draw trustworthy cause-and-effect conclusions.

A practical point is worth considering here: Every time a commercial for a product claims "these people used this product, and just look the results!" scientific reasoning says that no evidence for a cause-and-effect relationship has been offered, even when the sad people who chose a different product are shown for comparison. Without control over extraneous variables, there are likely to be many relevant differences between the people who used the product and those who did not.

The lack of control in quasi-experimental research and the inability to draw cause-and-effect conclusions raises an interesting question: Why would a serious scientist ever want to do quasi-experimental research? What purpose does it serve?

REASONS FOR CHOOSING QUASI-EXPERIMENTS: ETHICS AND PRACTICALITY

Ethics are, of course, an important concern for all researchers in psychology. Whether our studies are descriptive, correlational, experimental, or quasi-experimental, ethics will play a role in the types of questions we ask and how we attempt to answer them. The American Psychological Association has adopted five guiding principles for ethical conduct in research with human subjects: (1) Beneficence and Nonmaleficence, (2) Fidelity and Responsibility, (3) Integrity, (4) Justice, and (5) Respect for People's Rights and Dignity. Brief descriptions of these principles are provided below. For more information, visit apa.org/ethics/code and click on the link for "General Principles."

The principle of *Beneficence and Nonmaleficence* means that our research must produce some benefits, either by gathering information that can directly help people, or by meaningfully contributing to our understanding of the natural world. If there are risks associated with our research, the benefits must outweigh those risks, and no research should be done with the intent to harm. *Fidelity and Responsibility* means that we should be trustworthy and professionally responsible for our actions. *Integrity* requires that we provide accurate, informative accounts of our research in the service of truth, and that we are honest with our participants at all times. Where deceit is needed in order to test a hypothesis, any misinformation must be immediately corrected after observations are completed. *Justice* requires that we do not place unfair burdens of research participation on people who will not benefit from the information gathered, and that any benefits gained by the research are shared equitably. For instance, effective medications or treatments developed through human subjects research must be accessible to those who participated in the research. *Respect for People's Rights and Dignity* means that we respect and value the dignity and independence of our research participants above our research goals. Among other related concerns, in cases where gathering data has any impact at all on our participants, we must make sure that they are given sufficient information to make responsible decisions regarding whether or not to participate. They must also be informed and assured of their right to leave the study at any time without fear of negative consequences. Children in research must have the informed consent of a parent or guardian, and must be given the same assurances.

In keeping with those ethical principles, it may be unethical to purposefully expose people to some of the conditions we want to test. For example, given that we value human dignity above research goals, we could not test the effects of public humiliation on self-esteem with a true experiment. It would be unethical (and unkind!) to publicly humiliate people on purpose. Instead, we could use a quasi-experiment and measure self-esteem in people who have already experienced severe public humiliation compared to people who have not. We would do our best to make sure the comparison group shares relevant characteristics with the first group (e.g., age, number of positive social experiences). But no matter how many relevant characteristics we control, this is not a true experiment. Embarrassment is a quasi-experimental IV; we are not directly manipulating or controlling it. Instead, we are simply measuring the effects of a naturally occurring manipulation, just as we would in a correlational study. The only thing that separates this from correlational research is the purposeful selection of people for our comparison group who are matched by age and positive experiences to the experimental group. So we have some control over these extraneous variables, but not enough. Some would argue that this is just a correlational study. Because we did not randomly assign people to these two groups, we cannot suppose that the two groups are equal in any way other than the variables we purposefully matched. There are probably numerous hidden variables causing differences between our groups – we have no way of knowing. This is why quasi-experimental studies with two or more groups are often called ***nonequivalent groups*** research. Our groups may differ in socioeconomic status, the types of friends they have, or cultural awareness, at the very least. All of these would be **confounding variables.** Chapter 5

Because we cannot ethically expose people to a condition that could cause harm, nor randomly assign people to harmful versus non-harmful conditions, we are sometimes forced to use quasi-experimental research to address certain questions. Other examples include the effects of smoking, certain drugs, or poor air quality on human cognition or behavior.

Practicality or cost can also necessitate a quasi-experimental approach to test a hypothesis. It may be impossible, extremely difficult, or prohibitively expensive to experimentally test certain ideas. If we wish to test the hypothesis that optimism increases empathy, or that being elderly increases irritability (the "Hey-you-kids-get-off-my-lawn hypothesis"), or that registering with a political party increases voter participation, there is no way to randomly assign people to be optimists or pessimists, old or young, political-party affiliated or not. However, we can measure and compare empathy in samples of people who score high in optimism versus those who score low, or irritability in the elderly versus young adults, or voter participation in registered party members versus independents. Perhaps driving an electric vehicle (EV) increases recycling behavior (causal hypothesis), but buying an EV for each participant in the experimental group would be expensive. Instead, we could measure recycling behavior in people who drive EVs and those who do not. These two group are probably not equivalent: EV drivers may have been more likely to recycle than other drivers even before they drove an EV. In all of these examples, the two groups being compared are not equal, and are therefore called ***non-equivalent groups.*** Any pre-existing differences between non-equivalent groups are confounding variables that eliminate our ability to draw cause-and-effect conclusions, but the information gathered may still be useful, just as correlational data are useful.

When true experiments are not possible, quasi-experimental research is our next-best alternative. While the lack of control does present some problems for interpretation, the ability to explore questions that could not be asked with true experiments is extremely valuable. How else could we examine the effectiveness of large-scale programs designed to improve student learning in public schools? Or the effect of child abuse on psychological wellbeing? Or how to prevent child abuse and help those who have been affected? The list of valuable quasi-experiments is long and diverse. It's also important to remember that while a quasi-experimental study cannot strongly *support* a cause-and-effect hypothesis, it *can* help to rule one out. *A cause-and-effect relationship cannot exist without a correlation. So if there is no correlation (no support from a quasi-experimental study), there is, by default, no cause-and-effect relationship.*

BOX 7.1 - Types of Single-Group[3] Quasi-Experiments

This box imposes a somewhat arbitrary organization on the various types of quasi-experimental studies you might encounter as you read about research in psychology. In truth, there may be as many different iterations of quasi-experimental research as there are points along our control continuum. Categorizing these types of research into basic types is merely a way of organizing their underlying structures. It should also be noted that there are additional types of quasi-experimental research that do not fit neatly into any one of these categories, and that these techniques and others can be combined in a wide variety of ways.

1. The Single-Group, Posttest Only study either directly manipulates some event or takes advantage of a naturally occurring event and simply measures the dependent variable (DV) after exposure. This approach is often used in industry and education, when a program for improving some aspect of production or learning is tested. For various reasons, a comparison of the DV from before to after the new program, or with other businesses or schools that do not have this program is not possible, usually because data are not available. The complete lack of control over other variables that could impact the DV, and lack of information about whether the DV has changed at all mean that the results of this type of quasi-experiment cannot be considered evidence of a cause-and-effect relationship.

---

[3] Note that these three quasi-experimental designs can also be applied to research with two groups. See first paragraph of the next section, "Thinking Critically about Quasi-Experimental Research."

2. We can achieve a little more control with another type of single-group quasi-experimental study called a Single-Group, Pretest–Posttest study. In this case, the DV is measured first (pretest), then some manipulation (the IV) is introduced or occurs naturally, and the DV is measured again (posttest). Also frequently used in industry and education, this is essentially the same as the posttest only design, except that measurements of the DV can be compared from before to after the treatment. Would an increase in productivity or learning from pretest to posttest provide evidence for a cause-and-effect relationship? Sadly, no. First, the IV is only presented at one level, so there is no comparison condition. Only the DV is compared from before to after the IV occurred. It is possible, even likely, that when people are tested for the same thing twice, they will score higher the second time, regardless of whether or not the IV occurred between attempts. It is also quite likely that workers, teachers, or students will try harder when they know their performance is expected to improve. Therefore, we cannot conclude that the new program was the cause of any observed increase in productivity or learning.

3. Another quasi-experimental technique is the Single-Group Time Series study, which is very much like a pretest–posttest study, but with multiple pretests and multiple posttests. This is frequently used in marketing research. Measurements of the DV are often recorded for several weeks before the IV is introduced. This allows the researcher to establish normal, baseline behavior and avoids the problem of people just trying harder from one pretest to one posttest. After the IV is introduced (a new commercial or marketing strategy) or naturally occurs (a competitor opens), continuous measurement of the DV (sales per week) allows the researcher to observe the long-term effects of the IV. There is improved control over extraneous variables, as their natural fluctuations can sometimes be identified during the course of repeated observations, and accounted for when comparing the DV before and after exposure to the IV. This approach is also often used is in public policy research. For example, criminal activity is regularly monitored, and researchers examine changes in the data from before to after the introduction of new laws in order to assess the effects of those laws on crime rates. If crime rates drop after the introduction of a new law, this might be considered weak evidence for a cause-and-effect hypothesis. Admittedly, the evidence is stronger than other single-group quasi-experimental designs, but there are still confounds, particularly if the new law was introduced at the same time that some other event occurred, which may or may not have been noticed or tracked. Media attention to the crime problem at the same time the new law is passed, for example, might make potential victims more cautious, and therefore, can affect opportunities for criminal activity.

THINKING CRITICALLY ABOUT QUASI-EXPERIMENTAL RESEARCH

The single-group techniques described in Box 7.1 all lack the control over extraneous variables that comes with a comparison group. But those same techniques can also be expanded to include comparison groups, adding some level of control. That is, quasi-experimental studies can also be two group, *posttest studies*; two group, *pretest-posttest studies*; or two-group *time series studies*. But if participants are not randomly assigned to the comparison and experimental groups, then we have a *non-equivalent groups* quasi-experiment. While having a comparison group strengthens the test of the hypothesis, the fact that the comparison group is non-equivalent means that confounding variables will disqualify any evidence for a cause-and-effect relationship.

The key to getting the most out of quasi-experimental research lies in understanding the limitations and interpreting the results with caution and a persistent, scientific attitude. There are many different kinds of quasi-experimental studies; however, most of them are called quasi-experimental for reasons described previously, all related to a lack of experimenter control. To summarize, quasi-experimental studies may have one or more of the following characteristics:

(1) There is only a single group and no comparison group or condition, as when we ask a group of volunteers to try out a headache medicine and report on its effectiveness. In single-group studies, it should be clear that the lack of a control or comparison opens up the possibility that any observed "effects" might have happened without the experimental treatment. Other examples of single-group designs are listed in Box 7.1.

(2) The different levels of the independent variable are not purposefully manipulated. Instead, the levels of the IV occur naturally. It is always possible that some other event that the researcher might not know about coincides with the change in the IV, causing changes in the DV. In two-group designs with naturally occurring IVs, researchers select participants who differ with respect to the levels of some naturally occurring IV, usually trying to match the selected participants on some other important variables. The individuals selected for each group will have other differences, besides the levels of the IV. Those differences are confounding variables, making it impossible to draw clear cause-and-effect conclusions.

(3) There is no control over assignment of participants to different levels of the IV (no random assignment). This also results in non-equivalent groups, i.e., groups that differ in ways other than the independent variable. Again, in non-equivalent groups designs, we have no way of knowing the impact of pre-existing differences between groups on the measurement of the DV.

In conclusion, the only way to draw a strong cause-and-effect conclusion with one study is when that study is a well-designed, true experiment. Does this make it impossible to obtain strong cause-and-effect evidence for any hypothesis that can't be tested with a true experiment? No, not necessarily. While ethics and practicality may keep us from being able to do true experiments for some hypotheses, it is still possible to compile evidence from several quasi-experimental, descriptive, and correlational studies, as well as true experiments with other species or related variables, and arrive at a strong cause-and-effect conclusion. One example would be studies revealing that smoking causes cancer in humans. Obviously, for ethical reasons, we cannot manipulate the number of cigarettes smoked, or randomly assign humans to either smoking or nonsmoking groups. Instead, the Surgeon General's warning that smoking causes cancer is based on some true experiments showing that exposure to cigarette smoke causes cancer in laboratory animals, as well as molecular studies of the biological activity of carcinogens contained in cigarette smoke, and correlational and quasi-experimental studies in humans that statistically control for other known factors that could affect cancer rates, among other studies. The fact that all these various lines of evidence have repeatedly come to the same conclusion is very strong evidence for a cause-and-effect relationship between smoking and cancer in humans, even though no true experiments could be done to test that hypothesis.

Quasi-experimental research has been described in this chapter as research that attempts to study cause-and-effect relationships, but lacks proper experimental control. There are many different types of studies that would fall into this category, and one should keep in mind that any particular research technique can be modified in ways that increase control or relinquish it. In other words, the same basic quasi-experimental research design can be moved right or left on our control continuum (Figure 7.1), based on how much consideration is given to controlling or statistically correcting for extraneous variables. In general, as we improve control over extraneous variables, we can come a little closer to a true test of the cause-and-effect hypothesis (without ever reaching it until we do a true experiment). The ways in which control can be increased will be discussed in more advanced research design courses.

The true delight is in the finding out rather than in the knowing.
~Isaac Asimov

"I don't think only 2 can solve this."

CHART 7A – APPLICATION LEARNING OBJECTIVES

7A Sleep and Cognition Objectives	START HERE ▼ BEFORE READING THE NEXT SECTION AND DOING THIS RESEARCH Check how well you feel you can accomplish each objective.				FINISH HERE ▼ YOUR LAB PROFESSOR WILL TELL YOU WHEN TO COMPLETE THESE COLUMNS (IN LAB)			
	I don't know how 1	I know a little about this 2	I know enough about this to guess correctly 3	I know how to do this and/or have already done it. 4	I don't know how 1	I know a little about this 2	I know enough about this to guess correctly 3	I know how to do this and/or have already done it. 4
1 Based on research presented in your lecture textbook, describe two negative effects of sleep deprivation.								
2 Explain how a median split can be used to set up groups in a quasi-experiment.								
3 Gain experience with quasi-experimental research design and discuss one specific type of design and how to interpret the results.								
4 Identify confounding variables in quasi-experimental research.								

▼

After you complete this half of the chart, read pages 231-232. Do not complete the white half until asked to do so in lab.

STUDY 7A
SLEEP DEPRIVATION AND COGNITION [4]

© pathdoc/Shutterstock.com

"Work eight hours and sleep eight hours, and make sure they're not the same eight hours."

~ T. Boone Pickens,
American Capitalist

We've all been told that 7 or 8 hours of sleep every night is generally required for a healthy mind and body. But the demands of modern life, the stress of college, and the glare of an irresistible phone screen seem to conspire to rob us of a good night's sleep, night after night. Your lecture textbook devotes more than two full pages to the negative effects of sleep loss on cognition and health (see Myers and DeWall, pp. 102-105).

On page 103, Myers and DeWall cite research suggesting that the majority of students know that they are functioning "below their peak," but the evidence presented[5] is descriptive in nature, based on Gallup survey results. It merely describes the desire to "get more sleep on weekdays," and reports on students' perceptions of their own low level of functioning when they are tired. It is possible that these perceptions are influenced by popular culture and the often-repeated mantra that sleep deprivation "makes you stupid" (Carskadon, 2002[4], as cited in Myers & DeWall, 2018).

In this quasi-experimental study, we will test the hypothesis that sleep deprivation decreases cognitive performance in college students, using ourselves as the participants. Ethically, we cannot assign some students to get 8 hours of sleep while others are only allowed 4 hours. Even if it were ethical to ask students to lose sleep for science, it would be practically impossible to control without a sleep laboratory.

Important information continues after the data sheet on the back of this page. Keep reading…

---

[4] This study derives from an Introductory Psychology research project idea proposed by Ralph Barnes (Montana State University).

[5] For information on where to find these original sources (Mason, 2003, 2005; Carskadon, 2002), see the References section of Myers & DeWall (2018), pages R-58 and R-14, respectively.

Due to these ethical and practical concerns, we will use a quasi-experiment to test our hypothesis. The design of this study is a two-group comparison with participants assigned to non-equivalent groups based on a *median split*. That is, we will measure sleep deprivation on a scale, calculate the median score, then divide our participants into those who scored high in sleep deprivation (above the median) and those who scored low (below the median). We will then compare the cognitive performance of those groups using a PVT (Psychomotor Vigilance Test). We might also consider testing another hypothesis simultaneously, if time allows and the class is interested in testing other effects of sleep deprivation. For example, we could test the effects of sleep deprivation on working memory, happiness, irritability, or other easily measured dependent variables.

PROCEDURE 7A (DATA SHEET ABOVE)

1. Answer some online survey questions about how tired you feel (the Epworth Sleepiness Scale, or ESS), write your score on a small scrap of paper, fold it up, and drop it in the bag that will be provided to assure anonymity.
2. Visit the website sleepdisordersflorida.com/pvt1.html to take the Psychomotor Vigilance Test. It is a 2-minute test. Please do your best to stay focused on the white square, minimize blinking, and react as quickly as possible.
3. Record your score on the data sheet at the top of this page. It is at the top so that you can cut it out of this book without losing the footnote information on the back of this page. Scissors will be provided at each table.
4. While you complete Step 2, anonymous scores on the ESS will be ranked from high to low and the results of a median split will be announced in lab.
5. You will then be asked to record your scores on the PVT and ESS, circle the group to which your data belong and then hand in your data sheet anonymously.
6. A *t*-test will be used to compare PVT scores between groups.
7. Complete the Lab Record for Study 7A/B/C on page 245.

CHART 7B – APPLICATION LEARNING OBJECTIVES

7B Blood Sugar, Cognition, and Behavior Objectives	**START HERE** ▼ **BEFORE READING THE NEXT SECTION AND DOING THIS RESEARCH** Check how well you feel you can accomplish each objective.				**FINISH HERE** ▼ **YOUR LAB PROFESSOR WILL TELL YOU WHEN TO COMPLETE THESE COLUMNS (IN LAB)**			
	I don't know how **1**	I know a little about this **2**	I know enough about this to guess correctly **3**	I know how to do this and/or have already done it. **4**	I don't know how **1**	I know a little about this **2**	I know enough about this to guess correctly **3**	I know how to do this and/or have already done it. **4**
1 Briefly summarize research on the effects of sugar on behavior in children.								
2 Explain how the glycemic index of a food relates to blood sugar levels.								
3 Gain experience with quasi-experimental research design and discuss one specific type of design and how to interpret the results.								
4 Identify confounding variables in quasi-experimental research.								

▼

After you complete this half of the chart, read pages 235-237. Do not complete the white half until asked to do so in lab.

STUDY 7B
BLOOD SUGAR AND COGNITION

Image © Stockcreations/Shutterstock

IS THERE SUCH A THING AS A SUGAR HIGH?

Has anyone ever accused you of being on a "sugar high?" Have you ever felt energetic, or maybe jittery, after eating a candy bar? Perhaps based on these individual anecdotes, or maybe due to stressed out parents looking for some explanation for their stress, the claim that giving a toddler candy results in behavioral mayhem is one of those common sense ideas that has been circulating for generations. It is what some would call "common sense" (more on this in Chapter 8). However, as is often the case with "common sense," the idea doesn't hold up to scientific scrutiny. Wolraich, Wilson, and White (1995) conducted a combined analysis of nearly two dozen studies published between 1982 and 1994 and found no evidence that sugar has any negative effect on toddler behavior, though the authors could not rule out the possibility that certain children might have sensitivities to high-sugar diets that could potentially affect their behavior.

In fact, rather than revealing negative effects of sugar on behavior, most research conducted during the 1980s and 1990s points to a positive influence of glucose, in general, and negative effects of *low* blood sugar on cognition in children, which is why the United States Department of Agriculture (USDA) recommends that every child start the day with a healthy breakfast. Many studies have demonstrated that changing blood sugar levels can impact adult cognition as well. For example, a relatively recent study of college students (Morris, 2008) found that those who were given a glucose drink performed 20% better on a memory task than a control group that had been given a zero-glucose, artificially sweetened drink. Given the evidence that maintaining healthy blood sugar can improve thinking and memory, one might wonder why the USDA doesn't recommend candy for breakfast. The problem with candy and other high-sugar foods is that they tend to have a high *glycemic index*, meaning that they cause blood sugar to increase rapidly, then decline rapidly as the body moves the excess glucose into the liver for storage. With a few exceptions, foods that we typically think of as "healthy" tend to have a lower glycemic index. They release sugar into the blood gradually, for a more regulated, constant supply of glucose to the brain. Nevertheless, when blood sugar is low, even foods with a high glycemic index (GI) might temporarily improve cognitive function. Sadly, even if that hypothesis is true, intake of foods with high GI is not the way to a high GPA; other research also suggests that a regular diet of high GI foods is linked to diabetes and other metabolic health issues.

In research Applications A and B, quasi-experimental designs are used to study the relationship between blood glucose and cognition. As with many quasi-experimental studies, ethical considerations are an important reason to decide against using a true experiment to study this relationship. We will use nonequivalent groups research designs, giving participants the choice of whether to consume a high-sugar beverage, a zero-sugar beverage, or no beverage at all. Based on the APA's principles for the ethical treatment of human subjects (see pages 223/224), we do not wish to force students in this class to consume large amounts of sugar or artificial sweetener that they would not normally consume, and so we give every student the autonomy to choose a type of beverage, or to choose no beverage at all. Given that consuming no beverage should have the same effect on blood sugar as choosing a zero-sugar beverage, students who decide not to consume either beverage will be assigned to the zero-sugar (control) group. Application A uses a pure nonequivalent groups comparison, whereas Application B is a non-equivalent groups study that also uses the same time series research technique described in Box 7.1 for single-group studies.

Image © Cartoonresource/Shutterstock

"Maybe there's a reason our blood sugar is up."

PROCEDURE 7B WITH DATA SHEET

1. You will be asked to answer a few survey questions about when and what you ate before lab.
2. Twice during lab, you'll be asked to complete a brief online memory test. Follow instructions for recording your score, provided in lab. The two memory tests should be separated by about 20 minutes.
3. After the second memory test, non-equivalent groups will be formed before introduction of the two levels of the independent variable.
4. Approximately 15-20 minutes later, you'll be asked to complete the memory test a third time.
5. Approximately 20 minutes later, you'll be asked to complete the memory test a fourth and last time.
6. Data will be collected and entered into an MS Excel file, then combined across all labs to be discussed in next week's lab.

Data sheet for Study 7B   Participant # _____

"SCORE" = maximum number of correctly recalled items

		SimpleMath Memory
Attempt	Time	SCORE
First Pretest →		
Second Pretest →		
First Posttest →		
Second Posttest →		

List everything you ate or drank ***during the introduction of the independent variable.*** INCLUDE APPROXIMATE AMOUNTS!

_____ amt: _____   _____ amt: _____

_____ amt: _____   _____ amt: _____

_____ amt: _____   _____ amt: _____

_____ amt: _____   _____ amt: _____

_____ amt: _____   _____ amt: _____

CHART 7C – APPLICATION LEARNING OBJECTIVES

7C Self-Help and Social Support Networks Objectives	START HERE ▼ BEFORE READING THE NEXT SECTION AND DOING THIS RESEARCH Check how well you feel you can accomplish each objective.				FINISH HERE ▼ YOUR LAB PROFESSOR WILL TELL YOU WHEN TO COMPLETE THESE COLUMNS (IN LAB)			
	I don't know how **1**	I know a little about this **2**	I know enough about this to guess correctly **3**	I know how to do this and/or have already done it. **4**	I don't know how **1**	I know a little about this **2**	I know enough about this to guess correctly **3**	I know how to do this and/or have already done it. **4**
1 Accurately discuss the availability of self-help information and empirical research on whether or not it actually helps.								
2 Define a social support network and discuss its relationship to mental health.								
3 Gain experience with quasi-experimental research design and discuss one specific type of design and how to interpret the results.								
4 Identify confounding variables in quasi-experimental research designs.								

▼

After you complete this half of the chart, read pages 241-243. Do not complete the white half until asked to do so in lab.

STUDY 7C—SELF-HELP AND SOCIAL SUPPORT NETWORKS

Image © kentoh/Shutterstock

I went to a bookstore and asked the saleswoman, "Where's the self-help section?"
She said if she told me, it would defeat the purpose.   ~George Carlin

HOW MUCH DOES SELF-HELP HELP?

Placing a monetary value on the self-help industry in the United States would be difficult, and by most accounts, would probably result in an underestimate. As of July 2017, typing "self-help" into the search bar of one leading online bookstore produced 700,011 hits. These books promise to improve readers' self-esteem, organizational skills, love-life, friendships, financial status, brain power, and a whole host of other things people might not have even thought needed improving. Add the overwhelming number of websites with self-help content, and it becomes clear that there is no shortage of opinions on what is wrong with us and how to fix it.

What is unclear is the extent to which any of this information actually helps people. A handful of studies have shown some empirical support for the effectiveness of specific self-help books and information (e.g., Bjorvatn, Fiske, & Pallesen, 2011; Cunningham, Humphreys, Koski-Jännes, & Cordingley, 2005), but given the number of such books in existence and their growing impact on the U.S. economy, one would expect more attention to this question.

In this research, we will investigate a possible role for self-help advice in improving social support networks. A *social support network* consists of the people you turn to for help when you are dealing with something difficult or stressful. Friends, family, special acquaintances, groups, and communities to which we belong can all be part of a social support network. Whether you're in need of a loan, advice, or just someone to talk to, the feeling that you know someone who will try to help you is an important source of good mental health. Compared to people with strong networks of friends and family, people with less social support tend to have more difficulty dealing with stress. There are ways to build social support networks, and plenty of advice is offered on the Internet and in self-help books. In this study, we will first anonymously measure the average strength of the social support networks in your class, then expose the class to self-help information on how to build and extend social support networks. You'll have two or three weeks to try out any parts of the advice you care to try, after which we will measure the whole class's social support a second time to see whether there have been any changes.

IMPORTANT CAVEATS TO THIS RESEARCH

The idea that exposure to self-help information improves social support is a cause-and-effect hypothesis, so our quasi-experimental research cannot provide strong support for it, even if we do see the average number of support networks increase after exposure to self-help information. In that case, our main conclusion would be a possible link between exposure to self-help information and an improvement in social support, but the cause of that link would not be clear because there is no comparison group. On the other hand, if absolutely no relationship is found, or if social support decreases after exposure to self-help information, that could be evidence against the idea that exposure to self-help advice improves social support networks, because a cause-and-effect relationship, if it exists, would naturally produce a correlation.[36] Of course, whether our results agree or disagree with our hypothesis, all possible explanations for whatever we observe should be considered, including, but not limited to the accuracy of the hypothesis.

Another important point is that your data must be gathered anonymously. Data will be based on a short survey of social support strength, which is personal information that you should not feel obligated to share. You may, at any point during this study, decide NOT to contribute, and your decision will not affect your grade in this class. If you do participate, your answers will be completely anonymous. Scores for the whole class will be grouped to arrive at a class average. If you wish to know your personal score, you may request a copy of the scoring rubric from your instructor, but remember that this survey is meant to be informative, not diagnostic.

And then it occurred to him:
the world needed yet another book on leadership.

---

6 Remember from Chapter 3 (page 92) that the existence of a correlation does not mean there is necessarily a cause-and-effect relationship, but the existence of a cause-and-effect relationship DOES mean that there must be a correlation, because every time the cause changes, so must the effect.

PROCEDURE 7C

1.   You will be given a social support survey called the Interpersonal Support Evaluation List (ISEL) (Cohen and Hoberman, 1983). It has 40 statements that you should rate based on how well they apply to you, using a 4-point Likert-type scale, where 0 = definitely false, 1 = probably false, 2 = probably true, and 3 = definitely true. Read the statements carefully, as they are not all in agreement that 0 is bad and 4 is good. Sometimes, a 0 will mean that you have good support, and sometimes, it will mean that you have poor support. This makes it difficult for participants to fake having a good (or poor) score, and also makes it difficult for anyone to determine your total score just by glancing at your individual answers. It also means you should not try to get the highest or lowest total; just rate the truth of the statements honestly and to the best of your ability. The entire survey will take less than 15 min to complete.

2.   Submit your answers **anonymously**, according to the instructions provided by your lab instructor. Your lab instructor will electronically capture your answers only, with no identifying information, and paste them into a spreadsheet, so that all scores will be combined for the whole class BEFORE any individual scores are calculated. This will assure anonymity of your ISEL score.

3.   Once all scores have been recorded, you will be given a handout or webpage to go to for self-help advice on how to build social support networks, and told how and when and for how long you should attempt to follow some of the advice.

4.   At the end of the study, you will again complete the ISEL survey, which will again be anonymous and scored in the same way.

5.   Your instructor will provide the results of a statistical comparison between pretest and posttest ISEL scores for the class.

YOUR SURVEY ANSWERS

DO NOT WRITE YOUR NAME ON THIS SHEET AND DO NOT USE A DIFFERENT SHEET. UNIFORMITY HELPS MAINTAIN ANONYMITY.

1. _____
2. _____
3. _____
4. _____
5. _____
6. _____
7. _____
8. _____
9. _____
10. _____
11. _____
12. _____
13. _____
14. _____
15. _____
16. _____
17. _____
18. _____
19. _____
20. _____

21. _____
22. _____
23. _____
24. _____
25. _____
26. _____
27. _____
28. _____
29. _____
30. _____
31. _____
32. _____
33. _____
34. _____
35. _____
36. _____
37. _____
38. _____
39. _____
40. _____

GLOSSARY OF TERMS AND EXAMPLES

Where to find these terms: EP = *Experience Psychology!* (this book),
MD = Myers & DeWall, 2018 (lecture textbook). Figures are in EP.

Glycemic Index (GI): An indication of the speed with which sugar is released into the blood upon ingestion of a certain food. Foods with a high glycemic index cause blood sugar to increase quickly and by larger amounts, compared to foods with a lower glycemic index. High glycemic index foods also cause blood sugar to drop more quickly after it increases (due to stronger insulin response), whereas low glycemic index foods help maintain good levels of blood sugar for a longer time.

    Examples: According to the website of the Mayo Clinic, foods with a low GI (less than 55) include raw carrots, lentils, peanuts, grapefruit and skim milk. High GI foods (over 70) include potatoes, instant white rice, watermelon and popcorn. Most non-diet sodas have a GI of approximately 55.

    Where to find this term: EP 236

Median Split: A technique for creating categorical data out of interval data, so that ***non-equivalent groups*** may be formed to test a hypothesis. Participants are measured on some scale, then ranked from highest to lowest scores to determine the median score. Participants are then split into two groups: those who scored above or below the median. To maximize the signal (difference between means for the DV[(Chapter 5)]), those who score at the median are often dropped from the data analysis.

    Example: To separate participants for a study into optimists and pessimists, all participants might be given a test to assess their level of optimism. Researchers might then rank the participants from highest to lowest optimism scores, calculate the median score, and assign participants who scored above the median to the "Optimistic Group" and those who scored below the median to the "Pessimistic Group."

    Where to find this term: EP 232

Nonequivalent Groups: A study design that compares two or more groups that differ in important ways other than the levels of the IV. This is usually because participants were selected for the groups based on their pre-existing differences with respect to the IV, in order to measure the "effects" of their IV differences. Since the participants in these groups differ in multiple ways other than the levels of the IV, one cannot conclude that any observed difference in the DV was caused by differences in the IV.

    Example: A researcher is testing the idea that attending plays at the theatre makes people happier than going to the movies, so she takes surveys of happiness levels from people leaving live performances at a theatre and people leaving the movies. She compares them and finds that people leaving the theatre reported being happier than those leaving the movies. The groups she compared are nonequivalent. The stories they just watched were probably different, and there may be personality differences between theatre-goers and movie-goers, including a general disposition toward more or less happiness, regardless of whether one has just seen a play or a movie.

    Where to find this term: EP 224, 236, Box 7.1

Pretest–Posttest: A quasi-experimental study where the dependent variable (DV) is measured first (pretest), then the independent variable (IV) is either introduced or occurs naturally, then the DV is measured again (posttest). Changes in the DV from before to after the IV are used as evidence of a relationship between the IV and the DV. This research technique can be used with no comparison group (a single-group, pretest-posttest study), but is also often used with a non-equivalent comparison group and with a randomly assigned comparison group (true experiment).

    Example: A researcher wants to know whether having a pet decreases stress levels, so he asks a pet adoption agency to administer a survey of stress levels to first-time pet adopters before they take their new pets home (pretest). After one month of pet ownership (IV), each pet adopter completes the stress survey again (posttest). If stress levels have decreased, one might conclude that there is a relationship between pet ownership and stress levels, but cannot conclude that owning the pets *caused* the decrease, because there was no comparison group. Another explanation is that the mere process of looking for a pet increased stress levels, rather than the pet ownership decreasing stress.

Where to find this term: EP Box 7.1

Posttest Only: A quasi-experimental study where the dependent variable (DV) is measured only once, after the independent variable (IV) is either introduced or occurs naturally. If predicted scores are observed for the DV, this might be incorrectly presented as evidence that the IV affected the DV. Because there is nothing to which the scores may be compared, the evidence for a cause-and-effect relationship is nonexistent.

Example: Commercials where people show off how great their hair looks after using a certain product are attempting to convince viewers of a cause-and-effect relationship with a single-group, posttest only report. Sadly, many viewers have no information about basic research designs or how to interpret them, and do not recognize the complete lack of evidence for a cause-and-effect relationship. The actors may have had great hair before using that product, and professional hair stylists may have been hired to make their hair look great.

Where to find this term: EP Box 7.1

Quasi-Experiment: A study that attempts to examine a cause-and-effect hypothesis, but lacks control over important extraneous variables. The reasons for lack of control are varied and can include the lack of any control group or comparison group or condition, a naturally occurring (not manipulated) independent variable, comparison of groups that are not equal in terms of important extraneous variables, or a combination of the above.

Example: In a **nonequivalent groups** study, a quasi-experiment on the relationship between funding for field trips and student enthusiasm for school uses two different schools: one with funds for field trips, one without, and measures student enthusiasm by giving a survey to all the students in both schools. Note that students are not randomly assigned to a group that gets funding and a group that does not, so there is no control over other things that could affect student enthusiasm for school, like parents' and teachers' enthusiasm, school culture, and so on (these extraneous variables are confounding variables). Thus, if differences in the DV (student enthusiasm) are found, that is not evidence that funding for field trips caused those differences.

Where to find this term: EP 221-228, 231-232, 236, 242, Fig. 7.1, Box 7.1

Social Support Network: The people to whom one turns for help when problems arise, such as when there is a need for advice, money, or just someone to talk to.

Examples: Anyone you feel you could trust to help you when you need it could be considered part of your social support network. This includes friends, family, neighbors, fraternity or sorority members, church members or leaders, and any others to whom you can turn for help.

Where to find this term: EP 241-243

Time Series (single group): A quasi-experimental study where the dependent variable (DV) is measured repeatedly over time, and at some point during that time, the independent variable (IV) is either purposefully introduced or occurs naturally. Measurements of the DV continue, and if a change in the DV coincides with the introduction of the IV, this is interpreted as evidence of a relationship between the IV and DV. However, caution must be used, as it is possible that some other variable is causing changes in the DV.

Example: A bathroom tissue company believes that an ecofriendly stamp on their packaging will improve sales. Biweekly sales data are collected over the course of the whole year (time series data on the DV), and during that year, the new packaging is introduced (IV). A spike in sales is seen shortly after the packaging is introduced, and a few months later, sales remain higher than before the change. However, it is possible that a competing bathroom tissue company either went out of business or stopped or changed their advertising campaign, so one should exercise caution in assuming a cause-and-effect relationship between the new packaging and the increased sales. The time-series technique alone cannot provide sufficient evidence for a cause-and-effect relationship.

Where to find this term: EP 226, 236, Box 7.1

CHAPTER 8
ADVANCED TOPICS AND ANIMAL RESEARCH

CONCEPTS

APPLICATIONS

GLOSSARY OF TERMS AND EXAMPLES

CHART 8 - CONCEPT LEARNING OBJECTIVES

Chapter 8 Concepts / Objectives	START HERE — BEFORE READING THE NEXT SECTION Check how well you feel you can accomplish each objective.					FINISH HERE — AFTER YOU HAVE READ UP TO THE NEXT CHART Check how well you feel you can accomplish each objective, and fix any inaccurate answers on the left.			
	I don't know how **1**	I know a little about this **2**	I know enough about this to guess correctly **3**	I know how to do this and/or have already done it. **4**		I don't know how **1**	I know a little about this **2**	I know enough about this to guess correctly **3**	I know how to do this and/or have already done it. **4**
1 Explain how complex research designs can be built from the simple designs you have learned about previously.									
2 Explain how adding predictions to a study affects the probability of accidentally finding support for an untrue hypothesis.									
3 Distinguish between a one-way experiment and a two-way experiment.									
4 Describe at least two good reasons for doing animal research.									
5 Debunk three common complaints about research in psychology.									

		I don't know how 1	I know a little about this 2	I know enough about this to guess correctly 3	I know how to do this and/or have already done it. 4		I don't know how 1	I know a little about this 2	I know enough about this to guess correctly 3	I know how to do this and/or have already done it. 4
6	Explain how scientific reports incorporate principles of connectivity, replicability, integrity, and convergence.									

↓

After you complete this half of the chart, read pages 253-264. Then return to page 251 and complete the white half of this chart.

↓

After you complete this half of the chart, go to your assigned application chart(s) and complete the gray half. Then read about that study to prepare for the research you'll do in lab.

MORE COMPLEX EXPERIMENTS

In the last three chapters, we have tested cause-and-effect hypotheses with true experiments and quasi-experiments in which a single independent variable (IV) was manipulated in two ways (an experimental level and a control or comparison level), and the effect of that manipulation (the DV) was measured in only one way. If you read the published literature in psychology, you will find that this simple, two-group comparison with just one measurement of the effect is rare. The vast majority of experiments in psychology are more complex, with more than two levels of the IV, more than one DV or operational definition of the DV, or some combination of these. In fact, many published experiments have two or more independent variables. Sometimes, in the same experiment, one IV is tested with a **between-participants** design, while another is simultaneously tested **within-participants.** Table 8.1 shows some examples of more complex research designs.

Designing research is like building with Lego ® building blocks. The techniques and terms you have learned so far are a good starter set, and there are countless ways to combine them into new ideas and projects. This chapter will help you in your capstone project for this course, designing your own experiment. Since more complicated experimental designs are the norm, this chapter provides more information to carry beyond this course and help you think critically about the next level of research design and interpretation.

Table 8.1. Examples of ways that one could test the hypothesis that eating chocolate makes children hyperactive, with research designs leading to multiple comparisons.

Design Possibilities	Examples	Possible Multiple Comparisons
More than two levels of the IV	**Amount of Chocolate** No chocolate / 12 ounces / 24 ounces / 48 ounces 40 kids / 40 kids / 40 kids / 40 kids	Kids in the no-chocolate group will show less hyperactivity than the 24-ounce group and the 12-ounce group, but not compared to the 48-ounce group, since they could be feeling sick.
More than one operational definition of the DV	Hyperactivity could be measured by: 1. the number of times a child's buttocks leaves his/her chair. 2. the number of times a child's head moves. 3. the number of times a child speaks out of turn.	Chocolate will affect the ability to sit still and the number of times a child's head moves, but will not affect speaking out of turn.
More than one conceptual IV	_No Chocolate_ / _24 ounces_ Second Graders: 40 kids / 40 kids Eighth Graders: 40 kids / 40 kids	Chocolate will affect younger kids, but not older kids. Or, it will affect young kids more than it affects older kids (age of students is a quasi-experimental variable, see Chapter 6)
More than one conceptual DV	The hypothesis could be that chocolate affects both hyperactivity and mood.	Chocolate will make kids generally happier, but also more active.

While you are working on your own research, we will complete one more research project as a class -- an animal study with two IVs and more than one specific prediction. To properly interpret that research and your own, we must first understand how adding predictions affects the objective decision-making process.

ADDING PREDICTIONS IMPACTS OBJECTIVE DECISION MAKING

Back in Chapter 5, you read about an experiment testing the hypothesis that *classical music improves math performance* (page 145). It was a simple, two-group study where one group of children was exposed to classical music for 3 hr per day, while the other group was not, and all the children were given a math test. Questions were raised about whether this was the best way to test the hypothesis. If the classical music group did better on the math test than the no-music (control) group, could we conclude that it was the classical nature of the music, or might any music at all improve math performance? A suggested improvement was to expose several groups of children to different kinds of music, and compare math test scores among all those groups, rather than just compare classical music to no music. At the time, we said that this would add complications to the interpretation of our results, and left it at that. Now it's time to deal with those complications.

Each experimental prediction we've made so far has been *statistically tested* based on the odds of seeing it happen when the null hypothesis is true. In every case, we predicted a difference between two groups or conditions and then calculated the magnitude of the difference. We asked, assuming the null hypothesis is true, what are the odds that we would see that much of a difference? If the odds were poor (less than 5% chance), we rejected the null and said, "We have support for our research hypothesis." There was one hypothesis, one prediction, one odds-based test of the outcome.

But if we revised the classical music experiment to better test the hypothesis that it is the classical nature of the music that affects math performance, not just any music, then our single hypothesis would lead to several predictions: (1) Children in the classical music group would be expected to perform better than children in the control group. The classical music group would also be expected to perform better than a rock music group (2), a country music group (3), a rap music group (4), or a jazz group (5). We could add more different types of music, but we already have five predictions from one hypothesis!

Another possibility is that we might have two or more operational definitions of our DV (for example, two kinds of math tests for measuring math performance), leading to twice as many predictions for each group comparison. Sometimes, there are two or more conceptual DVs. For example, we might hypothesize that listening to classical music improves both math performance and rhythmic ability. And why not have two or three ways of measuring each of them? Given the difficulty of finding participants for one experiment, it is tempting to try to answer as many questions as we can with one experiment.

Unfortunately, multiple comparisons in the same experiment can pose a problem for our objective decision-making process, because *probability* is the basis on which we decide whether or not to reject the null hypothesis. The problem can best be understood with an example from dice-tossing.

Suppose you predict, before tossing one die, "I'm going to roll a 1." You have a 1 in 6 chance of being correct (about 0.17). But if you make three predictions, saying, "I'm going to roll a 1 or a 2 or a 3," there is now a 3 in 6 chance that at least one prediction will be correct. You have just increased the chances that the outcome will support your prediction, from a 17% chance to a 50% chance! (0.17 for a "1," plus 0.17 for a "2," plus 0.17 for a "3" ≈ 0.5). Instinctively, you can see how each prediction you make increases the chances that at least one of your predictions will occur, just by chance. Of course, if you predict that you will roll a 1, 2, 3, 4, 5, or 6, you have a 100% chance of being correct!

The example above is an oversimplification, but like the roll of a die, each time we test the null hypothesis, we are trying to determine the likelihood of seeing a truly random event turn out in a particular, predicted way (under the null hypothesis, observations should be truly random, not predictable). We must remember that every "statistically significant" outcome (prediction) has up to a 5% chance of happening just by chance when the null hypothesis is true, meaning we have a 5% chance of being *wrong* to reject the null hypothesis. We are accepting that risk when we apply our decision rule. But if we make *multiple* predictions, and *each one* has a 0.05 chance of being wrong, those chances of being wrong add up pretty quickly![1]

Consider again our experiment on classical music, where we compared classical music to no music, jazz, rock, rap, and country. In this case, we have six groups and five predicted differences, as listed above. For each prediction, our chances of wrongly rejecting the null hypothesis are 5%. Assuming the null hypothesis is true, the children in different groups would have no reason to perform differently on their math test, and yet, we would have a 23% chance of wrongly rejecting the null hypothesis on at least one prediction (using the adding rule described for the dice, 5% for each of five predictions would be 25%, but the adding rule doesn't exactly apply to hypothesis testing, so the actual risk of being wrong would be about 23%; see footnote).

In summary, when designing experiments, *we have to remember that the more predictions we make about how a random data set will turn out, the more likely it is that one of those predictions will be observed, not because it is true, but just by chance alone.* This increases our chances of erroneously rejecting the null hypothesis, and concluding that there is a real difference when in fact, there is not. In making just five simple comparisons, we went from having a 5% (1 in 20) chance of being wrong to having a 23% (nearly 1 in 4) chance of being wrong! This **inflated error rate** is not an acceptable standard for falsification.

Thankfully, there are several ways around this problem, and you will learn more about these statistical techniques in this chapter, and still more if you go on in psychology. For your last, whole-class research project in this lab, you will do an experiment with two independent variables, leading to three predictions, so you'll get a chance to see how one of these techniques works. It's called an **overall comparison**. Rather than test each difference between any two groups with one

---

[1] Statistically, the actual probability of wrongly rejecting the null hypothesis for multiple comparisons is not as simple as adding the individual probabilities, because we are no longer dealing with just one decision. Instead, we are now dealing with multiple, independent decisions. It's more like asking, what are the chances of getting at least one "3" on *two* rolls of the die? Each roll is an independent event, so we can't just add the probabilities; we have to take a different approach. Appendix A has more information on how to calculate the probability of one thing happening in multiple independent events, including rolls of the die and accidental rejections of the null hypothesis.

comparison at a time, it tests whether there are any differences at all among multiple groups, simultaneously.

The reason this works is because it substitutes one single odds-based decision in place of several. In an experiment with three conditions, labeled A, B, and C, you could ask, under the assumption that the null hypothesis is true, "What are the odds I'd see this much of a difference between A and B?" And "What are the odds I'd see this much of a difference between B and C?" And, "What are the odds I'd see this much of a difference between A and C?" Or you could ask just one question: "What are the odds that any of these three conditions would differ this much from any of the others?" That's basically what the overall comparison does. If the overall comparison is significant, then there is almost always at least one difference among the conditions. We still won't know where that difference is, but the significant overall comparison gives us statistical permission to make more comparisons to see where the difference is.

By limiting the number of decisions we make with the overall comparison, we partially avoid the **inflated error rate** that happens when we make multiple odds-based decisions. It's a clever little bit of statistical reasoning, to say the least. If, and only if, the overall comparison is significant, we can then make *pairwise comparisons,* pairing off each of our conditions and testing to see whether there are differences between them, to see which differences are significant. We still have to be somewhat concerned about the inflated error rate problem (there is a limit to the number of further comparisons we can make) but the problem is less drastic, since we're now reasonably sure that at least one significant difference exists.

INCREASING THE NUMBER OF IVs

In our previous experiments, we have investigated cause and effect relationships by manipulating one IV and measuring the effects on the DV. But life is complicated, and relationships often interact with one another. That is, whether or not a cause (A) affects something else (B) can depend on other factors. If those other factors are treated as extraneous variables, we do our best to hold them constant while we manipulate the A and measure B. However, if we suspect that another variable (C) will influence whether or not we can observe our cause-and-effect relationship between A and B, we can test that hypothesis. Rather than keeping that variable (C) constant, we can systematically manipulate it, so that we manipulate both A and C and measure B. In other words, we can design an experiment with more than one IV. Experiments with two IVs are called *two-way experiments*; if there are three IVs, it is a *three-way* experiment. Our previous experiments have been *one-way experiments* (one IV).

Doing a two-way experiment is a lot like doing two "mini-experiments" at the same time, with the same DV. We can still statistically test differences in a way that will tell us the effect of each IV alone, as though we did two separate experiments. But the advantage of combining them into one bigger experiment is that we can gain valuable insight into how these two IVs might *interact*. Does the effect of one variable depend on the level of the other variable? The ability to answer this question is the main reason we design experiments with more than one IV.

This is best explained with an example. Suppose we have a new drug, "X," which is hypothesized to decrease cholesterol. We've also been told that regular exercise decreases cholesterol. As you know, to test both of these claims, we could just do two separate experiments. Review the terminology (answers are in Appendix B):

1. To test the hypothesis that Drug X decreases cholesterol…
   a. What would be our IV? _____
   b. What might be two levels of the IV? _____
   c. What would be our DV? _____

2. To test the hypothesis that exercise decreases cholesterol…
   a. What would be our IV? _____
   b. What might be two levels of the IV? _____
   c. What would be our DV? _____

But suppose we hypothesize that Drug X will *only* decrease cholesterol *if* the patients exercise regularly. Those two experiments alone would tell us nothing about whether *combining* Drug X and exercise decreases cholesterol more than either one alone. We might be tempted to try four experiments:

1. Test Drug X vs. placebo in exercising patients (the placebo looks like Drug X but is inert)
2. Test Drug X vs. placebo in non-exercising patients
3. Test exercise vs. no exercise in patients who are on Drug X
4. Test exercise vs. no exercise in patients who are on a placebo

Let's assume this would require 100 participants per group (diet and lifestyle vary a lot in humans; all this variability requires many more participants in order to detect differences due to the drug or the exercise, if they exist). That's 200 participants per study, times 4 studies, which is 800 participants. If you've ever tried to collect signatures for a petition, you know how difficult it can be just to get people to sign their name to a cause; imagine trying to find 800 people who are willing to participate in your research by taking an untested drug and/or exercising daily!

But there is a more fundamental problem with performing four separate experiments: We could not test the hypothesis that the effects of Drug X *depend on whether or not the patient is exercising*. Here's why: Suppose experiment 1 shows that Drug X causes a significant decrease in cholesterol in exercising patients ($p < 0.05$), and experiment 2 shows that Drug X does *not* cause a significant decrease in cholesterol in patients who are *not* exercising (e.g., the p-value is 0.11). But is there a real difference between the way Drug X decreased cholesterol in exercising patients and the way it didn't (significantly) decrease cholesterol in non-exercising patients?

Remember, we based our decision about whether or not the drug works on probability. Differences we observed in experiment 1, with the exercising patients, showed a p-value of 0.04 (significant), while the difference we saw in the non-exercising experiment showed a p-value of 0.11 (not significant). We can conclude that Drug X worked for exercisers. And, we *cannot* conclude that it worked for non-exercisers. Using our objective decision-making process, the only difference between being able to conclude that something worked and *not* being able to conclude that it worked is which side of 0.05 we're on. Is there a real (significant) difference between probabilities of .04 and .11? Unless those differences are part of the same experiment, we really can't statistically compare them. Even doing experiments 3 and 4 would not allow us to ask whether Drug X makes *more* of a difference in exercisers than it does in non-exercisers. We cannot statistically test this question with separate experiments.

In cases where we want to hypothesize that two IVs interact (the effect of one IV is different for different levels of the other IV) we need a ***two-way design***, where we *systematically* manipulate the two IVs in the same experiment. In this case, we would manipulate *both* the level of Drug X and the level of exercise. The two-way experiment would look like this:

Second IV:
Exercise (two levels)

		Exercise	No Exercise
First IV: Drug X (two levels)	Drug X	**Group A** 100 people	**Group B** 100 people
	Placebo	**Group C** 100 people	**Group D** 100 people

This solves both of the problems we faced when doing four separate experiments. First, we no longer need 800 participants. In a single experiment with only 400 participants, we now have 200 people who get Drug X and 200 who do not. We also have 200 people who exercise and 200 who do not. Since the proportion of exercisers to non-exercisers is the same for those taking Drug X as it is for those not taking it, we can think of exercise as an extraneous variable that is balanced across drug treatment groups and ignore it when we test for the effect of Drug X alone on cholesterol. That is, we'll statistically compare the 200 participants who got Drug X (Groups A and B combined) to the 200 participants who did not (Groups C and D combined). The test of either IV alone, ignoring the manipulation of the other IV, is called a ***main effect***. Likewise, we can statistically test the main effect of exercise on cholesterol by comparing the average cholesterol levels of all 200 participants who exercised (Groups A and C combined) to the 200 participants who did not exercise (Groups B and D combined). By using a two-way design, we can test *two* hypotheses in *one* experiment with *half as many* participants! But wait! There's more…

This approach will also allow us to test the ***interaction hypothesis***. We can now test the idea that the effect of Drug X is significantly stronger in people who exercise than in people who don't. It's like an experiment repeated *within* another experiment: We're testing the same hypothesis (that Drug X decreases cholesterol) twice, simultaneously, under two different conditions (one with exercising patients and one with non-exercising patients). If the results with exercising patients significantly differ from the results with non-exercising patients, that's called an *interaction effect*. In a significant interaction, the results from the test of one IV are significantly different when tested at different levels of a second IV.

But can we still ask the same four simple questions that we would have asked with our experiments on page 257? Yes, we can, and we still have 100 participants per group! Experiment 1 on page 257 asks, "Does Drug X decrease cholesterol in exercising patients?" The test of that question is in the comparison of group A versus group C. Experiment 2 asks, "Does Drug X decrease cholesterol in non-exercising patients? To find out, we can compare group B to group D. Experiment 3 addresses whether exercise makes a difference for patients who are taking Drug X, and we can test that by comparing A to B. Lastly, does exercise make a difference in people who are not on any real medication? Compare C and D. Even though our experiment is a bit more complicated, we can still ask the simple questions.

As you can see, there are some new terms and new ways of thinking associated with the two-way design, but they all stem from what we already know about experiments with only one IV. These concepts will become clearer as we complete our next experiment, which involves two IVs and is therefore a two-way design. If you go on in psychology or another science, you will learn more about these and other types of experimental designs in later classes. Even if you never take another science course, completing this study will still help you understand the basics of how research with two or more IVs can be accomplished.

This brief introduction to more complex designs leaves out many other statistical considerations, but that will be true of any introduction. At this point, you have what you need to understand the basics of how psychological science is done. Our last two goals for this chapter, and for this course, are to address three common complaints about psychology and to provide information that will help you find, interpret and critically evaluate published research in psychology.

"THE PROBLEM WITH RESEARCH IN PSYCHOLOGY IS . . ."

In social situations, when people meet for the first time, they often ask, "So, what do you do?" For almost 20 years, I have been pleased to reply with, "I teach psychology." But I am not always pleased at the responses I get in return. People have actually said things like, "That's interesting, but so much of the research in psychology seems to be common sense." And, "It's too bad that the research in psychology is so artificial, right?" And my personal favorite, as an animal behaviorist, "What's up with all the animal research? Humans are nothing like rats!" There are many misconceptions about this field, and most of them stem from ignorance about how science is done, or that psychology is, in fact, a science. I sincerely hope that this lab course has given you the knowledge and the conviction to dispel such misconceptions if ever and whenever they are heard again. Toward that end, I will address these three issues here:

1. The "Common Sense" Problem

First, as you, the student of psychology, are now well-aware, we aren't trying to "prove" anything. In the example of research being criticized here, we seek evidence to test the idea that distractions impair driving performance. It is true that a distraction, by definition, diverts attention away from another task. But many drivers claim they can do other things while driving because they are on "autopilot." They say it's common sense: they've been driving for so long, they can do it without thinking. Is that even possible? Our so-called "common sense" research has determined that for the vast majority of people, it is not. Without this research, it would be more difficult to pass laws that save lives. Furthermore, while some might think it is "common sense" that hands-free phones are less distracting than hand-held phones, research in psychology has shown that this is not the case. Perhaps your own research in Application 7B found that conversation, even without holding a phone, impacted reaction times. These are testable questions, and basing our answers on actual observations rather than "common sense" might save lives.

> *All that research money on driving simulators, just to prove that distracted driving is bad driving? It's common sense!*

Image © Dmitry Natashin/Shutterstock

Before one suggests that scientists are asking questions that could be answered with common sense, one should first ask, "What defines common sense?" Although the term implies otherwise, "common sense" is not common to every situation or person. It is most often whatever sense best fits the situation in hindsight, and is rarely able to predict what will happen in a new situation. Assume, for example, Jack and Jill started dating during their senior year in high school, but Jill's parents disapproved and decided to keep them apart by moving to a different city. You might think it's common sense, "absence makes the heart grow fonder," and predict that they will find a way to stay in touch, maybe run away together, or maybe even elope in Vegas. But common sense also says, "Out of sight, out of mind." So maybe they will eventually meet new friends and start dating other people. Common sense is not a good basis on which to make predictions. For more information, read the section on "hindsight bias" in your lecture textbook (Myers & DeWall, 2018, pp 22-25 & 503).

2. The "Artificiality" Problem

> *You really think you can study human behavior in a lab? It's so contrived and artificial! People in a lab don't behave the way they would in the real world.*

Image © Dmitry Natashin/Shutterstock

Admittedly, there are some questions in psychology that are better answered with "field research" (i.e., research conducted in natural settings). And there are many, many field studies in psychology. But the fact that one cannot perfectly recreate an exact replica of a real airplane full of passengers in a laboratory should not preclude a laboratory study of how pilots handle stressful situations. Critics point to the lack of real-life complications in these laboratory studies and say, "that won't apply in real life—

it's a contrived situation." This criticism stems from a lack of understanding that the goal of all true experimentation is to test the existence of real cause-and-effect relationships, and this requires manipulation and control. We cannot manipulate the IV and control extraneous variables without creating a situation that is at least partially contrived.

This "problem" is not unique to psychology; experiments in all areas of science create artificial situations to test ideas. Chemists, for example, typically use purified chemicals that do not exist in pure form in nature. Most would not dismiss the chemist's conclusions on the basis that the research was artificial, or that it doesn't apply to chemical reactions in the real world. Yet, psychological research is often dismissed for being artificial or contrived. Perhaps this is due to the normal human tendency to reject or ignore evidence that challenges our previously held beliefs (see confirmation bias, pages 25 & 39), or perhaps people hold more deep-rooted beliefs about human behavior than they do about chemistry. Regardless, in psychology, just as in other sciences, what is exposed by artificial manipulation is *not* necessarily artificial, particularly if it can also be seen to apply in naturally occurring situations. Evidence from each experiment is just one piece of the puzzle that scientists use to collaboratively assemble an understanding of reality.

3. The "I Am Not a Rat" Problem

Whole books have been devoted to what we can learn about ourselves by studying rats and other animals. Lafayette College has at least two courses devoted to this topic (one in psychology and one in biology). In my own view (admittedly, as an animal behaviorist), taking other animals out of the study of behavior and cognition would be like trying to understand international government and law without the study of history or cultural differences. It is perhaps possible, but would be missing a great deal of the coherence and context.

I am not a rat. Humans are way more complicated! You can't learn anything about human behavior by studying rats!

Image © Dmitry Natashin/Shutterstock

Many psychologists study non-human animals. Some are simply interested in why animals do the things they do and/or how certain behaviors evolve (animal behaviorists and evolutionary psychologists). This type of research, with the goal of understanding more about a particular subject, is often called **basic research**. Others seek to improve the care and conservation of animals, to find better ways to train them, or to improve agricultural practices. This is called **applied research** because it is designed to provide information that can be directly applied to specific problems. Though they have different goals, basic and applied research are not mutually exclusive, since information obtained with either goal in mind can simultaneously achieve the other goal. That is, basic research often ends up finding applications that were not foreseen by the researchers, and applied research often leads to better basic understanding of the natural world. Whether basic or applied, many psychologists study non-human animals when their research questions cannot practically or ethically be answered with human participants. Like medical science, behavioral science is helped tremendously by a better understanding through the study of simpler systems. This will be illustrated in Application 8A.

As with human studies, before we do any type of research, it is important to consider the ethical implications. This is no less important in animal research, and perhaps more so because animals cannot speak up for their own interests or give us their informed consent to participate. You will find the APA's guidelines for ethical research on non-human animals at the following link:

apa.org/science/leadership/care/guidelines.aspx

All of these guidelines must be followed in this lab. You must familiarize yourself with these guidelines before you do animal research. Your instructor might also require other readings on animal research ethics, as you will be expected to make informed contributions to class discussions on the ethics of animal research in class.

READING AND WRITING SCIENTIFIC REPORTS: CONNECTIVITY, REPLICABILITY, INTEGRITY, AND CONVERGENCE

We end as we began, with an emphasis on science as a social and collective endeavor. None of what we do as scientists actually contributes to science until it is publicly communicated and scrutinized. It is through this collective process that we gain a better understanding of the natural world, and the central mechanism of this process is, of course, our ability to clearly and accurately report our work. The main reason we have asked you to complete lab records this semester was to provide opportunities for you to practice figuring out and clearly communicating the relevant aspects of your research. For working scientists, lab records secure the details needed to create clear and accurate reports, and those reports are the foundation on which science is built.

As in any profession, there are standards and expectations for reporting in science, and the whole process works best when those practices are followed. The types of required content and formats for presenting them have evolved over many years of public scientific discourse, and while the formats continue to evolve, the required content remains the same: **Introduction**, **Method**, **Results**, and **Discussion**. These content sections are intimately linked to four guiding principles of scientific reporting: *connectivity, replicability, integrity, and convergence*, respectively. Familiarity with these principles and how they are expressed through scientific reports will help you critically evaluate published research, and help you to write better lab reports yourself.

The **introduction** of a scientific report, as a whole, should suggest to the reader that the author of the report had *good reasons* for doing the research contained therein, and those reasons should recognize and give credit to what is known or suggested by the work of other scientists. In other words, the introduction establishes the *connectivity* of the ideas to current understanding on the topic and to the broader context from which the hypothesis is derived. Often, the author's own previous work will be cited, but it is never the only work mentioned. Educated consumers of science should realize that the need to establish connectivity does not mean that all new science must *agree* with other scientists to be accepted (quite the contrary!). Often, the work of other scientists sparks disagreement, and this is the point of connection. The principle of *connectivity* simply states that science does not originate as an idea plucked out of a scientific vacuum. As a consumer of science, it is important to be aware: Research that is presented as though the idea came out of a vacuum is probably vacuous. A good introduction stresses *where* the ideas for the reported research came from, and logically builds a rationale, either for this hypothesis or for this way of testing it, or both. The introduction ends with a paragraph about the hypothesis, how it was tested, and the predictions, all of which should logically flow from the connections to previous research. A lack of connectivity in the introduction should be a warning to the skeptical reader that the research might be based more on assumptions than on previous knowledge.

The **Method** section of a scientific report adheres to the principle of ***replicability***. All of the relevant details that will allow other researchers to replicate the study should be presented. For clarity and easy access to the kinds of information a reader might seek, this section is often (though not always) broken down into three subsections: *Participants*, *Materials*, and *Procedure*. The *Participants* subsection should describe the number, sex, age, and any other relevant details about the subjects in the study, including how they were selected or recruited and whether they were compensated for their participation. The *Materials* subsection provides descriptions of anything unique that was needed to conduct the study, including surveys, inventories, and any unusual equipment or software. The *Procedure* subsection should focus on how the researchers used the materials to collect data, including what participants were asked to do, in what order, and how they were instructed. It is also important that the report include information on how data were summarized and statistically analyzed, although this is sometimes reported as part of the **Results** section. Skeptical readers read the Method section as though they intend to replicate the study, and can determine whether all the relevant details have been provided. A thorough critique of a published Method section requires a fairly advanced level of experience with research designs and statistical techniques, but at a basic level, consumers of science should be able to tell when a research article is missing important information, such as the age and sex of the participants, how they were recruited, and whether or not they were compensated, particularly in research where compensation might affect how participants behaved in the study.

Although ***integrity*** is, of course, a guiding principle for all aspects of scientific research (the purpose of science is, after all, to collectively figure out the truth), it is particularly useful to think about this principle as we read or write a **Results** section. Results must be focused on an accurate account of precisely what was observed in the data, and the outcome of the statistical analysis that was the true test of the hypothesis. Due to the probabilistic nature of the evidence, honesty is critical in reporting the results. Remember that the data and the statistical tests must come after the predictions have been made, and if they did not, that must be reported. Back in Chapter 4, we learned that looking at the data before stating and statistically testing the predictions would be paramount to flipping a coin first and then claiming that the fact that it landed on heads is evidence that you knew it was going to be heads all along. The true evidence lies in whether or not the predictions made ahead of time were observed in the data. "Predictions" that come after we see the data and/or the analyses are not predictions, nor are they evidence; they are merely descriptions of observed patterns, and must be reported as such. Without the integrity to report these things honestly, researchers may find that their results are not replicable.

Another definition of the word integrity is the quality of being unimpaired and uncompromised. A container with no leaks has integrity. Although some scientific reports will combine the Results and Discussion sections, this is not the norm. There should be no interpretations of the *meaning* of the results in the Results section, just the observations, without opinions on why the statistics turned out as they did, or what any of it really means. Integrity, in this sense, is further upheld in the Results section by not letting interpretations creep into the presentation of observations.

Skeptical readers will therefore pay close attention, in the Method and Results sections, to the description of how the data were analyzed. If a researcher says that based on an observed pattern in the data, a statistical test was used to check for an apparent difference or relationship, then the conclusions based on that statistical analysis cannot be taken as evidence for or against the hypothesis, no matter how the researcher decides to interpret those results in the Discussion. Statistical analyses performed after the data were seen *can* be used to suggest further examination of an idea, but cannot be taken as scientific evidence for that idea. Looking at a pattern in the data and THEN running the analysis to test whether the pattern is significant is, unfortunately, a mistake that can make its way into published research.

In the **Discussion**, the reader should find the author's interpretation of the results. The Discussion should *not* simply repeat the results. Rather, the goal, in accordance with the principle of *convergence*, is to revisit the hypothesis, in full consideration of the body of evidence for or against it. The hypothesis should be a clear and central theme in the presentation of the evidence that is now being presented for or against it. If results supported the hypothesis, the author should clearly explain how, using plain language, as though the reader is a skeptical stranger who wants to know what observations led to the author's conclusions. If results differed from specific predictions or did not support the hypothesis, testable explanations for the differences should be presented. Limitations of the current study, in terms of research design, potential confounding variables, and/or generalizability of the findings, should also be discussed, and, where possible, other published research that provides insight into these concerns should be referenced.

As scientists, we seek to use our varied perspectives and pieces of evidence to converge on the truth about reality. We are attempting, through our Discussion sections, to collaborate with other scientists, to describe and test ideas in multiple ways and use the evidence to converge on the best hypotheses. Thus, it is not enough to simply interpret the results. A good discussion expresses *convergence* by bringing together the current evidence with evidence from varied sources. Taken together, what does the body of research, including this study, now suggest about the hypothesis, and related ideas, and the bigger context to which the hypothesis contributes? How do other hypotheses compare? Do the current observations agree or disagree with others'? If there are disagreements, the discussion should attempt to explain them. Do the differences suggest that a change in thinking might be warranted? The answers to these questions may become the basis for future research.

Future research is the perfect segue to one final note from me to you...

Long after you leave this course, and whether or not you major in psychology, you will continue to see reports of research in this field, if not in scientific journals, then certainly in the popular media. We —the Psychology Department of Lafayette College, your lab assistant and I— hope your experiences in this lab course will leave you with the skills and knowledge needed to critically evaluate those reports, to understand the basics of the science behind them, and to appreciate the scientific approach to answering questions about the natural world, especially about the behavior of humans and other animals.

CHART 8A - APPLICATION LEARNING OBJECTIVES

8A Social and Biological Effects on Crayfish Aggression Objectives	START HERE ▼ BEFORE READING THE NEXT SECTION AND DOING THIS RESEARCH Check how well you feel you can accomplish each objective.				FINISH HERE ▼ YOUR LAB PROFESSOR WILL TELL YOU WHEN TO COMPLETE THESE COLUMNS (IN LAB)			
	I don't know how **1**	I know a little about this **2**	I know enough about this to guess correctly **3**	I know how to do this and/or have already done it. **4**	I don't know how **1**	I know a little about this **2**	I know enough about this to guess correctly **3**	I know how to do this and/or have already done it. **4**
1 Explain the role of social hierarchies in decreasing the intensity of fighting behavior among non-human animals, and discuss how this applies to humans.								
2 Operationally define crayfish aggression and submission.								
3 Apply a two-way experimental design to test an interaction hypothesis.								
4 Handle crayfish with appropriate concern for each animal's welfare.								
5 Interpret results (provided in the form of graphs and p-values) and draw appropriate conclusions from a two-way experiment.								

▼

After you complete this half of the chart, read pages 267-276. Do not to complete the white half until asked to do so in lab.

Acknowledgments

This experiment is based on research by former Introductory Psychology students at Lafayette College, Easton, PA. Parts of the original experiment were designed by Chelsea Michael ('09), as part of an EXCEL scholarship research project, Spring 2008. Lafayette students, in the interim, have collected data that led to the hypotheses begin tested in this experiment. All crayfish photographs © Carolyn Buckley.

8A: SOCIAL AND BIOLOGICAL EFFECTS ON CRAYFISH AGGRESSION

All Crayfish Photographs in this Chapter © C Buckley, 2013.

"You wanna piece a me?"

WHY FIGHT?

Animals, including humans, fight for a lot of reasons, but most often, the reason is limited and/or valuable resources. In humans, this could mean land, food, shelter, or even gold. According to one report on the California Goldrush (Wiegand, 1998), "In just one July week in 1850 in Sonora, two Massachusetts men had their throats slit; a Chilean was shot to death in a gunfight, and a Frenchman stabbed a Mexican to death. Marysville reported 17 murders in one week, and at the height of the Gold Rush, San Francisco averaged 30 new houses —and two murders— a day."[2]

Goldrush or not, people still fight over resources. Other animals also fight over resources (shelter, food, and available mates). But fighting is dangerous – potentially deadly – and takes time and energy away from more important activities associated with survival and reproduction. Therefore, although social animals can (and sometimes do) kill one another during fights, many different species of animals, including humans, have evolved to use social hierarchies (dominant or subordinate social status, relative to others) to avoid fighting to the death. Once a hierarchy is established, dominant individuals get the best resources, and subordinates take whatever is left, usually without complaining or further fighting. Throughout the animal kingdom, in species that use social hierarchies, by far the most common way to establish dominance is via aggressive posturing (i.e., relatively mild fighting or aggressive threats and displays). To explore the factors that impact aggressive behavior, we can't ask humans to fight, so we will use a non-human animal model: the Red Swamp Crayfish, *Procambarus clarkii*.

---

[2] calgoldrush.com/part1/01overview.html#storylink=cpy

CRAYFISH FIGHTING ETIQUETTE

In crayfish, fights usually follow a similar pattern or series of predictable stages (Brusksi & Dunham, 1987). First, one crayfish approaches another to begin the interaction. This is followed by one or both of the crayfish displaying a threat, called a "**meral spread**" (Figures 8.1 and 8.2A), where it will raise its chelae, spread them open ("muscle-man" fashion), and open its claws. If the fight continues, they will turn to face one another and begin to poke or jab each other with their chelae (Figures 8.3 and 8.4). They may "**interlock**" chelae and push one another (Figure 8.5). While interlocked, if two males are fighting, one male might flip the other one onto its back (Figure 8.6). This is part of normal mating behavior, but is also used by males to establish dominance (Issa & Edwards, 2006). These behaviors will continue until one crayfish loses the fight. The loser retreats, generally in one of two ways: it will either perform a quick **tailflip**, propelling itself away from the other crayfish (Figure 8.7); or it will back up or walk away with its chelae extended straight out in front of it, closed claws, its tail extended and its body low, close to the substrate (bottom of the tank or gravel) (Figures 8.2B and 8.8). The winner may convey its dominance to other crayfish often through a "**flexed posture**," where the individual stands on the tips of its legs and its tail is stretched out with the tip of the tail bent at a 90 degree angle, holding the abdomen up off the substrate (walking legs and tail positions are similar to the meral spread, shown in Figure 8.1).

Figure 8.1 (above). Meral spread.

Figure 8.2 (above). Crayfish A is displaying a meral spread, while B is in a submissive posture.

Figure 8.3 (left). Crayfish A appears to be trying to poke the other crayfish in the face.

Figure 8.4 (right). Crayfish A is jabbing the other crayfish with its left cheliped.

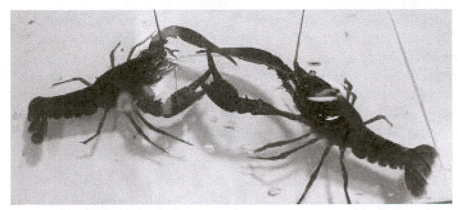

Figure 8.5 (left). These crayfish are in an "interlocked" position, where each holds the other's claws. This position may be held for several minutes. The crayfish will push and pull against each other while their chelae remain interlocked.

Figure 8.6 (left). One crayfish has just flipped the other onto its back. When this happens, the flipped crayfish usually becomes subordinate.

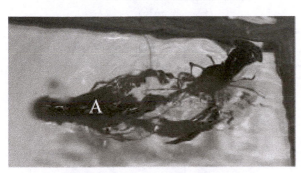

Figure 5.7 (above). Crayfish A is retreating with a quick tailflip.

Figure 8.8 (above). A subordinate posture.

RESEARCH ON CRAYFISH AGGRESSION BY LAFAYETTE COLLEGE PSYC 110L STUDENTS

Research on animals can help us understand the biological systems that are directly responsible for the behaviors we observe. Crayfish convey social status to each other using chemical cues, such as urine, and visual cues, such as threatening displays. In this research, Lafayette students have examined the social and biological systems that regulate threatening displays in crayfish.

In humans and many other species, we know that social experience (winning or losing fights) affects aggressive posture. Winners raise their arms in victory, spreading them widely above their heads. Those who lose tend to round their backs, slump their shoulders, and drop their chins. In crayfish, aggressive threat displays (Figure 81.) and submissive postures (Figure 8.8) have been studied extensively. Just like humans, crayfish that win a fight show more aggressive postures afterward, and those that lose show fewer aggressive postures. Because crayfish have a much simpler body plan than humans, we can determine the precise muscles that are used to act aggressively, and we have learned at least some of the neural and hormonal changes that happen during fighting. What we are still working out is to what extent hormonal changes during fighting might influence aggressive postures. Do crayfish hormones influence their aggressive postures, and does that depend on their social experiences? This a great question for a two-way design!

For the past several years, students at Lafayette College have tested the hypothesis that social experience and hormone levels interact to affect aggression in crayfish with a simple, two-way experiment. They measured aggressive postures in pairs of crayfish, then allowed the crayfish to fight long enough to determine a clear winner (dominant crayfish) and loser (subordinate crayfish). Half of the dominants and half of the subordinates were then treated with Octopamine (OA, a neurohormone similar to norepinephrine, delivered by injection). The other half of each group received inert saline injections (in case just being injected affects behavior). Lastly, they measured aggressive posturing a second time to see how it changed as a result of the various combinations of social experience (defined by winning or losing the fight) and OA levels (defined by injections with or without OA). The design of that experiment is summarized below:

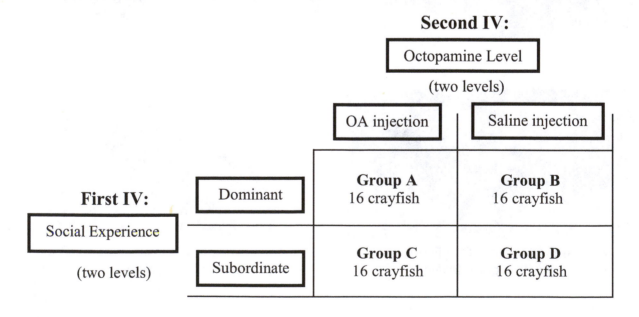

The neurohormone OA, when injected into crayfish, tends to decrease aggression. We tested the *interaction hypothesis* that this effect depends on the social experience of the crayfish, and predicted that dominant crayfish would respond to OA injection by decreasing aggression, but subordinate crayfish would not. We predicted a significantly greater effect of OA on dominant crayfish than on subordinate (an *interaction effect*).

Since Fall of 2008, over 600 crayfish have been observed by Lafayette students in Introductory Psychology labs across 12 replications of this experiment. Often, the results were exactly as predicted, and we found statistically significant support for our hypothesis. Sometimes, differences between groups were not significant, or hurricanes or poor crayfish supplies kept us from being able to conduct this research. Figure 8.9 shows all available data, good and bad, combined into one graph and one statistical analysis. As you can see, the results, overall, support our interaction hypothesis.

Figure 8.9. Combined results after 12 replications of the experiment described on page 270. Dominant crayfish were significantly less aggressive after injection of OA (compared to injection of saline), while Subordinate crayfish were not. The interaction was significant, *p* < .05. Error bars show the "Standard Error of the Mean" (SEM) for each group. SEM is a way of estimating variability that you will learn more about if you take Quantitative Methods (Psyc 120). Each group includes more than 150 crayfish, which is why the error bars are so small. SEM is not the same as SD.

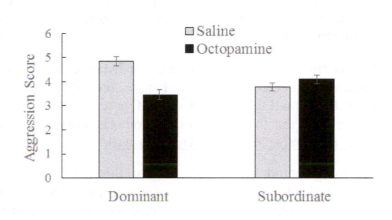

In an actual Results section of a lab report, we would write:

"A significant interaction was observed between social status and OA treatment, $F(1, 633) = 21.61$, $p < .0001$. Compared to the control treatment of insert saline, Octopamine injections significantly decreased aggressive responses to unexpected touch in dominant crayfish, $F(1, 633) = 28.53$, $p < .001$, but did not affect aggressive responses in subordinate crayfish, and $F(1, 633) = 1.50$, $p = .22$ (Figure 8.9)."

In the Discussion, we would interpret the <u>meaning</u> of those results <u>in the context of a discussion about the hypothesis</u>, using plain language (not statistical terminology). We would also discuss alternative interpretations and ways of testing them. We might say something like this:

"In crayfish, as in humans and many other species, gaining dominant social status by winning a fight increases aggressive posturing. Losing crayfish become subordinate and display fewer aggressive postures. We hypothesized that Octopamine (OA, a biogenic amine) plays a role in modifying aggressive postures after fighting, based on status as a winner or loser. Specifically, we tested the hypothesis that OA levels naturally decrease as crayfish become dominant, and increase as crayfish become subordinate, and that high levels of OA serve to block aggressive posturing in crayfish that are losing the fight. This was supported by our observation that compared to inert injections of saline, treatment with OA decreased aggressive postures in dominant crayfish, but did not change the behavior of subordinate crayfish. This observation makes sense if naturally low levels of OA in dominant crayfish allow them to display aggressive postures. Injecting OA would block that ability. If subordinate crayfish build up high levels of OA as they lose a fight, injecting more OA would not be likely to have strong effects on further aggression, which is already blocked.

Although social status was determined by the crayfish themselves, not randomly assigned, the fighting pairs of crayfish were weight-matched before fighting, and a comparison of those that became dominant to those that became subordinate showed no differences in their aggressive posturing before fighting. While it is possible that there is some inherent difference in crayfish that become dominant which renders them more sensitive to treatment with any biogenic amine than crayfish that become subordinate, it is more likely that OA itself is playing a role. One way to further examine the role of OA in this context would be to test the effects of phentolamine, an OA receptor blocker, on aggressive posturing in dominant and subordinate crayfish. If a lack of OA increases aggression in winning crayfish, then administering an OA blocker should have no effect on dominant crayfish. However, in subordinate crayfish, with high natural levels of OA, an OA-blocker should increase aggression. In other words, obtaining the opposite results to our OA study with an OA blocker would add further support to the general hypothesis that OA is playing a role in socially-induced displays of aggression."

In this study, we are still testing the hypothesis that OA levels naturally change with social experience, decreasing as crayfish become dominant and/or increasing as crayfish become subordinate, and that high levels of OA serve to block aggressive posturing in crayfish that are losing the fight. In general, our hypothesis remains that *social status and OA levels interact to affect aggressive threat displays in crayfish.*

Having gathered some evidence for this hypothesis, we now turn to the follow-up study, recommended in the discussion of our previous research on page 271. Note that our study, even though it was replicated several times, is *not proof that our hypothesis is correct*. As suggested in the discussion, there are other explanations for our observations. We now turn to the suggested experiment that could further support our hypothesis.

Since conceptual variables are pulled directly from the hypothesis, and we are testing the same hypothesis, we still have two causes (two IVs). The conceptual IVs in the italicized, underlined version of our hypothesis above are easy to spot – they precede the word "affect." Social Status and OA Levels are the two IVs. The effect (DV) is aggression.

We will operationally define Social Status, as "Dominant" and "Subordinate" (winners and losers).[3] We will operationally define levels of OA, as "injection of OA blocker" and "injection of vehicle (the same solution, but without the OA blocker)." We will measure our DV (aggression) using a technique called "Response to Unexpected Touch (RUT)" (Song, Herberholz, & Edwards, 2006), which you will learn about in lab. We predict an interaction effect between OA blocker injection and social status, such that blocking OA will increase aggressive RUT in subordinate, but not dominant crayfish. To review this information, go back to the in the boxes in diagram of our two-way previous two-way design on page 270, and recreate it with the correct labels for our new study. Answers are in Appendix B.

---

[3] As noted in the discussion above, social status is not a true IV, in the sense that we, as experimenters, cannot directly manipulate it. The crayfish themselves will determine whether they end up dominant or subordinate. You should recognize this as a "quasi-experimental variable." Gender is another example of a quasi-experimental variable that is often used in two-way designs.

HOW TO SAFELY HANDLE A CRAYFISH

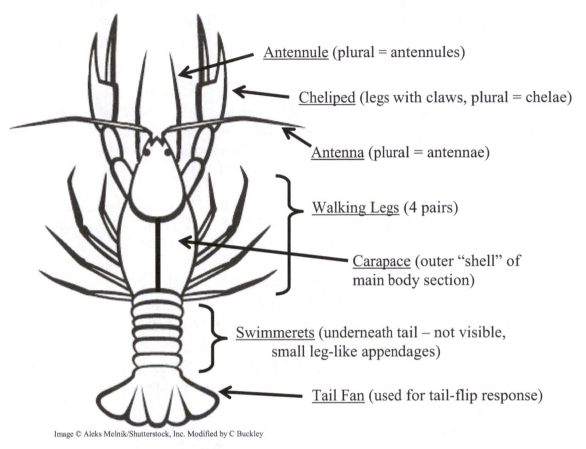

Antennule (plural = antennules)

Cheliped (legs with claws, plural = chelae)

Antenna (plural = antennae)

Walking Legs (4 pairs)

Carapace (outer "shell" of main body section)

Swimmerets (underneath tail – not visible, small leg-like appendages)

Tail Fan (used for tail-flip response)

Image © Aleks Melnik/Shutterstock, Inc. Modified by C Buckley

Figure 8.10 – Basic crayfish anatomy.

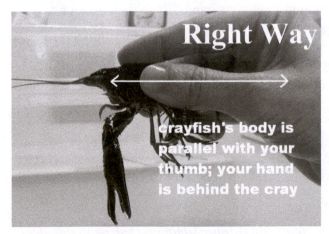

Right Way

crayfish's body is parallel with your thumb; your hand is behind the cray

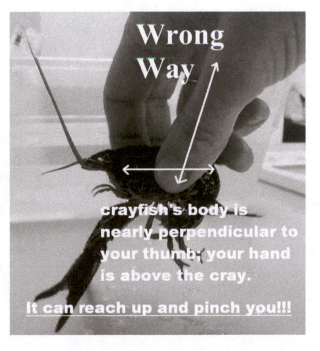

Wrong Way

crayfish's body is nearly perpendicular to your thumb; your hand is above the cray.

It can reach up and pinch you!!!

Figure 8.11 – How to hold a crayfish.
Above (correct): Thumb is parallel to crayfish carapace. It cannot pinch you in this position. Right (incorrect): Thumb and fingers are above crayfish body. It can easily reach above its head and grab your skin with its chelae.

Crayfish have no internal bones, just an exoskeleton. You will hold the crayfish using your thumb and middle finger on either side of the *carapace* (see Figures 8.10 and 8.11). **If you squeeze it too tightly, the exoskeleton will crack!** If the skin of your fingers turns white at the pressure points where you are holding the crayfish, you are holding it too tightly! A feather-light hold is all that is needed and all that should be applied.

It will be easier to get a correct hold on the crayfish if it is *not* in the water. Plastic tongs maybe be used to catch the crayfish and set it on a table. Then, coming from directly behind the crayfish (not from above), apply gentle pressure with your pointer finger on top of the carapace, close to the head. This will keep the crayfish from flipping itself backward to pinch you as you gently close your thumb and middle finger on either side of the crayfish.

If you hold it as gently as you should, there is a chance that it will slip out of your hands (or the tongs you might be using to pick it up). DON'T WORRY ABOUT THAT. Crayfish can handle falling on the floor a lot better than they can handle being squeezed too tightly.

If a crayfish falls on the floor and grabs the carpet,
DO NOT pull on the crayfish to get it to let go!
The same goes for skin or anything else the crayfish grabs!

NEVER PULL A CRAYFISH AWAY FROM ITS "OBJECT OF DESIRE."
MOST CRAYS WOULD RATHER LOSE A LIMB THAN LET GO!

...Then how do you get the crayfish to let go?

Carpet: Place a piece of notebook paper in front of the cray. Wait a few seconds. Then nudge its tail or touch its sides. It will let go in order to turn and face your hand. Push the paper under the claws. This will keep it from grabbing the fiber again when you try to pick it up.

Paper Towel: Completely let go of the paper towel. Give it to the crayfish, and move your hands away from the front of the crayfish. Wait a few seconds. Then nudge its tail or touch its sides. It will let go in order to turn and face your hand.

Skin: Do not pull on the crayfish! That will hurt more than it helps! Put a notebook or any flat object underneath the cray's walking legs and (as difficult as this might be), wait at least a second or two. Then nudge its tail or touch its sides. It will turn to face the part of its body that was touched, letting go of whatever is in front of it.

Always remember that you are dealing with a living, breathing animal that probably feels threatened by your attempts to touch it. It did not ask to be here, and it deserves your patience and respect. **Purposefully harming these animals in any way is absolutely unacceptable and will result in immediate dismissal from the lab.**

PROCEDURE 8A

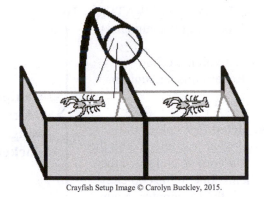

Figure 8.12. How to set up **two** crayfish for simultaneous measurement of RUT.

Crayfish Setup Image © Carolyn Buckley, 2015.

1) Choose a pair of crayfish. One will have a single white dot, and the other will have two dots on its back. On the front of each crayfish's container you will find a piece of tape with the crayfish's ID number and body weight. Record these on BOTH the white lab record worksheet AND the yellow data sheet.

> **Record Crayfish ID's and Body Weights.**

2) **Remove the white covers from the containers**. Take both crayfish, in their containers, into a cubicle, and place each one behind a black divider. Set up the red light so that it is shining on both containers, and the dividers so that the crayfish cannot see each other or you, as shown in Figure 8.12 above.

3) Turn off the room lights and close the door so that the only light is from the red lamp. Keep computers and cell phones turned **OFF.** Start the stopwatch.

4) After 2 minutes, use the probes to touch the crayfish once on <u>THE SIDES</u> of their backs, as demonstrated in lab. BE SNEAKY. The crayfish should not see the probe coming. Record the <u>first reaction</u> of each crayfish on the yellow data sheet, on the side that says, "YOUR OWN…" The pair of observers should agree on what the *first* reaction was, as **only one box can be checked on each row of the data sheet.**

5) Wait 2 minutes, then repeat step 4 until you have 5 readings for each crayfish. This should take about 10 minutes.

> **Measure Baseline Aggression (using RUT)**

6) Turn the room lights on. Obtain one clean container with clean, **dechlorinated** water and place it underneath the angled mirror.

7) <u>NOTE THE TIME.</u> Put both crayfish into the new container of clean water **at the same time**, facing each other. Place ONE black divider around the front of the container, and sit down to watch the crayfish interact in the mirror. *The black divider is important; it will block out any distractions for the crayfish.*

8) Observe the crays together for 30 minutes. While observing:

A) **Count aggressive and submissive behaviors for each crayfish on the lab record worksheet.**
B) **Toward the end of the 30 minutes, decide which crayfish is dominant and which one is subordinate. Record this on the Yellow Data Sheet.**
C) **Rate your confidence in this decision on the Yellow Data Sheet.**
D) <u>**Do not share this information with students outside your own group!**</u>
They will be observing your crayfish later on, and knowledge of their social status will bias their observations!

> **Determine Social Status**

9) Return the crayfish to their CORRECT separate containers. <u>LEAVE THE WATER</u> in the container that both crayfish were in together (you will be using it again later).

10) Based on the body weights of your crays, calculate the correct volume of the substance to be injected: Weight of crayfish times 0.005. Record this amount on your Yellow Data Sheet.

11) Bring your crayfish (in their own containers) and the **completed** first half of the Yellow Data Sheet to your instructor for injections. <u>Record what was injected on the bottom of the yellow data sheet</u>, then bring them back to your cubicle and place them behind the black dividers (as in Fig. 8.12) to rest. Leave them alone in the cubicle. Leave the light on, but close the door, and <u>set your stopwatch for 15 minutes</u>. Your group should work in the main area of Room 300 on your lab record during this time.

Manipulate OA response using OA blocker

12) After the 15-min rest period, go back to <u>YOUR OWN</u> crayfish. Move the container that the crayfish were fighting in **away from the mirror**, aim the red light at it and place one black divider around it. Make sure the container is NOT under the mirror, and IS under the red light. Then put both crayfish back into the shared container **at the same time**, facing and touching each other.

13) Leaving the lights on, observe the crays. As soon as they begin fighting, separate them with the wire grid. If they do not interact within 2 minutes, take them out of the water and place them back together again at the same time, facing and touching each other and wait one more minute. Then use the wire grid to separate the crayfish, regardless of whether they are interacting. Now turn off the room lights, turn on the red light, and leave the room.

Prepare YOUR crayfish for blind observations

14) Find another team that is at the same point in their data collection. When you enter their room, **close the door and keep the lights off.** Start your timer and <u>repeat Step 4</u>, but record these data on the OTHER side of the yellow data sheet. **Don't forget to circle the letter of your new cubicle** in the appropriate space on the yellow data sheet.

Measure Post-Treatment Aggression (RUT) for ANOTHER group's crayfish

15) Clean up and hand in completed Yellow Data Sheets.

Please, please-please-PLEASE read the stuff in the box! I'm beggin', over here…

These crayfish will behave as they do in nature; they can be extremely aggressive, and can severely injure or kill each other! If a fight escalates to the point where one appears to be injured or is being relentlessly chased and beaten, use the tongs to separate them, then remove the weak or injured crayfish and inform your lab instructor, who will provide further instruction.

Cartoon Crayfish Image © ilkka Kukko/Shutterstock, Inc. Modified by C Buckley

LAB RECORD FOR STUDY 8A, PART 1 (PART 2 IN LAB)

Purpose and hypothesis: *We have found that in dominant crayfish, but not in subordinates, OA decreases aggressive postures. The purpose of this study is to further test the* **hypothesis** *that the effect of OA on aggressive postures is mediated by social status. We hypothesize that natural OA increases as crayfish lose fights, causing less aggressive posturing. If this is true, blocking OA receptors in subordinate crayfish should cause them to display more aggression than untreated subordinate crayfish, while OA blocker should have no effect on aggression in dominant crayfish. We are manipulating the combination of social status and treatment with OA-blocker to see whether there is an interaction effect.*

Conceptual independent variables: 1. _____

2. _____

Which independent variable is quasi-experimental? _____

We define the *dominant animal* as the one that displays more threatening behavior toward the other, and the *subordinate animal* as the one that displays more submissive behaviors. These notes will help other researchers know what to look for so that they can replicate our labeling of dominant and subordinate animals.

DETERMINING SOCIAL STATUS

Behavior	Does the behavior indicate Dominance or Subordinance? Write "D" or "S."	As you watch the crayfish interact, keep a tally in the appropriate box for the number of times you see each cray exhibit each behavior:	
		Tally this behavior for One-Dot Crayfish	Tally this behavior for Two-Dot Crayfish
Walking (forward or backward) away from another crayfish			
Meral Spread			
Approaching and/or poking the other crayfish from the side			
Tail-flipping			
Flipping another crayfish on its back			

Operational definitions of the conceptual independent variables (each has two levels, A and B):

IV One, Level A: _____ Level B _____

IV Two, Level A: _____ Level B _____

Conceptual dependent variable: _____

What is the operational definition of dependent variable (how are we measuring the response to the manipulation of our two independent variables)?

_____

Subjects: *Genus and species* _____

We will use ____ animals of both sexes, but fighting pairs will always be same-sex and weight-matched, plus or minus 10 %. Animals are housed individually in 6" X 12" X 5" deep plastic containers for at least one week before testing, given food (algae wafers) every two days, and fresh water every two weeks. They are kept on a 12/12 light/dark photoperiod.

Equipment: _____
_____
_____
_____

Procedure: Each pair of crayfish are same-sex and size-matched to within 10% of each other. They have been housed individually for at least a week before the study began. Both were labeled:

Crayfish ID number ____ was labeled with 1 white-out dot on its back. Body wt was _____ g.
Crayfish ID number ____ was labeled with 2 white-out dots on its back. Body wt was _____ g.

Describe procedure for this experiment **in general**. Include relevant information that clarifies the logic of the experiment, not just what you did with your crayfish. Stay focused on the test of the hypothesis. Include details only if they could affect the outcome of the study.

_____
_____
_____
_____
_____
_____
_____
_____
_____
_____
_____
_____
_____
_____

CHART 8B - APPLICATION LEARNING OBJECTIVES

8B Your Own Research Objectives	START HERE BEFORE READING THE NEXT SECTION AND DOING THIS RESEARCH Check how well you feel you can accomplish each objective.					FINISH HERE YOUR LAB PROFESSOR WILL TELL YOU WHEN TO COMPLETE THESE COLUMNS (IN LAB)			
	I don't know how **1**	I know a little about this **2**	I know enough about this to guess correctly **3**	I know how to do this and/or have already done it. **4**		I don't know how **1**	I know a little about this **2**	I know enough about this to guess correctly **3**	I know how to do this and/or have already done it. **4**
1 Formulate a cause-and-effect hypothesis regarding human behavior.									
2 Use PsycInfo or another database to find original research articles on a topic of interest and be able to summarize the important findings.									
3 Design an original experiment to test your hypothesis and the materials needed to collect data.									
4 Explain the role of the Institutional Review Board in assuring ethical conduct in psychology research.									
5 Collect data, organize them in MS Excel, create graphs, and interpret results of a statistical analysis from *p*-value (provided).									

		I don't know how **1**	I know a little about this **2**	I know enough about this to guess correctly **3**	I know how to do this and/or have already done it. **4**		I don't know how **1**	I know a little about this **2**	I know enough about this to guess correctly **3**	I know how to do this and/or have already done it. **4**
6	Present your research project using PowerPoint and standard scientific reporting guidelines, with slides organized to briefly present introduction, method, results and conclusions.									

After you complete this half of the chart, read pages 281-284. Do not to complete the white half until asked to do so in lab.

STUDY 8B - YOUR OWN RESEARCH

Before each study this semester, you have been given background information within each chapter, often with references to published articles on the topics we've studied. Those articles and the chapters of this book have provided the context for each research project, illustrating the importance of educating oneself on a topic before attempting to design research.

Your final project will be designed by you and your group, so at least two of the articles to which you will connect your research ideas are yet to be uncovered. Lecture content and lab discussions will provide some context, but you and your group will use our library's resources to find a few scientific reports that are relevant to your topic of interest, and then formulate a hypothesis and design a way to test it. As a group, you'll prepare all your materials, including an application to the Institutional Review Board. You'll obtain approval, collect data, interpret your results (statistical results will be provided by your professor), and present the completed project to your lab class. *Each member of the group will **independently** write his or her own full lab report on your research.*

PSYCINFO: FISHING FOR INFORMATION IN A SEA OF KNOWLEDGE

With thousands of psychology-related articles published worldwide, finding the information you want can be overwhelming. A broad Internet search may turn up a few articles, but most of them will not be original research published in peer-reviewed journals, which is what you must use for your research. "Google scholar" can help, but is limited in its search techniques. To get better, more comprehensive coverage of all published articles, the **PsycInfo database** will be useful, and as you find articles that are related, even tangentially, to your topic, you can skim the Introduction and Discussion sections in html format and link easily to other articles that could be more relevant, using the Reference list to find them. Or, you can just skim the Reference list for relevant titles, and/or use authors' names to search for more articles on the same topic.

As you search and sift through the tons of research articles in psychology, we hope you will come to realize why we must stress standardization in scientific reporting. In so many ways, standardization makes finding the information we need a lot easier! Here are just some things you may notice as you sift through this database:

1) Long, informative, accurate titles make it easier to find relevant information, compared to brief titles that tell you only the main topics and lead you into a dead-end search, chasing down an article that you thought was exactly on your topic, only to find out it was actually a study on hippos or penguins. No kidding. That has happened to me. More than once.

2) Introductions that demonstrate the principle of connectivity (see page 262-263 & 285) will lead you back to original sources for information and can show you the progress that has been made in testing your hypothesis.

3) A well-written method section will lead you precisely to the information you want about how research related to your topic has been conducted.

4) Results sections that stick to results will give you exactly what you want to know about which differences or comparisons were significant, and will not confuse the numbers with their interpretations. This is purposeful, and allows you to make some decisions on your own before you read the author's interpretation.

5) Figures and their captions will be clear and concise, allowing you to visualize the important findings at a glance.

6) Discussion sections with clear, plain language will explain exactly what the authors concluded from their results and the evidence for those conclusions. Using the principle of convergence, they will bring together other research and inform you of the status of their hypothesis as of the date their article was written. They will also usually suggest great ideas for future research.

7) Reference lists in APA format will give you all the information you're looking for about how to find related articles, without having to search for missing pieces.

In lab, you will get a brief introduction and some assistance in using PsycInfo, which is very much like using any other internet search engine, but with more options. Also don't forget that you can switch back and forth; go from finding articles using the database to finding more database search terms using the articles.

Your PLA is an advanced student in psychology or neuroscience, and is an excellent resource to help you use the database to its full advantage. Our Reference Librarians at Lafayette are also happy to help you find what you're looking for.

IRB APPROVAL

Before conducting any research using human subjects, you must obtain approval from the Institutional Review Board (IRB). This is true whether you do the research on your own or at the National Institutes of Health, at any pharmaceutical company, at Lafayette College or at any other research institution. The following information on IRB approval at Lafayette College applies to the Fall 2019 and Spring 2020 semesters, and is accurate as of the printing of this book. However, please be aware that standards for IRB approval at Lafayette College are revisited regularly to assure best practices. If changes occur, your lab professor will inform you.

Since there are so many research projects conducted in our Psychology Department at Lafayette College, we currently have "blanket approval" for our Introductory Psychology projects, with certain important stipulations: 1) That IRB approval forms are completed in full and reviewed and approved by TWO members of the Psychology Department. 2) That the proposed project poses no risk to participants, or absolutely minimal risk that is more than offset by benefits of the research. 3) That all other APA guidelines for ethical conduct for research involving human subjects are strictly followed (see pages 223 & 224 and other required reading provided by your lab instructor). If (and only if) your proposed project *clearly* meets the standards set forth by these stipulations, your lab professor will approve it, at which point it must be taken to another professor in the Psychology Department at Lafayette College for a second approval. If any modifications are recommended, these must be discussed with your lab professor BEFORE any data collection may begin. Every psychology faculty member, including your lab professor, reserves the right to deny any research project that does not, in his or her opinion, clearly meet these standards.

If all this sounds overly serious, please know that the seriousness is not exaggerated. When it comes to ethical conduct in the treatment of research participants, the Psychology Department is very serious, indeed. For this reason, you should not blame your lab professor for being "overly picky" about your IRB forms. He or she is not allowed to sign them unless they meet the standards outlined above, and although it occasionally happens, no professor wants to waste time signing a form that is later denied by someone else.

Because your research will ask people to participate, rather than simply observing behavior in response to some manipulation (as in a field study), you will also need to prepare an informed consent form and a debriefing statement. The forms you need to obtain IRB approval and informed consent will be provided by your lab professor, both in template form and with completed examples so you can see what they should look like when you submit them. If all goes well, conducting your own research will be an exciting and eye-opening experience.

PROCEDURE 8B
(more information will be provided by your lab instructor)

This project will span the entire second half of the semester. The following steps will be spread out over several weeks, starting sometime around the middle of the semester. Meetings with your group between labs will be necessary. Depending on how your project unfolds, between-lab meetings with your PLA and/or professor may also be necessary.

1. Read through the abstracts provided online for your lab section and rank the top five in terms of how interesting the topics are to you. Based on this ranking and the rankings of others, your professor and PLA will work together to assign research topics to groups, with the goal of giving everyone a topic that they find inherently interesting.

2. Each group member will be responsible for finding and reading (being prepared to briefly summarize) another relevant research article for your group's project.

3. Your group will get together to discuss the research you've found, brainstorm new hypotheses based on that research, and discuss ways of testing them. The better you connect your new ideas to published findings, the easier it will be to write up your research for your final lab report.

4. As a group, you will design your own research and gather or design materials to collect data to test one of your hypotheses.

5. Before you can do the research, you'll have to complete an IRB application and get your research approved. About 80% of the time, this also requires revising your materials after IRB review in order to obtain approval.

6. Your group will then schedule data collection appointments in other labs, collect data and enter and organize them in MS Excel, interpret an analysis of your data, and draw conclusions. During data collection week, you will also have the opportunity to be a participant in many other research projects being conducted by students in other sections of lab.

7. On the last day of lab, your group will give group scientific PPT presentations, where you will communicate your research and your conclusions. As a class, we will bask in the glory of all the learning we did!

8. Each individual will use the feedback from the presentation to revise a draft of his/her own lab report (in APA format) on this research, due 48 hours after your presentation.

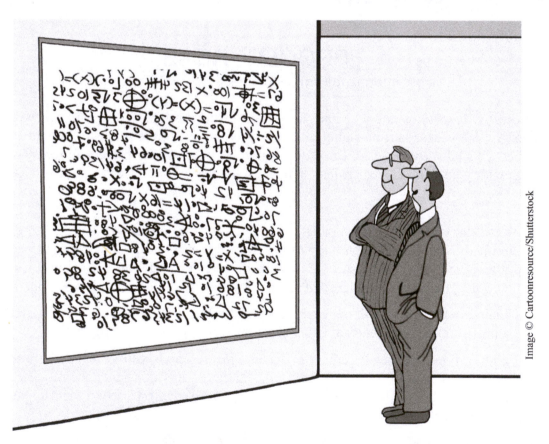

"When you put it like that, it makes perfect sense."

GLOSSARY OF TERMS AND EXAMPLES

Where to find these terms: EP = *Experience Psychology!* (this book),
MD = Myers & DeWall, 2018 (lecture textbook). Figures are in EP.

Applied Research: Research designed to provide useful or practical solutions to problems.
   Examples: Cancer research. Animal welfare research. Environmental issues research.
   Where to find this term: EP 261

Basic Research: Research designed to provide information for the sake of better understanding.
   Example: The Hubble Deep Space telescope. Myers & DeWall (p 14) give many examples of basic research, but it is important to remember that much basic research in psychology may start out basic and then become practical in unpredictable ways.
   Where to find this term: EP 261

Connectivity: The guiding principle of science that suggests that when we plan research, we should examine what is currently known on the topic and tell how our ideas are related to the bigger picture of what is known, what has been suggested, and what is not known. We should explain how our new ideas relate to other ideas, where our ideas came from, and the reasons our work is important in the bigger context. This principle is most clearly expressed in the Introduction section of our scientific reports.
   Example: A researcher who wishes to test the hypothesis that pigs can fly would have a hard time establishing connectivity in his or her introduction. This is not necessarily a matter of the truth of the hypothesis; it is a matter of what is currently known. The hypothesis that pigs like flying in airplanes would be an easier topic. To establish connectivity, one could draw on literature from the neuroendocrinology of joy, how it can be measured in animals, and the frequency with which pigs are shipped by airplane.
   Where to find this term: EP 262-263, 281

Convergence: The guiding principle of science that says that reporting should focus on how the results and conclusions of a study fit into the bigger context of the idea being tested and how the evidence converges on the truth. This principle is most clearly expressed through the Discussion section of a scientific report, which interprets the results in terms of whether or not they support the hypothesis and to what extent, but also examines how the results compare to similar studies, and attempts to explain any differences in terms of their relevance to the hypothesis and to the bigger context.
   Example: A researcher finds that the correlation coefficient for SAT scores and college GPAs for a very large sample of students is 0.16. Because the sample is so large, this correlation is significant. In the discussion, the author should cite other relevant research, keeping in mind that the hypothesis is part of a bigger picture of the truth about the relationship between SAT scores and college success, and that science is attempting to converge on that truth. For example, other correlations reported in the published literature should be discussed, and attempts should be made to explain contradictory findings. There might be discussion about whether the SAT score can or should be used to predict individuals' chances of succeeding in college, other ways of measuring success in college, or the variability of GPA as a measure of success.
   Where to find this term: EP 262, 264, 282

Inflated Error Rate: Refers to the fact that when we make more than one prediction in a single experiment, we have an increased chance of accidentally rejecting the null hypothesis, even though it is actually true. Normally, with just one prediction (a simple, two-group comparison), we reject the null hypothesis if our results have less than a 5% chance of happening when the null hypothesis is true. This means that we have a 5% chance of being wrong, because up to 5% of the time, our results should occur *even though the null hypothesis is true*. If we have a 5% chance of being wrong each time we make a decision about our data, and we make several such decisions, then the odds that we will be accidentally wrong at least once are increased (inflated).

    Example: In an experiment testing the effect of rewards on student volunteerism, a researcher predicts that a group of children given 50 cents each time they volunteer to do a classroom chore will volunteer more often than children given no reward. He predicts a difference between the reward and no-reward groups, and has a 5% chance of being wrong when he has evidence to reject the null hypothesis. If that same experiment is done with 3 groups (no reward, 50 cents, and a dollar), he might predict differences between each level of reward (0 versus 50 cents, 0 versus $1.00, and 50 cents versus $1.00). For each prediction, he would have a 5% chance of wrongfully rejecting the null, and the inflated error rate would be 14% (Appendix A explains why it is not 15%).

    Where to find this term: EP 255-256

Integrity: The guiding principle of science that says that results should be reported honestly and directly, with no negative findings withheld and no unsubstantiated opinions presented. This principle is most clearly expressed through the Results section of a scientific report, which provides the precise outcomes of our measurements in quantifiable terms, and compares those measurements using statistical tools that force objective decisions.

    Example: In the Results section of a scientific report, the authors are obliged to use and report straightforward, logical, appropriate statistical tests for their research. Any failure to do so should be detected by reviewers before publication. Indeed, many papers in peer-reviewed journals are rejected from publication on the grounds that the statistics are inappropriate for the method used or type of data collected. Unfortunately, there is little that can be done to assure that the results being reported are not the only significant results from multiple attempts (i.e., that negative results are not being left out of a report). The high expected standard of objectivity is why integrity is particularly critical in the Results section (see example for ***replicability***).

    Where to find this term: EP 262-264

Interaction Effect: In experiments with more than one IV, this is when there is a "difference between differences," such that the effect of manipulating one IV depends on the manipulation of another IV. If IV-one has two levels, A and B, and the difference between A and B depends on some other factor (IV-two, which we also manipulate), then we have an interaction effect.

    Example: Twenty people were asked to "arrive hungry" for a party, and 20 other people were asked to please be sure to eat before arriving. Ten people from each group were sent to a room with either small or large plates at the buffet table, and the amount of food consumed for each person was secretly videotaped and later measured. When people were hungry, they ate about the same amount, regardless of plate size. But well-fed people ate significantly more when the plate was large. This is an interaction effect, because whether or not plate size affected the amount eaten depended on how hungry people were (see ***interaction hypothesis***).

    Where to find this term: EP 259, 271, 272

Interaction hypothesis: A declarative statement about a cause-and-effect relationship, stating that the relationship depends on some other independent variable.

  Example: The easiest way to think of an interaction hypothesis is to first start with a simple cause-and-effect hypothesis: For example, "Using smaller plates causes people to eat less." Then ask yourself, "Does that depend on something else?" Perhaps hunger mediates whether or not plate size affects consumption. That would be an interaction hypothesis. Hunger would be one IV, and plate size would be another. The amount consumed would be the DV (see *interaction effect*).

  Where to find this term: EP 258, 271

Main Effect: In experiments with more than one IV, this is when there is a significant difference between two levels of one IV when the other IV is completely ignored (all levels of the other IV are combined as though they were not manipulated).

  Example: To test the *interaction hypothesis* example given as an example in that entry above, 20 people were asked to "arrive hungry" for a party, and 20 other people were asked to "please be sure to eat before arriving." Ten people from each group were sent to a room with either small or large plates at the buffet table, and the amount of food consumed for each person was secretly videotaped and later measured. If we compared the 20 hungry participants to the 20 well-fed participants (ignoring what size plates everyone was given), and found that hungry participants ate significantly more than well-fed participants, that would be a main effect (of hunger). Similarly, if we ignored whether people were hungry or well-fed, and found that people who used large plates ate significantly more than those who used small plates, that would be a main effect (of plate size).

  Where to find this term: EP 258

One-way (Experimental Design): An experiment with one IV that has three or more levels.

  Example: Our driving study had one IV (distraction) with only two levels, but if we had added another level of distraction, such as a control condition where we measured reaction time with no talking at all, it would have been a one-way experiment.

  Where to find this term: EP 256

Overall Comparison: A way of dealing with *inflated error rate* when we want to make multiple predictions. Rather than compare each group to each other group, we first ask whether there are any significant differences anywhere among multiple groups. This turns multiple decisions into one decision. If the overall comparison is not significant, we cannot perform more comparisons. If it is significant, we can make further *pairwise comparisons* to see where the difference is, since an overall comparison will reveal whether there is a difference, but not where the difference is.

  Example: In the study described in the example for *inflated error rate*, where the researcher wants to compare no reward to a small reward, no reward to a large reward, and a small reward to a large reward, the researcher would first do an overall comparison to see whether any one of those three comparisons would yield a significant difference in volunteerism. If the overall comparison is not significant, then no further comparisons can be done. If the overall comparison is significant, then there is probably at least one difference among the three comparisons, and further **pairwise comparisons** would be used to determine where the difference(s) is(are).

  Where to find this term: EP 255-256

Pairwise Comparison: A statistical comparison between two groups or conditions. In other words, a comparison between a *pair* of groups or conditions. This term is not used to describe comparisons in a simple, two-group experiment, but is used when there are multiple comparisons to make, as a way of distinguishing this from other types of comparisons that can be made in the same experiment.

Example: If a researcher sets up an experiment with four groups, and expects Group A to be different from B, C, and D, there will first be an overall comparison. If that is significant, there will be three important **pairwise comparisons**: A to B, A to C, and A to D.

Where to find this term: EP 256

Replicability: The guiding principle of science that says that under the same conditions, a scientific finding should be reproducible. This principle is most clearly expressed through the Method section of a scientific report, which must provide sufficient detail regarding how a study was conducted so that others who attempt the same study could reproduce the finding.

Example: Unfortunately, many studies that found promising treatments for cancer have not been replicable, for a variety of reasons. Some of these have to do with the many different types of cancer; some deal with the lack of detail regarding how data were collected and from whom; some are caused by differences in other data collection techniques; and some, undoubtedly, are due to natural, probability-based errors in rejecting the null hypothesis when it is actually true. It is also likely, unfortunately, that some studies have failed to find significant differences multiple times, but were successful once, and only the significant findings were publishable. This is a subject for a whole course on the philosophy of science. For now, in general, just remember that the better the Method section, the more likely the research will stand up to tests of replicability.

Where to find this term: EP 262-263

Three-way (Experimental Design): An experiment with three IVs. Each IV may have two or more levels.

Example: A researcher hypothesizes that a particular drug (A) will decrease alcohol consumption, but only if taken in within an hour before alcohol is offered, and if taken with food. Three IVs (the drug, the time it is taken, and whether or not it is taken with food) would be systematically manipulated, and alcohol consumption would be measured.

Where to find this term: EP 256

Two-way (Experimental Design): An experiment with **two** IVs. Each IV may have two or more levels.

Example: One type of therapy is hypothesized to be more effective at preventing panic attacks than another, depending on the amount of pre-therapy biofeedback training provided. One hundred and fifty people with panic disorder sign up for the experiment. Seventy-five people receive one type of therapy, and 75 people receive the other. Each group of 75 is split into three more groups of 25, and each of these three groups receives either 0, 1, or 4 hours of biofeedback training before their first therapy session. Frequency and intensity of panic attacks are measured for all participants over the next 4 weeks. This example has two IVs (therapy and amount of biofeedback training). Therapy has two levels, and biofeedback training has three levels.

Where to find this term: EP 256, 258-259, 270, 272

Appendix A
INFORMATION AND APA STYLE GUIDE

Here you will find an APA-Light Style Guide (pages 290-297). But first...

FOR THE MATH-MINDED: THE PROBABILITY OF WRONGLY REJECTING THE NULL HYPOTHESIS FOR MULTIPLE COMPARISONS

For math-minded folks who want to know why we never have a 100% chance of being wrong when we reject the null hypothesis:

Every decision we make about whether our data support our prediction has a preset probability that we will be wrong if we reject the null hypothesis. By consensus, this acceptable probability of being wrong is usually set at 5%. If we make multiple predictions about the same data, and our acceptable probability of being wrong for each prediction (i.e., each comparison) is 0.05, then the probability of being wrong for any number of comparisons in the same data set would be calculated as $1 - (1 - 0.05)^c$, where "c" is equal to the number of comparisons we make. For example, when we make two comparisons, the probability of incorrectly rejecting the null hypothesis would be $1 - (1 - 0.05)^2 = 0.0975$. Not quite 10%, but close. If we make 20 comparisons, the chances of being wrong on at least one are $1 - (1 - 0.05)^{20} = 0.64$, or 64%, not 100%. Why is this different from the die example given on pages 127-128 (and Box 4.3) and again on page 255? In that example, we were simply illustrating a straightforward additive probability situation, with an exhaustive list of all possible outcomes. One roll of a single, six-sided die must turn up one of six ways. If we predict a 6, we have a one in six chance of being right ($1/6 = 17\%$). If we predict a 5 OR a 6, we have a two in six chance of being right ($2/6 = 33\%$). If we predict that it will be a 1, 2, 3, 4, 5, OR 6, we have a six in six chance of being right, or 100%. We used that example on page 255 in order to illustrate the basic concept of additive probabilities in the simplest case. However, hypothesis-testing is a little different – we are not predicting an exhaustive list of all possible outcomes. Instead, each prediction is treated as an independent event with a 5% chance of occurring. We can change our die example so that it is truly analogous to hypothesis-testing; instead of predicting a 6 with one toss of the die, we would predict a 6 on at least one of any number of tosses. Each toss would be an independent event with a 0.17 (one in six) chance of occurring. Then the probability of being right would be $1 - (1 - 0.17)^n$, where "n" is the number of tosses. In this case, even if we tossed the die six times, we would not have a 100% chance of getting a 6. Instead, the probability of getting at least one 6 would be $1 - (1 - 0.17)^6 = 67\%$, not 100%.

Isn't probability fun? If you want more information on probability and dice, a good source is: http://mathforum.org/library/drmath/sets/select/dm_dice.html

WRITING AN APA-LIGHT STYLE LAB REPORT: GENERAL RULES

NOTE: "APA-Light" Style is uniquely designed for Psych 110L students based on two things: 1) the rules of presentation for scientific reports described in *The Publication Manual of the American Psychological Association, 6th Ed.,* (2010), published by the American Psychological Association , and 2) Common issues in scientific writing at the introductory level. Although similar, APA-Light Style is NOT identical to APA Style, and future courses may not adhere to all the guidelines below.

1. WORK INDEPENDENTLY! COLLABORATION WITH ANYONE OTHER THAN YOUR PLA OR PROFESSOR IS INAPPROPRIATE AND WILL BE REPORTED TO THE DEAN.

2. Express thoughts clearly and precisely, using standard (proper) written English. Make sure each sentence has *useful* information in it. Omit irrelevant information and avoid redundancy. ***Shorter is always better, provided no important information is missing.***

3. No title page. (Real APA Style requires a title page; "APA Light" will focus on other sections.) Your name goes on the back of the last page only, along with this statement: "By signing below, I confirm that this work is my own, and that I have not received help from anyone other than my PLA or professor." Please print and sign.

4. Put a RUNNING HEAD at the upper left corner and a page number in the upper right corner of every page (a sample running head is shown above and on all pages from here to page 297). It is a short title, up to 50 characters, that makes sense on its own. For example, for a paper about the effects of television on aggression, the running head "TELEVISION ON AGGRESSION" does not make sense, but "TELEVISION AND AGGRESSION" does. Use the same font and font size as the rest of the paper, but ALL CAPS. Use your word processing "header" function. If you don't know how, ask your PLA for help.

5. Evenly double space *everything* and use the same font size and style throughout. Start every section right after the previous section, *only one* double-spaced line below. There should be no extra spaces between paragraphs, headings or subheadings. The only acceptable extra space is when a section ends near the bottom of a page and there is no room to start the next section. If there is no room for text under the heading, insert a page break and start the new section (with the heading) on the next page. Careful: MS Word automatically adds extra space between paragraphs. You must change its settings. If necessary, ask your PLA for help.

6. Use citations where needed, in APA format, and include a References section, also in APA style (see pp 285 & 286 of this book).

7. Use PAST TENSE for all information that pertains to the past, especially when describing the research you are reporting. Even in the introduction, speak of your study in past tense. It is over, and you are reporting your results. Do not say "this study will..." Again, this study is OVER. You should even use past tense to describe ideas you had before you did the study (i.e., the hypothesis you tested, not the hypothesis you will test).

8. Proofread your work before submitting it. Multiple errors and/or lack of clarity will affect your grade.

9. NO QUOTES ALLOWED. Explain everything *in your own words*, from start to finish. The only exception to this is that you may quote your own Materials, e.g., "Our survey asked, "How much do you like cake?""

10. Submit the whole report on time, with all elements in the order they are listed below, and with all section headings correctly formatted (use bold or regular font, flush left or center, as described below). Proper order and font style are outlined here:

   a) The title of the report is centered at the top of the first page and *not* bold. Do not write "Introduction."
   b) **Method** (heading is centered, **bold**).
      Subsection headings (**Participants, Materials, Procedure**) are flush left and **bold**.
   c) **Results** (heading is centered, **bold**)
   d) **Discussion** (heading is centered, **bold**)
   e) References (heading is centered, NOT bold)
   f) Figures and captions (*"Figure 1."* is flush left and *italicized*, with a period after the number. The caption is not a sentence, but a brief description of the variables shown in the graph. Like a sentence, it starts with a capital letter and ends with a period. See section on Figures and Captions, pages 296 & 297.)

Lab report page numbers belong in the top right corner (see above), not at the bottom of the page.

WRITING AN APA-LIGHT STYLE INTRODUCTION

☐ 1. Write the title as the heading for this section. The recommended title length is no more than 12 words and all the words should be useful in summarizing the main point of the report. Make it as informative as possible. Phrases like "A Study of" are obvious and should be avoided. Use the same font size and style as the rest of the report. Center and double-space the title, and capitalize major words in the title.

☐ 2. Start the introduction immediately after the title (no extra space, just double-space like the entire report).

☐ 3. Introduce the problem. In no more than one short paragraph, draw the reader's attention to the main topic of the research. State the general purpose of the research you did. Provide the big-picture (context).

☐ 4. Develop the background and rationale. Explain what the reader needs to know in order to understand the research you did. Based on the principle of connectivity, your research should not sound like a random study that came out of nowhere. If you found no other studies that tested the same hypothesis, then discuss any that have presented conclusions that could logically lead to the formulation of your hypothesis. Describe the connections. Provide *relevant* information regarding how other researchers came to their conclusions that either directly tested the same hypothesis, or produced ideas that led to your new hypothesis. *Only include as much detail as is needed to help the reader understand where the hypothesis came from, and/or why it needed new or further testing.* It may help to describe how previous findings (from background research) could be interpreted differently or improved upon, but only insofar as those shortcomings provide a good reason(s) for the research you did. Keep any criticisms of other research professional and *only discuss problems with other research if your own research attempts to fix those problems.* Criticism of other researchers for not testing your hypothesis (if that was not their goal) is not valid criticism.

☐ 5. State the goals (either together with the hypothesis or as separate ideas). While the rationale is the *reason* for the research, goals are statements about what you (the researchers) tried to do. In other words, a *goal* is *what* you wanted to accomplish; a *rationale* is *why* you wanted to accomplish it.

☐ 6. In the *last paragraph of the introduction*, you must do three things:

　　☐ a) State the hypothesis clearly. Remember to state it in terms of conceptual variables.
　　☐ b) Briefly (but logically) describe how it was tested. In one or two sentences, describe what your research involved. What were participants asked to do and under what conditions? For experiments, describe how participants were split up for the levels of your IV (the operational definition of the IV should be easily understood without actually saying, "our operational definition was..."). Same for DV and its measurements. For correlational studies, describe how variables were measured (briefly). The most important point here is that the reader sees the logic in your test of your hypothesis.
　　☐ c) State predicted outcomes. Predictions must be stated in past tense, and in terms of operational definitions, not conceptual variables (see page 114 of this book, Fig. 4.4). If they are not completely obvious, then go back to your rationale and make sure that you have thoroughly explained the rationale for your hypothesis, so that the reader is not left wondering "why would you predict THAT?"

WRITING AN APA-LIGHT STYLE METHOD SECTION

☐ 1. USE PAST TENSE for ALL SUBSECTIONS (**Participants**, **Materials** and **Procedure**).

☐ 2. When writing numbers: For all numbers *10 and above*, use numeric form. For example, write out "nine," but use the number for "10." Exceptions: Always write out a number if it starts a sentence (you can't capitalize a number in numeric form). Always use numeric form if a number precedes a unit of measurement or represents a value on a scale, or is a fraction, decimal, or percentage. Avoid starting sentences with these types of numbers because they would have to be written out (see previous exception). These rules apply to numbers in all sections of a report, but are mentioned here because this is where they are often broken.

Lab report page numbers belong in the top right corner (see above), not at the bottom of the page.

☐ 3. **Participants** subsection: Describe the group of people who participated in the study.
☐ a) Include the number, gender and age range of participants and any other information pertinent to their performance in this study (for example, that they were students in an introductory level psychology class). Use general terms (e.g., not "Psych 110," but "introductory psychology).

☐ b) Describe how participants were recruited. If anyone was excluded, explain why. Tell whether or not participants were compensated and how. For example, if participation was mandatory for a class grade, that should be clearly stated.

☐ 4. **Materials** subsection: Describe what was used during data collection.

☐ a) Describe measurement tools (surveys, inventories) and any other materials that were uniquely needed for your study. Describe the **tools**, <u>not</u> what the participants did with them. A good rule of thumb is to avoid even using the word "participants" in the Materials section, but especially avoid using it as the subject of any sentence.

☐ b) Avoid exhaustive lists when brief descriptions with a few examples will make the point. If materials can be adequately described in general terms such that a person of reasonable intelligence could replicate your work, then detailed lists are not needed.

☐ c) Do *not* include human body parts or common things like pens, paper, or MS Excel, but do include any *specially designed* surveys or data collection tools.

☐ 5. **Procedure** subsection: Describe all relevant aspects of how the study was conducted.

☐ a) Provide a summary of the research procedure. Be concise but provide enough detail that another researcher could replicate the study.

☐ b) Any information or instructions given to participants that could impact their behavior during data collection should be noted. Details of the instructions that would not affect the results of the study should not be included.

☐ c) Treat this report as real research, ***not a class project***. Do not talk about "the professor" or "the students" within the procedure subsection. Use "we" or "the researchers" to refer to people who collected or analyzed data, and use "participants" to refer to those who provided data.

☐ d) Describe the data handling, i.e., how the data were summarized and analyzed.

WRITING AN APA-LIGHT STYLE RESULTS SECTION

☐ 1. USE PAST TENSE!

☐ 2. Describe the *results* only, <u>in terms of operational definitions and measurements (e.g., frequencies or means), not conceptual variables.</u>

☐ 3. Refer the reader to any relevant graphs that illustrate the results. Refer to graphs as "Figure 1," "Figure 2," etc., *in the order they are mentioned*, and make sure the actual graphs are in the same order. Always capitalize "Figure" when you use it as a label (proper noun). For example, "the figure shows…" and "as Figure 1 shows…" are correct, but "as figure 1 shows…" is incorrect.

☐ 4. Whenever a mean (M) is reported, it must be accompanied by a standard deviation (SD) in parentheses. The subject or object of the sentence can be the mean, but the standard deviation is always parenthetically reported with the mean. For example:

The mean shoe size was 9.5 (SD = 1.2) for males, and 7.6 (SD = 1.1) for females.

Standard deviation is always parenthetical. Do not say, "The standard deviation was...."

☐ 5. Whenever statistical significance is mentioned, it must be supported mathematically with statistical evidence, always reported in the same (standardized) way. For example:

| **Sentence mentions significance** | **Ends with a comma, then statistical evidence** |

There was a significant positive correlation between height and shoe size, $r(42) = .64, p < .05.$

| Statistical test used was r | Degrees of freedom was 42 | Calculated value of test was .64 | Probability of getting that value if null hypothesis is true (p) was less than .05. |

☐ 6. If the evidence shows *no* significance (i.e., we cannot reject the null hypothesis), then we still report it, but we report the exact value of p instead of saying that it was less than .05. For example:

There was no significant correlation between hair length and shoe size, $r(42) = .03, p = .83.$

☐ 7. Do not put all statistical evidence in parentheses, only degrees of freedom. Follow examples in 5 & 6 above.

☐ 8. Means (with SDs) and information about statistical significance *can be* included in the same sentence, and means *can be* reported parenthetically, with SDs. For example:

Shoe size for males (M = 9.5, SD = 1.2) was significantly larger than for females (M = 7.6, SD = 1.1), $t(42) = 3.56, p < .05.$

☐ 9. Italicize letters representing calculated values (M, SD, r, t, F, p), but not numbers. See points 5 & 6 above.

☐ 10. In the Results section, do not interpret the meaning of the results, and do not discuss whether or not they support the hypothesis (save those comments for the discussion section).

WRITING AN APA-LIGHT STYLE DISCUSSION

☐ 1. In the first paragraph, restate the hypothesis in the context of a discussion of whether or not it was supported.

☐ 2. Discuss the actual observations from the current research that support or fail to support the hypothesis.
   ☐ a) Use *plain language (not technical terms or undefined acronyms).* E.g., "control condition" is a technical term. Rather than "in the control condition," say, "when participants did not watch violent television..."
   ☐ b) Do *not* include statistics.
   ☐ c) Do *not* assume the reader has read the rest of the paper. The observations should stand on their own as logical evidence for or against the hypothesis, without the reader having to refer back to other sections of the paper to interpret them.
   ☐ d) Do *not* simply repeat results. Results have already been reported in the Results section in technical terms. The Discussion is supposed to *interpret* the observations in plain language and explain what they mean with respect to your hypothesis.

☐ 3. Elaborate on the most interesting results (observations). Describe *what* you thought was interesting, not *that* you thought it was interesting. (Let the reader decide how interesting it is.) Where observations disagreed with predictions, try to logically explain the observations based on methods used, past research, or other observations. That is, try to offer testable explanations for unexpected results (if there were any).

☐ 4. Compare the current research to previous research, but only as it relates to the evidence for or against the hypothesis, or clarifies the meaning of the results of the current study.

☐ a) Do not compare just for the sake of comparison. For example, don't just point out that someone else used different methods than your study. (The reader might ask, "So what?") If they used different methods *and came to the same conclusion*, state that clearly, because it relates to the combined evidence for or against the hypothesis.

☐ b) If your results conflict with previous research, differences in methodology can be very important, especially if they can be used to logically explain the different results.

☐ 5. Briefly describe TWO limitations in the design or execution of the study that might have undermined the reliability or the validity of the operational definitions or the ability to interpret or generalize the results. Do not describe more or fewer than *two* limitations. Choose the *two* most important.

☐ a) Do not "announce" limitations. For example, it is not necessary to say, "There were two limitations in the design of this study." Instead, simply describe the limitations. The reader will recognize them as limitations when you describe them.

☐ b) Be sure to explain how each limitation might have influenced the outcome or conclusions.

☐ 6. In the last paragraph, answer the following questions: What does the evidence (combining other research with the results of this study) say about the hypothesis? What is the big-picture importance of the combined research on this hypothesis or topic?

☐ 7. Also in the last paragraph, suggest a good direction for future research on this hypothesis or topic. This should be a "big picture" idea, not simply repetition of the same study without the limitations.

APA-LIGHT STYLE JOURNAL CITATIONS
MUST BE INCLUDED IN INTRODUCTION AND DISCUSSION

"Citations" are written within the text of your report, whenever you write about something that is not your own idea or your own work. In published reports, sources can vary from book chapters to government documents to websites, but by far the most common sources cited in scientific reports are journal articles. So for this class, we'd like you to cite only peer-reviewed journal articles, using APA-Style.

For citations in general:

☐ 1. Unlike MLA, there is no page number included in APA-Style citations, unless you are using a direct quote. Since you may not use ANY direct quotes in your lab reports for Psych 110L (see "General Rules, page 290), you should not include page numbers in your citations.

☐ 2. Refer to the work using *only the last names of the authors* and the *year* of the publication, which should be in parentheses if it is not part of the sentence (see Rule 4 of this section). Format depends, to some extent, on the number of authors, as described after Rule 5 of this section.

☐ 3. *Citations should not include*: page numbers, first names or initials, article titles, or where the research was done (unless the location is relevant to the idea being discussed, for example, when comparing results in one city to results in another).

☐ 4. Present the author names in one of two ways:

☐ a) As part of the sentence in which the citation is made, for example:

"Finkle, Watson and Belthaz (2003) tested the effect of alcohol on decision-making."

OR

☐ b) As part of the parenthetical publication year information, either at the end of the sentence or immediately after the work is mentioned, for example:

"A study on the effects of noise on concentration (Albright & Matz, 2010) reported that..."

☐ 5. The order of the authors' last names in the citation must match the order given in the publication and in the Reference list.

For TWO authors:

☐ 1. Use both authors' last names every time the work is cited, with an ampersand (&) between them (if citation is in parentheses) or the word "and" between them (if the author's names are part of the sentence).

For THREE, FOUR, or FIVE authors:

☐ 1. The first time the work is cited in your paper, include the last names of ALL authors, with commas between authors' names, except the last two, which should have an "&" between them (if in parentheses) or "and" (if the authors' names are part of the sentence). In the Reference List, be sure to list ALL author names, no matter how many there are.

☐ 2. On subsequent citations after the first, use only the first author's last name and "et al." followed by the year.

For SIX OR MORE authors:

☐ 1. Use only the first author's last name and "et al." followed by the year. In the Reference List, be sure to list ALL author names, no matter how many there are.

WRITING AN APA STYLE REFERENCE LIST

The "References" list is the list of sources that comes immediately <u>after the Discussion, but BEFORE the figures and their captions</u>. We will focus on how to format a reference to a journal article, as that is the type of source we would like you to use for this course. If necessary, proper formatting for other types of sources can be looked up in the APA Manual or online at APA.org, or check with your professor or PLA.

☐ 1. Follow all style points in the example on the next page, including using a "hanging indent," double-spaced. Each source starts flush left, and subsequent lines for that source are indented.

☐ 2. The entire Reference list should be in alphabetical order based on the last names of the first authors of each article. This refers to the entire LIST of sources. As noted above, authors for each entry must be in the same order as the publication. Use only the first authors' last names to alphabetize the Reference list.

☐ 3. Each reference must be cited somewhere in the report, and every citation must be in the References list, and all information (publication dates, spellings, order of names) must match exactly.

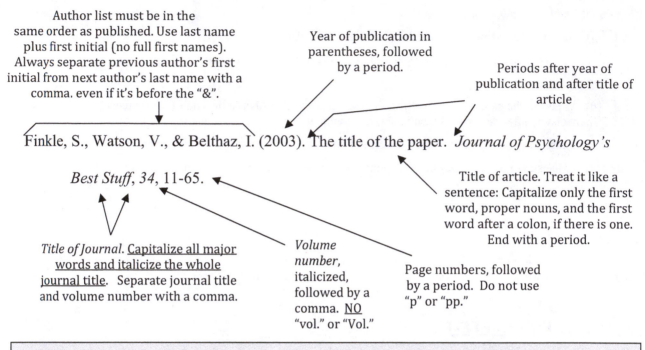

Author list must be in the same order as published. Use last name plus first initial (no full first names). Always separate previous author's first initial from next author's last name with a comma. even if it's before the "&".

Year of publication in parentheses, followed by a period.

Periods after year of publication and after title of article

Finkle, S., Watson, V., & Belthaz, I. (2003). The title of the paper. *Journal of Psychology's*

Best Stuff, 34, 11-65.

Title of article. Treat it like a sentence: Capitalize only the first word, proper nouns, and the first word after a colon, if there is one. End with a period.

Title of Journal. <u>Capitalize all major words and italicize the whole journal title.</u> Separate journal title and volume number with a comma.

Volume number, italicized, followed by a comma. <u>NO</u> "vol." or "Vol."

Page numbers, followed by a period. Do not use "p" or "pp."

RULES FOR APA-LIGHT STYLE FIGURES AND FIGURE CAPTIONS

1. **Every figure has its own page**. Figures should be the last thing in the report, after the Reference list.

2. Formatting an APA-Style figure:

   a) Most important: Keep it simple and clear. All other rules are based on that one.

   b) Major axis lines are required. There should be no other unnecessary lines, no boxes or borders around the chart area or the plot area, and no 3D effects. Include nothing that could distract from the meaning of the graph itself. Clear the plot area of gridlines. No other lines are allowed unless they are needed to give additional meaning to the graph.

   c) There should be no title, and nothing above the figure but the standard APA header and pagination.

   d) No legend (extra labels besides axis labels) *unless needed* (more than one IV or DV). If a legend is needed, place it in the closest open space *within the plot area*. There should be no box around it.

   e) Use black, white, gray, or a simple diagonal stripe pattern for columns in bar charts, and simple squares, dots or diamonds for scatterplots.

   f) Label both axes clearly, but briefly. Use the Figure Caption as a more detailed title to explain the meaning of labels (see # 5 below). Capitalize the first letter of all major words in the axis labels (and legend, if needed).

2. Unlike other sections of the report (e.g., Method, Results, Discussion), there is no section heading for the figures (i.e., do not write "Figures" at the top of the page), but DO keep the running head and page number at the top of each figure page.

3. UNLIKE the sample below, each figure must be ALONE on its OWN PAGE. There should be no other figures or text except the running head [as shown above] and the Figure Caption, just beneath the figure.

4. Figures must be in the <u>same (numeric) order that they are referred to in the text</u> of the report (usually in the Results section).

5. The Figure Caption is basically a detailed title for the graph, placed under the graph:

☐ a) It should be a brief description of the variables represented in the graph, usually starts with the dependent variable, and should provide just enough information for the reader to quickly understand what the graph is showing (see example below). Statistically significant differences are okay to include, but not necessary in Intro Psych. <u>See your professor or PLA for proper formatting if you want to include <i>p</i>-values</u>.

☐ b) It should be underneath the figure and double-spaced.

☐ c) The caption is a description, not a sentence, but it should start with a capital letter and end in a period. Like a sentence, you should capitalize only the first word and any proper nouns.

☐ d) As shown in the example below, use regular (not bold or italicized) text for the caption itself, but use <i>italics</i> for the figure caption label, and follow that with a period, not colon or dash.

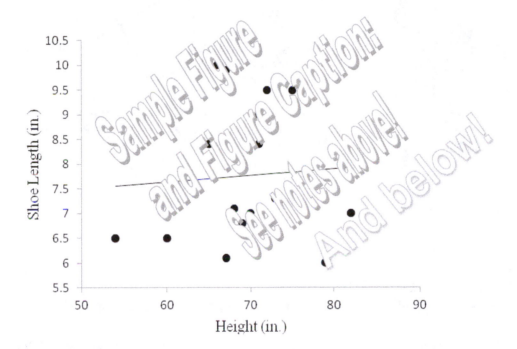

Figure 1. Relationship between height (in inches) and shoe length from heel seam to toe seam (in inches) for male participants.

<u>NOTE</u>: The example above is a scatterplot, used to report the results of a correlational study. Correlational studies (and scatterplots) show relationships between variables. It is not appropriate to describe experimental data (i.e., a bar graph) as "The relationship between...."

FROM PAGE 50 – Piaget's research was analog observation, and Goodall's research was naturalistic observation.

FROM PAGE 51

Image © Yellowj/Shutterstock, Inc

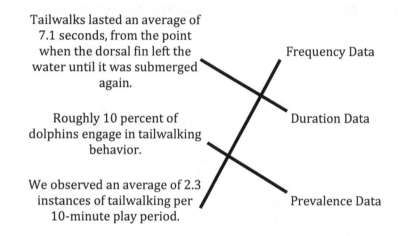

Tailwalks lasted an average of 7.1 seconds, from the point when the dorsal fin left the water until it was submerged again.

Roughly 10 percent of dolphins engage in tailwalking behavior.

We observed an average of 2.3 instances of tailwalking per 10-minute play period.

Frequency Data

Duration Data

Prevalence Data

FROM PAGE 86

1. c   2. b

FROM PAGE 145

To test the hypothesis, "Exposure to classical music improves math performance,"

1) The independent variable is *Classical Music (or, exposure to classical music)*
2) The dependent variable is *Math Performance*
3) There are many extraneous variables including age, IQ, math aptitude, previous education…

FROM PAGE 147

To test the hypothesis, "offering ice cream at the dining hall increases the dining hall's popularity,"

1) The independent variable is *offering ice cream at the dining hall*
2) The dependent variable is *the dining hall's popularity*
3) There are many extraneous variables including *day of the week, weather, other offers at nearby restaurants, other offers at the dining hall…*
4 & 5) One would need at least two levels of the independent variable: *1) offering ice cream, 2) not offering ice cream,* but it is also possible to test three levels: *1) no ice cream, 2)*

hard ice cream, 3) soft-serve ice cream (or more levels…. As long as each level answers an important question). There are other ways to test this, but note that if you get too creative (e.g., vanilla ice cream vs chocolate vs chocolate chip, you might get further from testing the actual hypothesis, which is not about flavors.

6) Again, there are several ways to do this, but one could measure *the number of students who enter the dining hall, or the number of students who actually eat at the dining hall, as some may enter and not eat (more valid, but harder to measure), or the number of students who stay at the dining hall for more than 5 minutes…*

7 & 8) Your operational definitions would be the same as your answers to 5 and 6 above.

FROM PAGE 148

To test the hypothesis that "ginseng improves memory," *the conceptual independent variable would be ginseng* and *the conceptual dependent variable would be memory*. The operational definition of ginseng is *a 12-oz serving of tea with ginseng versus a 12-oz serving of tea without it*. The operational definition of memory is *the number of words recalled*. Extraneous variables include *the amount of tea, the length of time between memorization and recall, the games played during that time, the number of words used*. Note that these are all the same between groups. If they were not, they would be confounding variables. The null hypothesis would be that *ginseng has no effect on memory*.

FROM PAGE 172

If we assume the null hypothesis is true, we would predict that *there would be no difference in the time it takes to complete the task with words versus without words*.

FROM PAGE 187

The null hypothesis is that *relaxing just before an exam has no effect on exam performance*.

The conceptual IV is *the relaxation period just before an exam*.

The conceptual DV is *exam performance*.

The levels of the IV are: *15-min relaxation just before the exam*, and *no relaxation just before the exam* (that is, *studying right up to starting the exam*).

The DV is operationally defined by *the score on the exam*.

The prediction is that *students who relax for 15 min just before the exam will get higher exam scores than students who study right up to starting the exam*.

Prof. Stewart can conclude that *relaxation just before an exam improves exam performance*.

There are several extraneous variables, including *how long students sat in the exam room before the 3-hr exam period started, how much they studied before coming to the exam, and how well they were each doing in the class*. Note that these are probably about the same between groups due to random assignment. One that is very well-controlled is *how much time they sat in the exam room between the start of the 3-hour exam period and actually taking the exam (75 minutes for both groups)*.

An important variable that could be a confounding variable is *what they were thinking about during the 15 min of rest. Those who rested first knew they had more time to study, so they might not have thought as much about the exam while they relaxed. Those who relaxed just before the exam might not have truly relaxed. Although Prof. Stewart tried to distract them from studying during the relaxation period, they might have been silently reviewing content that they just studied, and this could explain why they got higher scores than the group that had no opportunity to silently review what they had just studied.*

FROM PAGE 257

1. To test the hypothesis that Drug X decreases cholesterol…
   a. What would be our IV?   *Drug X*
   b. What might be two levels of the IV?   *1. Drug X   2. No Drug X (Placebo)*
   (Placebos look like drug X pills but have no drug X or other active ingredients in them)
   c. What would be our DV?   *Cholesterol levels (measured from blood samples)*

2. To test the hypothesis that exercise decreases cholesterol…
   a. What would be our IV?   *Exercise*
   b. What might be two levels of the IV?   *1. Routine exercise 2. No routine exercise*
   c. What would be our DV?   *Cholesterol levels (measured from blood samples)*

FROM PAGE 272 (REDO OF CHART ON P 270)

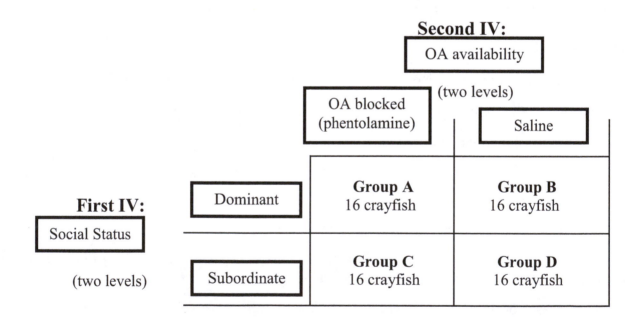

REFERENCES (IN APA MANUSCRIPT STYLE)

Alm, H. & Nilsson, L. (1995). The effect of a mobile telephone task on driver behavior in a car following situation. *Accident Analysis and Prevention, 27*, 707–715.

Beck, K., Yan, F., & Wang, M. (2007). Cell phone users, reported crash risk, unsafe driving behaviors and dispositions: A survey of motorists in Maryland. *Journal of Safety Research, 38*, 683–688.

Bjorvatn, B., Fiske, E., & Pallesen, S. (2011). A self-help book is better than sleep hygiene advice for insomnia: A randomized controlled comparative study. *Scandinavian Journal of Psychology, 52*, 580–585.

Boroditsky, L. (2001). Does language shape thought? Mandarin and English speakers' conceptions of time. *Cognitive Psychology, 43*, 1–22.

Cacioppo, J. (2007). Psychology is a hub science. *APS Observer*, 20(8). Retrieved from psychological science.org /observer

Cohen, S. & Hoberman, H. (1983). Positive events and social supports as buffers of life change stress. *Journal of Applied Social Psychology, 13*, 99–125.

Craik, F. & Tulving, E. (1975). Depth of processing and the retention of words in episodic memory. *Journal of Experimental Psychology: General, 104*, 268–294.

Cramer, S., Mayer, J., & Ryan, S. (2007). College students use cell phones while driving more frequently than found in government study. *Journal of American College Health, 56*, 181–184.

Cunningham, J., Humphreys, K., Koski-Jännes, A., & Cordingley, J. (2005). Internet and paper self-help materials for problem drinking: Is there an additive effect? *Addictive Behaviors, 30*, 1517–1523.

Deary, I., Whiteman, M., Starr, J., Whalley, L., & Fox, H. (2004). The impact of childhood intelligence on later life: Following up the Scottish Mental Surveys of 1932 and 1947. *Journal of Personality and Social Psychology, 86*, 130–147.

Elliott, E. & Dweck, C. (1988). Goals: An approach to motivation and achievement. *Journal of Personality and Social Psychology, 54*, 5–12.

Fredrickson, B. & Roberts, T. (1997). Objectification Theory: Toward understanding women's lived experiences and mental health risks. *Psychology of Women Quarterly, 21,* 173-206.

IJzerman, H., & Semin, G. R. (2009). The thermometer of social relations: Mapping social proximity on temperature. *Psychological Science, 20,* 1214–1220.

Issa, F., & Edwards, D. (2006). Ritualized submission and the reduction of aggression in an invertebrate. *Current Biology, 16,* 2217-2221.

Jung, M. & Hallbeck, M. (2004). Quantification of the effects of instruction type, verbal encouragement, and visual feedback on static and peak handgrip strength. *International Journal of Industrial Ergonomics, 34,* 367–374.

Kakalios, J. (2011). *The amazing story of quantum mechanics: A math-free exploration of the science that made our world.* London, UK: Duckworth Publishers.

Kidwell, B., Hardesty D., & Childers, T. (2008). Consumer emotional intelligence: Conceptualization, measurement, and the prediction of consumer decision making. *Journal of Consumer Research, 35,* 154–166.

Klauer, K. (1984). Intentional and incidental learning with instructional texts: A meta-analysis for 1970–1980. *American Educational Research Journal, 21,* 323–339.

Massy-Westropp, N., Gill, T., Taylor, A., Bohannon, R., & Hills, C. (2011). Hand grip strength: Age and gender stratified normative data in a population-based study. *BMC Research Notes, 4,* 127–131.

McGue, M. & Lykken, D. (1992). Genetic influence on risk of divorce. *Psychological Science, 3,* 368–373. Morris, N. (2008). Elevating blood glucose level increases the retention of information from a public safety video. *Biological Psychology, 78,* 188–190.

Papadatou-Pastou, M. & Tomprou, D. (2015). Intelligence and handedness: Meta-analyses of studies on intellectually disabled, typically developing, and gifted individuals. *Neuroscience and Biobehavioral Reviews, 56,* 151-65.

Pitney, W. & Ehlers, G. (2004). A grounded theory study of the mentoring process involved with undergraduate athletic training students. *Journal of Athletic Training, 39*, 344–351.

Redelmeir, D. & Tibishirani, R. (1997). Association between cellular-telephone calls and motor vehicle collisions. *New England Journal of Medicine, 336*, 453–458.

Reiss, S., Peterson, R., Gursky, D., & McNally, R. (1986). Anxiety sensitivity, anxiety frequency and the prediction of fearfulness. *Behavioral Research Therapy, 24*, 1–8.

Roy, M. & Liersch, M. (2014). I am a better driver than you think: examining self-enhancement for driving ability. *Journal of Applied Social Psychology, 43*(8), 1648–1659.

Ruebeck, C., Harrington, J., Jr., & Moffit, R. (2007). Handedness and earnings. *Laterality, 12*, 101–120.

Schilder, J., IJzerman, H. & Denissen, J. (2014). Physical warmth and perceptual focus: A replication of IJzerman and Semin (2009). *PLoS ONE 9(11)*. Article ID e112772.

Sherman, P. & Flaxman, S. (2001). Protecting ourselves from food: Spices and morning sickness may shield us from toxins and microorganisms in the diet. *American Scientist, 89*, 142–151.

Song, C., Herberholz, J., & Edwards, D. (2006). The effects of social experience on the behavioral response to unexpected touch in crayfish. *The Journal of Experimental Biology, 209*, 1355-1363.

Strayer, D. & Drews, F. (2004). Profiles in driver distraction: Effects of cell phone conversations on younger and older drivers. *Human Factors, 46*, 640–649.

Strayer, D., Drews, F., & Johnston, W. (2003). Cell phone-induced failures of visual attention during simulated driving. *Journal of Experimental Psychology: Applied, 9*, 2–23.

Strayer, D., Drews, F., & Crouch, D. (2006). A comparison of the cell phone driver and the drunk driver. *Human Factors, 48*, 381–391.

Strayer, D. & Johnston, W. (2001). Driven to distraction: dual-task studies of simulated driving and conversing on a cellular telephone. *Psychological Science, 12*, 462–466.

Stroop, J. (1935). Studies of interference in serial verbal reactions. *Journal of Experimental Psychology, 18*, 643–662.

Turner, J., Erseck, M., & Kemp, C. (2005). Self-efficacy for managing pain is associated with disability, depression, and pain coping among retirement community residents with chronic pain. *The Journal of Pain, 6*, 471–479.

Vliek, M. & Rotteveel, M. (2012). If time flies, are you more fun? The relative effect of expected exposure duration on the evaluation of social stimuli. *European Journal of Social Psychology, 42*, 327–333.

Wolraich, M., Wilson, D., & White, J. (1995). The effect of sugar on behavior or cognition in children—a meta-analysis. *Journal of the American Medical Association, 274*, 1617–1621.

Zagorsky, J. (2007). Do you have to be smart to be rich? The impact of IQ on wealth, income and financial distress. *Intelligence, 35*, 489–501.

Acknowledgments: This work, and this laboratory course in general, would not be possible without the previous and continued efforts of past and present faculty of the Psychology Department of Lafayette College, Easton, PA, especially those who have contributed to the ideas and text contained herein, most notably: All my former PLAs (too numerous to mention by name, but you know who you are), Jessica Redding, Jeannine Pinto, Wendy Hill, Jennifer Talarico, Andy Vinchur, John Shaw, Alan Childs, Michael Nees, Lauren Myers, Sue Wenze, Ann McGillicuddy-DeLisi, Susan Hannan, Rob Lipinski, Ralph Barnes, Jennifer DeCicco, Karyn Gunnet-Shoval, Courtney Ignarri, Eric Spiegel, Kat Longshore, Kara Enz, and Meghan Caulfield. Special thanks also to "The Psych 110L Committee," including Susan Basow, Jamila Bookwala, and Luis Schettino, and (again) to all the wonderful PLAs who have contributed so many thoughtful ideas and comments that have made this course better. Thank you to Lisa Gabel, Bob Allan, and Michelle Tomaszycki for support and encouragement, and to JoAnn Cannon, Rob Bouton, Fabienne Duré, and Amber Lachowicz for technical support. I know I mentioned him once already, but a second, big thank you to Ralph Barnes; the value of his ideas, discussions, support and contributions cannot be overstated. Sincere thank you to Kendall Hunt Publishers for investing in this project and in me, to Bev Kraus for making it all so much easier, and to Bob Largent for expertly overseeing the project. And of course, to my family, whose continued support is the only reason I ever get anything done. Thanks, Dave, Tristan, Caitlin, Trudyann, and Rudy! Any errors or failures to properly credit ideas that may have originated with others reflect my own mistakes, absolutely unintentional. Please direct comments or concerns directly to the author at buckleyc@lafayette.edu. Your comments and suggestions for improvement are welcome and appreciated.

Thank you, Lafayette Students! I hope that you found this course to be a meaningful and valuable learning experience!

CPSIA information can be obtained
at www.ICGtesting.com
Printed in the USA
LVHW012346290719
625732LV00002B/2/P